Circle Works

Transforming Eurocentric Consciousness

Fyre Jean Graveline, PhD

Fernwood Publishing • Halifax

Editing: Donna Davis
Cover illustration: Fyre Jean Graveline and Valerie Francis
Illustrations: Valerie Francis, Amber Moon Graveline and Fyre Jean Graveline
Design and production: Beverley Rach

Printed and bound in Canada by: Hignell Printing Limited

A publication of:
Fernwood Publishing
Box 9409, Station A
Halifax, Nova Scotia
B3K 5S3

Fernwood Publishing Company Limited gratefully acknowledges the financial
support of the Ministry of Canadian Heritage and the Nova Scotia Department of
Education, Cultural Affairs.

Canadian Cataloguing in Publication Data

Graveline, Fyre Jean.

    Circle Works

    Includes bibliographical references.
    ISBN 1-895686-30-X

1. Native peoples -- Education (Higher) -- Canada.*
2. Eurocentrism -- Canada.   3. Native peoples -- Canada. *
4. Education, Higher -- Canada.   I. Title.

E96.G72 1998   378'.017'0971   C97-950233-0

Dedication

TO THOSE WHO HAVE GONE BEFORE ME,
THANK YOU FOR WALKING THE PATH
AND LEAVING A TRAIL.

TO THOSE YET TO COME AFTER ME,
HEED THE WORDS OF OUR SISTER IN THE STRUGGLE:
"RESISTANCE WALKS ACROSS A LANDSCAPE
OF FIRE ACCOMPANIED BY HER DAUGHTERS
PERSEVERANCE AND DETERMINATION"
(CONNIE FIFE 1992: 31).

Contents

Introduction

We all currently share location in a world in which an increasing number of people are affected by widespread homelessness, joblessness, illiteracy, crime, disease (including AIDS), hunger, poverty, drug addiction, alcoholism and other illness-producing habits. Our degradation as humans is vitally interconnected with the continuing destruction of our Mother Earth, upon whom our existence depends. The Aboriginal peoples of North America are seriously affected by all of these calamities and reportedly have the highest incidence of all social disorders. While some equate the advancement of the Western way of life as progress, we must nonetheless acknowledge these calamities as products of "late multinational capitalism" (Wallace 1991: 6).

As a Métis woman, I am located in the intersection of Aboriginal and Western cultures. I walk with a foot in both worlds. I draw upon my Traditional Aboriginal "knowing" to assist me in surviving the nightmares of contemporary society. As "critical educator," I have struggled continuously to understand and challenge the existing relations of Western patriarchal capitalist domination. In this text I explore how these relations are manifested and can be challenged structurally and interpersonally within a classroom context. I reflect on my own successes and struggles as I "walk my talk" in a contemporary classroom.

Critical teaching, as understood and documented in this text, represents my "life work." As a community member who is enacting her desire to become especially knowledgeable about certain aspects of the world and its fundamental relationships, I am responsible for giving back to the community that which I am learning, in thought as well as in action. It is an act of reciprocity. As an Aboriginal educator, I am painfully aware that "schools have shown themselves to be ideological processing plants" (Maracle 1988: 113). I wish to contribute to education as the "practice of freedom" (Freire 1972), rather than as an act of repression (Brandt 1986), colonialism (English-Currie 1990) or imperialism (Carnoy 1974). hooks expresses a similar belief in relation to African American struggles:

> It is our collective responsibility both to ourselves as black people and to the academic communities in which we participate and to which we belong, to assume a primary role in establishing and maintaining academic and social spaces wherein the principles of education as the practice of freedom are promoted. (1988: 65)

I recognize and teach that "forms of consciousness are power structures" (Merchant 1989: 19). The very foundations of our everyday realities—space, time and relationships—are all contested terrain. The "ecological conscious-ness" of our Ancestors has been bombarded by the Eurocentric philosophies that are necessary to support industrial capitalism. Aboriginal beliefs are no longer shared by all North Americans, but our people and our Traditions continue to exist. Tradition is not lost if it can be remembered and revitalized to symbolize a possible future.

This work documents an effort to interrupt current Aboriginal/European power relations by transforming "business-as-usual" (Ellsworth 1989) by altering the prevailing social relations in a Western classroom. Developing an alternative Aboriginal teaching model and enacting it within "a single class-room cannot overcome the realities of a racist, heterosexist, patriarchal capital-ist society" (Briskin 1990: 14). I do believe, however, that we must engage all sites as potentially emancipatory. Resistance remains possible in the face of domination. My overall transformational vision scrutinizes the foundations of the currently dominant Western educational models, where educational con-cepts and practices that emphasize individual adaptation and skill development are matched to the current realities within public institutions. Our institutions operate within the context of market forces. "The acquisition of qualifications necessary both to participate in the labour market and to maintain oneself in public life, is the order of the day" (Jansen and Wildemeersch 1992: 10). This impacts on the curriculum and climate in all educational contexts: "the disguised values, norms and meaning of economical, political, and socio-cultural institutions are not the object of debate and contestation" (Jansen and Wildemeersch 1992: 10). "Efficiency" and "effectiveness" are framed as self-evident and self-reinforcing goals. As educational workers we are enlisted to help people adapt to these standards by improving their "personal" survival strategies. By not openly educating about some people's everyday privilege, which is enacted economically, politically and socially through dominant cultural forms and through overt acts of supremacy, the hegemonic power of Eurocentrism is validated rather than challenged. In educational theory and practice we assimilate to these norms by imposing them and then supporting people to adapt to these demands, rather than introducing new paradigms of knowledge.

My need to retheorize pedagogy has arisen through many years of encountering and mediating the oppressive relations in existence between Western educators and Aboriginal peoples. As educators located within Eurocentric institutions in Canada, our most immediate material circumstances are constituted by state bureaucratic structures. Any bureaucratic organization "depends on a hierarchy of authority, control and salary" (Gilroy 1990: 59). Our bodies of knowledge can be understood as "structures of discourse and regulation which aid in the establishment of forms of social management which have moved from the direct repression and punishment of deviants to their care, discipline and 'humane' control" (Leonard 1990: 16).

As educators, we must examine our part in maintaining this discourse. Competency-based educational models proliferate in schools. Competence means not only learning specific skills, but also acquiring the knowledge or theory base of the discipline, almost all of which is generated by middle-class, urban, White, male theorists. Skills and curriculum are based on notions of commonality within the human experience, and they tend to apply personal solutions to socio-structural problems. Little awareness of cultural diversity is present. Few culturally diverse members are represented as educators, and even fewer alternatives to Eurocentric models of education are available as curricula.

A skills-based definition of what is "required" for "competent" practice leads to an adoption of "power over" strategies in the classroom. Jarvis (1985) theorizes that the more control we seek to exercise over the body of knowledge, the more likely the educator's role will be an exercise of control over the learners. Ben Carniol (1990) links the need for control directly to our role as state employees. The desire to take a more "radical" approach is always mediated by the demands of "commodification" of the learning site. In all forms of institutionally located education, students and teachers are pressured to learn and teach what is considered marketable. When the state is acknowledged as the major employer, the issue of social control of the curriculum becomes undebatable.

The intention of this text is to explore a pedagogy of resistance that can be applied across disciplines and contexts rather than one that is lodged in grievances particular to one discipline or site. I wish to actively encourage critical engagement in an analysis of the Eurocentric foundations of Western educational models and to offer the possibility of an alternative paradigm. I am concerned with education's role in maintaining or challenging existing social and political structures of domination as they are divided along race and cultural lines. More specifically, I am interested in exploring the legitimacy of Aboriginal, holistic paradigms within some of the diverse frameworks available to us as educators; experiential learning, and feminist and anti-racist pedagogies will be emphasized. This text provides challenges at the theoretical level and strategies to implement in our classrooms. Moreover, this project is part of the global decolonization effort to challenge Westerners about "what they have to say" about the history and cultures of "subordinate" peoples (Said 1993: 195). It intends to help "establish the cultural integrity of noncanonical culture" (Fox-Genovese 1991: 202).

Within a Western School site, I am constructed and construct myself in the language of "minority teacher" (Ng 1991). In its standard sociological usage, the term "minority" refers to people who are relatively powerless in the hierarchy of power and authority. In Western scientific, capitalist discourse, numbers talk. According to Brandt, "[T]he almost exclusive recruitment of White teachers to the profession . . . ensures the perpetuation of White interests, cultural assumptions and the racial status quo of 'White' authority and 'Black' subordination" (1986: 128).

Collins (1991) aptly describes the position as that of an "outsider within." This position allows us a "distinct view of the contradictions between the dominant group's actions and ideologies" (Collins 1991: 11), including the "theories put forward by such intellectual communities" (Collins 1991: 12). According to Carty, daily lived experiences of racism and sexism render our lives "less embedded in the linguistic and institutional hierarchical structures which define academia" (1991a: 22). Our "subjugated knowledges" do not depend "solely on the dominant society's thought validation process" (Carty 1991a: 22). Eurocentric male dominance of the terrain has meant the construction of White/male as "the reference point of all knowledge" (Carty 1991a: 22). Only one cultural reality is universalized, one language is spoken: "the abstract mode of talking" (Holloway 1992: 269). The pressure to assimilate is constant. Schools are, by design, highly assimilatory institutions. As Raymond notes, "one of the recurring dangers that one faces in [the] quest for residence in the academy is immediate or gradual assimilation" (1985: 50).

Joe David, a Mohawk artist, warns us of the signs of acculturation in our work. "By being influenced by government propaganda," he says, "by making polarized political analysis, by being vague or—worst of all—by making satire out of the pain, fear and despair of our brothers and sisters, we do the government's job of 'white-washing' history, of belittling the issues" (David 1992: 140). Loretta Todd, a Métis artist, expresses this concern:

> How can we, then, create our own scholarship and practice of art and aesthetics in the face of what would appear to be positions that are opposed to our worldview, and where there is a real risk of assimilation, at worst, or serving the agenda of the dominant culture's own critics at best? (1992: 76)

While the terrain is contradictory and promotes fatalistic assimilation, I take heart from hooks. "Even in the face of powerful structures of domination," she says, "it remains possible for each of us, especially those of us who are members of oppressed and/or exploited groups . . . to define and determine alternative standards, to decide on the nature and the extent of the compromise" (hooks 1988: 81).

I am taking an "oppositional" stance. I acknowledge my intention to oppose in the education system whatever I perceive is operating to "oppress, repress or disenfranchise" (Brandt 1986: 125) me and the members of other cultural Communities. Much of Traditional Aboriginal teaching is oppositional. Our teachers help us to see "the upside down, the opposite, and the other balances of things around us and our human ways of acting and talking" (Beck and Walters 1977: 22). Thus I, too, take an oppositional stance; I learn and teach through reversal and embrace the Ikomi prophecy of "white man as Trickster" (Keeshig-Tobias 1992). This opposition will be located in the historical and contemporary resistance efforts of many others.

Power is embedded in the context of the School setting and invested in my role as educator within that site. Critical educators affirm, as does the Assembly of First Nations (1988), that all education is political. Freire warns us that: "the more conscious and committed they are, the more they understand that their role of educator requires them to take risks, including a willingness to risk their own jobs" (1985: 180). He claims that "[e]ducators that do their work uncritically, just to preserve their jobs, have not yet grasped the political nature of education" (Freire 1985: 180). Freire's words reflect my lived experience as an Aboriginal, feminist, anti-racist, critical educator, part of a very small numerical "minority" within a patriarchal, Eurocentric School context. Freire does not overestimate the risks, or the pain. Ng reports: "[F]or critical teachers, especially feminist teachers, attempts at critical teaching can be acutely painful experiences" (1991: 106). We must continuously ask ourselves: for whom and on whose behalf are we working? Building ongoing, supportive alliances is a critical necessity.

Chandra Mohanty also theorizes school as a political and a cultural site: "Thus, teachers and students produce, reinforce, recreate, resist, and transform ideas about race, gender and difference" (1994: 147). She reveals current agendas regarding the "self and collective knowledge of marginal peoples and the recovery of alternative, oppositional histories of domination and struggle. Here, disciplinary parameters matter less than questions of power, history, and self-identity" (Mohanty 1994: 147).

"Demystification" or "prophetic criticism" is proposed by Cornel West as a mode of theoretical enquiry, which unveils the "complex dynamics of institutional and other related power structures in order to disclose options and alternatives for transformative praxis" (1993: 213). In his view human agency is accented. According to Jay, "[A]gency appears in the way I take a social construction personally, as my duty, my responsibility, my ethos, my law, my enemy, or my love" (1995: 118). West believes that

> [p]rophetic critics and artists of color should be exemplars of what it means to be intellectual freedom fighters, that is, cultural workers who simultaneously position themselves within (or alongside) the mainstream while clearly aligned with groups who vow to keep alive potent traditions of critique and resistance. (1993: 216)

Peter McLaren concurs, stating that "[w]e should not forfeit the opportunity of theorizing both teachers and students as historical agents of resistance" (1994: 213). Trend also expresses the view that teachers and students have "a role in the making of their world and they need not accept positions as passive spectators or consumers" (1992: 150). "Resistance," Mohanty says, "lies in self-conscious engagement with dominant, normative discourses and representations and in the active creation of oppositional analytic and cultural spaces" (1994: 148). She believes, and I agree, that our "subjugated knowledges" need to be defined pedagogically in order to transform educational institutions.

Through this book I intend to document the reality that it remains possible for teachers to resist acculturation through redefining and enacting alternative curricula and pedagogies. In surviving the contradictory and assimilatory terrain of Schools, I have returned to the power of Aboriginal Traditional ways. Many people say that when they have been taught strong principles in the Traditional way, and have had even a glimpse of their tribe's guiding sacred vision, they are better able to cope with and live well in today's changing world (Beck and Walters 1977). Gerald McMaster, a Plains Cree, and Lee-Ann Martin, a Mohawk, argue that "rather than perpetuat[ing] an 'academic' colonialism, Aboriginal communities need to articulate their own scholarship that validates indigenous systems and philosophies" (1992: 21). In addressing Indigenous peoples around the world, Jeannette Armstrong, an Okanagan author and educator, states that "[q]uality education must be based on indigenous educational methods not only to ensure our survival as indigenous peoples but for our very existence as humans" (1987: 14).

Many Aboriginal people in the contemporary era are returning to the belief systems of our Ancestors to find solutions to the many and varied problems facing us today as individuals, as Community members, as Nations and as cohabitants of Mother Earth. This text is an effort to describe and embody a vision expressed by many healers, teachers and visionaries. As Twyla, a Cree medicine woman, says, "Medicine ways will give our people a feeling of belonging again. They will come together in a circle, caring for each other, helping each other" (in Steiger 1984: 195). Brooke Medicine Eagle, a Métis shaman, expresses a common sentiment:

> I have a lot of gratitude to my native elders. Dancing in circles, going into sweat lodge, all of those things were banned and people were killed who tried to hold these simple beautiful ways. My gratefulness is to those who had the heart and courage and love and spirit to bring those things to us. We are babies just beginning, but the knowledge is ancient in our bodies. We are just remembering. (in Cahill and Halpern 1992: 128)

Elders' advice is still regularly sought in coping with the dilemmas facing us. People come to ask Elders for advice because they can usually find an appropriate narrative or song to broaden the framework for thinking about a question, both when trying to explain some past decision and when encountering ideas new to us. Our Elders model an intellectual drive to formulate consistent links between "old ways" and "new ways" (Cruikshank 1992; Meili 1991). This quest permeates my "life work" and this account. As Minh-ha so aptly puts it: "i do feel the necessity to return to my so-called roots, since they are the fount of my strength, the guiding arrow to which i constantly refer before heading for a new direction" (1989: 89). As a mother, teacher, healer, scholar and activist, I wish to contribute to the revitalization of our Aboriginal culture. The linking of Traditional worldviews with knowledge of alternative and contemporary educational models that challenge the continuing impacts of colonization will contribute to the revitalization of cultural beliefs in our everyday lives.

Setting the Terms will help establish the common language and historical context necessary to appreciate the significance of the challenge to Western educational processes presented in this Model. I wish to help establish a framework that articulates the historical and ongoing relations between Aboriginal and non-Aboriginal people and institutions. Resistance is theorized as ongoing and fundamental to the current renaissance of our culture today. This text, as a representation of the "Native perspective," is framed as an act of resistance in opposition to the current status quo. I will review the complexity and interconnectedness of forms of Aboriginal consciousness relied on by the original inhabitants of North America. Through words of Aboriginal shamans, teachers, healers, Elders and other visionaries, "the Indian way" as it is being retained in the modern age will be constructed. The role of Aboriginal Tradi-

tional pedagogies, upon which this model of teaching was constructed, evolved and evaluated, will be emphasized.

Throughout the remainder of the text I rely on the Medicine Wheel, which to the Plains people is the "sacred centre" of the community. Paula Gunn Allen, a Laguna teacher, describes it as "a tangible object seen as possessing nonrational powers to unite or bind diverse elements into a community, a psychic and spiritual whole" (1986: 80). The Medicine Wheel in this case is used as the organizing frame for the curriculum of a particular Cross Cultural Issues course. I rely on it metaphorically and practically to describe, through the analysis of data,[1] one of the efforts I have made to introduce Aboriginal Tradition into a Western classroom context. Through the Medicine Wheel, the Model-In-Use[2] is explicated as a holistic teaching and healing process. Journeying around the Wheel, in the East I explore the multiple ways in which consciousness or knowing evolves in the process. The content taught through the Model is reviewed, along with one primary tool of consciousness-raising: First Voice.

Introduction

Circling to the South, I discuss how Aboriginal culture—philosophy and pedagogy—is introduced into the classroom context. Specific attention is given to the Talking Circle. Shifting to the West, I explore the various practices In-Use to build relations with the Communities[3] within and outside the classroom. The North focuses on the enacted aspects of the Model; learning by doing and taking an activist position are emphasized.

Simple description of my efforts is insufficient. The multiple layers of contradiction evident in introducing a teaching Model based on Aboriginal egalitarianism into a Western hierarchical context are explored separately. Contradictory elements in each Direction of the Wheel are delineated. The text concludes with the visions participants and I share in using and analyzing the Model. Our visions are a necessary beginning. This work, I hope, will be an opening to new ideas and models of teaching, so I end with hopeful possibilities for new beginnings.

Notes

1. In the text, all data, that is the voices of students and community members, are indicated by a distinct type face.
2. "Model-In-Use" is a Model from which I am presently teaching/learning through application.
3. "Communities" refers to the culturally diverse communities represented in this work: African Canadian, Aboriginal, Acadian, Asian and Lesbian and Gay.

Setting the Terms

Be Aware
Spirits of the Ancestors
Fuel our Will to Survive.
Aboriginal peoples
Have been Murdered . . . Denigrated . . . Acculturated . . . Problematized
Viewed as Static . . . Understandable through Categorization.
Acknowledge what our Ancestors
Our selves . . . our children . . . suffered and continue to suffer
Through "well-meaning" efforts
To make us speak . . . Dress . . . Eat . . . Worship . . . Live . . .
Like our oppressors.
Attempt to Assimilate

So that the children and unborn
Will not suffer as they had . . . as we have.
This effort springs out of a Need to Survive.
We desire to be treated Humanly.
Recognize . . . even when we Adapt
To dominant cultural ways
We are often still Excluded . . . Despised
Ridiculed for our "Difference."
Despite the language of
"Equal rights" . . . "Multiculturalism" . . . "Inclusion"
We are Not included.

This text is about beliefs people hold and enact In-Relation to others. It is an effort to explore changes in individuals' levels of conscious awareness. Structurally, I seek to challenge the forms of Western education that currently privilege the objective/rational/linear approach to knowing. I do this through theorizing and enacting a Model that is personal, holistic and circular. The teaching experience, and my analysis of it, is current, ongoing and evolving. I accept Said's analysis that "[n]o experience that is interpreted or reflected on can be characterized as immediate, just as no critic or interpreter can be entirely believed if he or she claims to have achieved an Archimedean perspective that is subject neither to history nor to a social setting" (1993: 32). I wish to fully understand the pastness of the past and its influence on the present-becoming future.

This work is subject to both history and social setting, as I aim to revitalize Ancestral Aboriginal Tradition within a contemporary Western School. I am working within the contradictory conditions given to me by my history, environment, social structure, worldview and social relations with other peoples. This work is guided by my images and assumptions, by my ideas about reality, by my consciousness. For me as a Métis, Aboriginal Traditional worldviews and White Eurocentric hegemony are competing and contrary energy forms. It is upon this terrain that this teaching/learning project was constructed, enacted and analyzed. So to understand it requires a sense of locatedness within the historically constructed but ongoing relations between our peoples.

To frame the scope of this undertaking and lodge it within existing critical theory requires a clarification of terms. As language is a cultural signifier and many terms have multiple and loaded meanings, specific language has been selected to communicate the complex ideas under study. These words will be defined and contextualized for use in the remainder of this text.

Beginning with definitions of consciousness, worldview, Traditional, culture and bicultural, I will turn to an exploration of "the Indian way" and "the White way" as two competing belief-sets, both historically and in today's society. I will then establish the historical and contemporary structural parameters that contextualize this work through a discussion of imperialism, colonialism, Eurocentrism, hegemony, appropriation and authenticity. Pedagogical violence as it was enacted historically will be briefly noted, as it influenced and continues to impact on all of our educational lives as Aboriginal teachers and students. Fundamentally, it is necessary not only to label but to challenge these realities. Resistance will be retheorized, laying the foundation to establish this work as a contemporary act of Aboriginal resistance to prevailing Eurocentric worldviews.

There will be no effort made to present a rational, objective or verifiable historical treatise. Rather the subject matter is being constructed as "ethnoscience"—defined by Blaut as the study of beliefs and "belief-holding groups" (1993: 32). An ethnographic approach explores "the people who believe a given idea, who communicate it to others as a belief. The question of whether a person believes in the validity of an idea is not at all the same as the question whether the idea is in fact a valid one" (Blaut 1993: 31).

Consciousness

Our understanding of events and the environment around us inform and are informed by our consciousness. Consciousness, an active and changing state—simultaneously both constitutive and constituting of our identities—is "the totality of one's thoughts, feelings and impressions, the awareness of one's acts and volitions" (Merchant 1989: 19). Consciousness is both individual and group and is shaped by both environment and culture. For Merchant, "[a] society's symbols and images of nature express its collective consciousness" (1989: 19). She reminds us that "forms of consciousness are power structures":

> When one worldview is challenged and replaced by another during a scientific or ecological revolution, power over society, nature, and space is at stake. Symbol systems, metaphors, and images express the implicit ethics of elites in positions of social power. (Merchant 1989: 22)

Theorizing consciousness in this way allows it to be collectivized beyond the individual and understood in terms of its social construction and its changeability over time and context. Aboriginal consciousness prior to colonial intervention has been named "mimetic." It was based on the insight that information comes from all sources, from all senses. "The Indians' face-to-face, oral-aural mode of transaction had been fully integrated with the other senses in daily survival" (Merchant 1989: 96). Sight, smell, sound, taste and touch were interconnected in a total "participatory consciousness" (Merchant 1989: 20). When Europeans took over Aboriginal lands, they introduced a form of consciousness based primarily on vision: "an observer distant from nature . . . knowledge modeled on perspective . . . a distant God substituted for the spirits within animals, trees, and fetishes" (Merchant 1989: 58). Knowing, for these colonists, was tied to the eye: "seeing is believing." This represented a shift from the integrative consciousness of Traditional peoples. Interconnectedness as a worldview was challenged by the domination of the colonizing mentality.

Current (dominant) forms of North American consciousness can be understood in terms of history and have changed over time through the interactions between Aboriginal and Western cultures. Europeans have sought to take power over Aboriginal forms of consciousness in order to meet their own social, economic and political agendas. The imposed shift in forms of cultural consciousness was a highly stressful process, which was actively resisted by some and acquiesced to by others. As E.P. Thompson states, "[T]he stress of the transition falls upon the whole culture: resistance to change and assent to change arises from the whole culture" (1991: 382). Unequal power relations defined this process.

Understanding consciousness as a form of historically and socially mediated cultural expression allows one to make distinctions between people and their systems. This makes room for alliances across racial and cultural divides. As Armstrong cautions, "[D]o not make the commonly made error that it is a people that we abhor, be clear that it is systems and processes which we must attack. Be clear that change in those systems will be promoted by people who can perceive intelligent and non-threatening alternatives" (1990b: 145).

Worldview

Collective consciousness can also be expressed as worldview. "A worldview is a set of images and assumptions about the world . . . . Since a worldview is knowledge about the world, what we are talking about here is epistemology, the theory of knowledge" (Kearney 1984: 10). Worldview is defined by Ortiz, a Tewa historian, as "a distinctive vision of reality which not only interprets and orders the places and events in the experience of a people, but lends form, direction, and continuity to life as well" (in Beck and Walters 1977: 5).

Traditional

In his definition, Ortiz reveals the link between worldview and Tradition. "Worldview provides people with a distinctive set of values, an identity, a feeling of rootedness, of belonging to a time and a place, and a felt sense of continuity with a tradition which transcends the experience of a single lifetime, a tradition which may be said to transcend even time" (in Beck and Walters 1977: 5).

The construct "Traditional" links geographical space and worldview. If the inhabitants of an environment have inhabited it for several generations or more, they will have come to perceive it and relate to it in a Traditional way. "This way of perceiving the environment is nothing more nor less than their worldview" (Kearney 1984: 119). How humans live on and use the Earth is foundational to any worldview analysis.

Merchant defines the ecological paradigm as having the following components:

> (1) [E]verything is connected to everything else in an integrated web; (2) the whole is greater than the sum of the parts; (3) nonhuman nature is active, dynamic, and responsive to human actions; (4) process, not parts, is primary; and (5) people and nature are a unified whole. (1989: 263)

She continues: "In the ecological model, humans are neither helpless victims nor arrogant dominators of nature, but active participants in the destiny of the webs of which they are a part" (Merchant 1989: 270). She proposes ecology as a "new worldview" that could "help resolve environmental problems rooted in the industrial-mechanistic mode of representing nature" (Merchant 1989: 270). The modern language of ecology makes "new" the Traditional worldview. Compared to the many thousands of years in which the general features of Aboriginal thought and society existed, the contemporary worldview is but a brief experiment (Kearney 1984). Ecology is visible in our Elders' stories, framed by the recurring theme of connection to people and the land over lifetimes. Paula Gunn Allen, a Laguna teacher, captures the relationship of movement and Tradition in this way: "The tribal systems are static in that all movement is related to all other movement—that is, harmonious and balanced or unified; they are not static in the sense that they do not allow or accept change" (1986: 56).

Culture

It is within this framework that the construct "culture" arises. Kahn defines culture broadly as "the environment in which things grow . . . . A person's environment determines much of what she is able or not able to do, to feel, to think" (1991: 325).

In Traditional times, culture was transmitted intergenerationally through imitation in song, myth, dance, sport, gathering, hunting and planting. "Oral-aural transmission of tribal knowledge through myth and transactions between animals, Indians, and neighbouring tribes produced sustainable relations between human and nonhuman worlds" (Merchant 1989: 20). Ancestors were once engaged in an intimate survival relationship with nature. But culture is not static; it is a "dialectic relation between individual and collectivity, and between collectivity and history" (Kearney 1984: 5). Cultures exist in history and are constantly self-creating by the necessity to respond to given conditions.

Indeed, few peoples make their own history and create their own culture. Shifts are often In-Relation to external conditions, and often in reaction to imposed hierarchical relationships. "Inevitably the more wealthy and powerful," Kearney asserts, "are most able to shape society in their interest and in response to the resistance offered by the less wealthy and powerful" (1984: 6).

Aboriginal Elders believe culture is enacted in our daily lives and evolves in connection to our environment. Culture is about Tradition, reaffirming our ties to Ancestral worldviews. Collins confirms that Afrocentric scholarship also reflects longstanding belief systems among African peoples: "The continuation of an Afrocentric worldview has been fundamental to African-Americans' resistance to racial oppression" (1991: 27). "Idea systems and culture in general, while having a certain autonomy are primarily responses—continuities—of that which has gone before" (Kearney 1984: 5). Culture then is both subject to the influences of domination and a tool of resistance.

Biculturality

Understanding the evolutionary nature of culture allows us to see that being Traditional in the modern context does not mean that Aboriginal people will return, or are able to return, to a way of life embodied by our Ancestors many moons ago before Europeans controlled our physical environment. As Barman, Hebert and McCaskill document:

> Canada's aboriginal peoples are not returning to a previous era; rather they are affirming their identity by selecting aspects of the old ways and blending them with the new . . . . In many Indian communities, people are emerging with bicultural identities, with an identity firmly anchored in the traditional cultural world of their people and a consciousness of the skills necessary to succeed in the dominant society. (1987: 5)

Bicultural consciousness is produced by the reality that Aboriginal identities in the contemporary Canadian context, whether by inclusion or exclusion, are all defined, identified and controlled by the Indian Act. According to Joane Cardinal-Schubert, a Cree artist, to be a Native in colonized Canada

> is to be in a position of powerlessness, to have absolutely no control over your identity . . . . The government declares by number who is Native and who is not and these numbers were, and continue to be, referred to as treaty and status numbers to indicate your 'official' and legal status as an Indian or Native. Under this system, whole families have been decimated for generations. (1992: 132)

Vine Deloria Jr. also comments on this modern-day cultural reality: "People are not allowed to be Indians and cannot become whites. They have been educated, as the old-timers would say, to think with their heads instead of their hearts" (1994: 242).

Categories such as "White" or "Indian" are not "natural" divisions, but rather are products of history and politics. As Jay confirms, this does not make such categories "false, unimportant, or unnecessary, but it does mean that we must accept some responsibility for them, whether we wish to advocate or deconstruct them" (1995: 119). Racial and cultural qualifiers "not only name but help shape the groups to which they are attached" (Jay 1995: 119). Certainly, analysis of the vocabulary associated with various racial groups, both historically and in contemporary society, reinforces this. Language and the power of attaching labels to identity is very much an ongoing political issue.

"The Indian Way"

Although consistent efforts have been made by authorities to officially construct our identities for us, we can resist by continuing to do things in "the Indian way." As Maeg says:

> If we are to be successful to any measure then we will have to be sure that we see the whole question we are faced with and deal with all of it in an Indian Way. It is the resistance of our forefathers and the continued resistance of our fathers that has left us with something to call ours. (in Armstrong 1988: 225)

"The Indian way" is a colloquialism embedded in the psyches of many Aboriginal people. It reflects a commonsense acknowledgment of a distinct worldview. Spoken among community members, it embodies an act of opposition, a method of communicating everyday resistance In-Relation to the "White way." It can be understood as an expression of the "lifeworld" as known to Native people, a signifier of an internalized identity intact in modern America. Many "inside" jokes and stories, which continue to evolve intergenerationally, have reinforced the dichotomized difference between the "Indian way" and the "White way" that was introduced through colonization. According to Said, "[W]e are still the inheritors of that style by which one is defined by the nation, which in turn derives its authority from a supposedly unbroken tradition" (1993: xxv).

We need to exercise caution in positing an "essential" Aboriginal identity. Qualifiers like "the Indian way" may act to obscure the variety of conditions—geographic, economic, cultural—and the complexity of influences interacting to inform the lived experience of an Aboriginal person in contemporary society today. While anthropologists have identified at least eight distinct culture areas in North America, Native peoples identify more than 300 distinct tribal groups. As Gotowiec and Beiser observe, "[C]ompounding socio-historical differences, individual choices to live on or off reserve, to follow traditional cultural values, majority-culture ways, or varying combinations of both, create an extremely diverse reality of aboriginal life in North America" (1994: 7).

It is possible to distinguish Aboriginal identity through physical appearance, to trace bloodlines and tribal affiliation and to identify those who grew up in predominantly Native communities. While Aboriginal people have been victimized by oppressive ideologies and practices in their many forms, and are implicated, directly or by association, in the current politics of First Nations, the focus of this text is more specifically on the retention and enhancement of Aboriginal consciousness. Many who follow the Traditional path claim to recognize ourselves in Ancestral tales. If we proclaim or are proclaimed to be Aboriginal, we know, are seeking or are mourning our Aboriginality. Many are calling on Ancestral memory, through ceremony, for our connection to this knowledge base. We are, as a people, reweaving the intricate web of our Traditional ways by doing things "the Indian way."

"The White Way"

To those who are still attuned to "the Indian way," the ways of the European colonizer are vivid in the stories of loss and are an integral part of the stories retained. As Russell Means, a Lakota activist, articulates, although European, Western and White may be used interchangeably, it is not specifically the race that is targeted. Rather, we are referring to "a mind-set, a worldview that is a product of the development of European culture. People are not genetically encoded to hold this outlook; they are acculturated to hold it" (Means 1980: 28). Jay theorizes "White" as a construct that "designates the supposed common culture binding diverse European immigrants" (1995: 124). He believes that since European ethnic and national groups did not constitute a common culture, "historiography had to invent one for them to help justify the project of colonialism and the institution of slavery" (Jay 1995: 124). Following Blaut (1993), Said (1993) and many Aboriginal writers, words like "European," "Western," "White" and "colonial" will be understood as code words for the currently dominant belief system. How this belief system has been implicated in the erosion of the unity and the diversity of Aboriginal Traditional worldviews will be one thread in the weaving of this text.

Eurocentrism

West contends that a knowledge of Eurocentrism's history is a necessary component of "a new cultural politics of difference" (1993: 204). McLaren concurs: we need to call attention to the "dominant meaning systems," which are "ideologically stitched into the fabric of Western imperialism and patriarchy" (1994: 214). Following Blaut (1993), Eurocentrism will be used as a label for all the beliefs, covert and expressed, that propose and/or reinforce past or present superiority of Europeans over non-Europeans. Some theorize it as sort of a prejudice, an "attitude" that could be eliminated along with racism and sexism.

> Eurocentrism is not just a matter of attitudes in the sense of values and prejudices, but rather a matter of science, scholarship, informed and expert opinion. Eurocentrism guides what is accepted as "empirical reality," "true," or "propositions supported by the 'facts.'" (Blaut 1993:9)

According to Clifford, the notion of evidence is bound by a "literalist epistemology"; it has "to exist or not exist as an objective documentary fact" (1988: 340). Yet what is most central to Aboriginal and many other cultures' existence was never written: "the surviving facts are largely the records of missionaries, government agents, outsiders" (Clifford 1988: 340). These "facts" are taken as verified "truth." One must reveal Eurocentrism to understand why it is very difficult to advance analysis that relies on an alternative set of beliefs and on a rearticulation of the commonly understood version of the "facts."

Academics and others are accustomed to ethnographic encounters that reveal the cultural belief sets of Aboriginal and other peoples. They are unaccustomed, however, to the application of similar analysis to "the White way." According to Blaut, when an ethnographic approach is applied to understanding and challenging White culture, "the results are disturbing and the enterprise itself seems somehow improper" (1993: 32). Some European descendants may wish to prevent the construction/unveiling of Eurocentrism as a globally dominant force. Reverence for diversity (ethnic, class, mind-set) is said to be ignored within this "essentialized" European construct. Some propose that the Europeans' descendants living on the North American continent today have evolved philosophically and technologically from their Ancestors. What about the ongoing exploitation of Mother Earth's resources to maintain a global, market-driven, export economy?

Eurocentrism, then, is "a 'unique' set of beliefs, and uniquely powerful because it is the intellectual and scholarly rationale for one of the most powerful social interests of the European elite" (Blaut 1993: 10).

Imperialism and Colonialism

Said's definitional work is clear. "'Imperialism' means the practice, the theory and the attitudes of a dominating metropolitan center ruling a distant territory; 'colonialism,' which is almost always a consequence of imperialism, is the implanting of settlements on distant territory" (Said 1993: 9). The connection between imperialism and colonialism is described succinctly: "At some very basic level, imperialism means thinking about, settling on, controlling land that you do not possess, that is distant, that is lived on and owned by others" (Said 1993: 7). According to Blaut, "[B]etween 1810 and 1860 or thereabouts Europeans subdued most of Asia, settled most of North America, and began the penetration of Africa" (1993: 22). The process of denying Aboriginal title and ownership and bestowing European place names exemplifies the appropriation and possession that was central to the European approach to space. As McMaster and Martin ask, "Why would colonists assume these lands were unclaimed and unnamed?" (1992: 12).

To engage in colonialism requires particular notions of the relationship between self and other. As Kearney tells it, "The individualistic Self is predisposed to competition and struggle with other persons and with the Other in general" (1984: 77). Throughout the colonization process there was a convergence of views in Europe about the nature and historical dynamics of the others—the "non-European world." As Said expresses it, "Throughout the exchange between Europeans and their 'others' that began systematically half a millennium ago, the one idea that has scarcely varied is that there is an 'us' and a 'them,' each quite settled, clear, unassailably self-evident" (1993: xxv). Taking their cues from a linear, mechanistic model, they theorized culture itself as evolutionary; from its very "primitive" beginnings, it progressed through European influence to a more "advanced" state—"a necessary though painful process for the non-Europeans" (Blaut 1993: 25). It was through the lens of capitalist profit that ideas about culture and people of other cultures were clarified, reinforced, criticized or rejected (Said 1993). As Blaut points out:

> Colonialism in its various forms, direct and indirect, was an immensely profitable business and considerable sums of money were invested in efforts to learn as much as possible about the people and resources of the regions to be conquered, dominated, and perhaps settled, and to learn as much as possible about the regions already conquered in order to facilitate the administration and economic exploitation of these regions. (1993: 23)

Colonial administrators and missionaries everywhere were required to submit detailed reports about Native legal systems, land tenure rules, production, reproduction, socialization, spiritual practices and much more. It is crucial to remember that most of what was learned and recorded and is now taught about Aboriginal peoples came from biased sources: "Europeans with very definite points of view, cultural, political, and religious lenses that forced them to see 'natives' in ways that were highly distorted" (Blaut 1993: 24). Europeans collected and used this information to meet their own ends, "explaining and justifying the individual acts of conquest, of repression, of exploitation. All of it was right, rational, and natural" (Blaut 1993: 26). Gloria Cranmer Webster, a Kwaquitle artist, expresses her understanding of the colonial worldview: "It was as if by thinking of our people in the worst possible terms, the white people could justify attempting to take complete control of our lands and our lives without reference to their own concept of justice" (1992: 30).

Many authors are working to unveil and better resist domination through an examination of Western language. McMaster and Martin provide a succinct summary of some relevant concepts:

> Humanism elevated the human being above all species, supported the imperative of human domination and justified the new age of imperialism. Rationalism's pragmatic approach created a milieu of curiosity, restlessness and the need to explain and explore. This culture of science

effectively reduced nature to a secular, rather than sacred, realm, and had long-lasting results in both technology and philosophy . . . . Finally materialism, the celebration and possession of material goods, dominated the ethical and religious frameworks of European society. (1992: 12)

Humanism, rationalism, "scientism" and materialism are all components of modernism. Todd reflects on the relationship of modernism and colonialism:

At the same time that modernism came into being, colonialism was intensifying. The colonies offered room for expansion and capital—including human capital—to fuel those technological developments . . . . Ironically, while Western thought was experiencing an Enlightenment and even revolution within its own cultures, it was also practising genocide through colonialism. (1992: 73–74)

The colonial period of European consciousness was characterized by objectification—an ideology that revered the domination by (European) humans of all life forms. Through this lens, all the beautiful and bounteous Gifts of Earth Mother became only objects for exploitation. The early colonial forms of consciousness evolved, continuously interlocked with the rise of capitalism. Capitalism emphasized efficient management and control of nature through the "development of mechanistic science and its use of perspective diagrams" (Merchant 1989: 22). "[T]he mechanistic model served to legitimate the human prediction, control, and manipulation of nature" (Merchant 1989: 199). European "progress" and increased wealth were achieved through the extraction of resources from the Earth by the "most efficient and profitable method" (Merchant 1989: 202). "The fences, fields, houses, roads, canals, and railroads that mapped the surface of the soil constrained it within grids imprinted by human minds that were guided by the goals of capitalist production" (Merchant 1989: 260). Evidence is plentiful to indicate how far industrial societies have become habituated to the industrial time sense. "Mature industrial societies of all varieties are marked by time-thrift and by a clear demarcation between 'work' and 'life'" (Thompson 1991: 399).

Pedagogical Violence

The Eurocentric colonial worldview allowed for and continues to perpetuate the pedagogical violence institutionally directed against our Aboriginal Ancestors and ourselves. We have been chronically excluded from educational systems and oppressed by dominant pedagogical forms. Education has classically and colonially been one tool by which industrial forms of consciousness were and are expanded beyond the dominant elites to include most others. Martin Carnoy argues that Western formal education came to most countries as part of imperialistic domination:

> It was consistent with the goals of imperialism: the economic and political control of the people in one country by the dominant class in another. The imperial powers attempted, through schooling, to train the colonized for roles that suited the colonizer. (1974: 3)

Blaut tells us that, "[s]trictly speaking, missionaries and colonial administrators were in the business of diffusing Europe to non-Europe" (1993: 24). This has historically been the case for Aboriginal peoples. Jo-Anne Fiske lodges residential schools within the service of the colonial order:

> The federal government saw them as essential to altering the Aboriginal economic order and to assimilating Aboriginal peoples into the dominant society; the missionaries saw them as necessary to transforming the Aboriginal moral order and to creating a segregated Christian society. (1991: 134)

Colonial forms of education, particularly residential schools, have contributed greatly to the efforts to eradicate Traditional forms of Aboriginal consciousness. The Ancestral practice of education as integral to daily life and to family and communal relationships shifted radically through colonial pedagogical measures. Merchant summarizes:

> The downfall of the Indians' memorized oral tradition and its replacement by a European system of thought, science, and education was a major epistemological transformation . . . . Seeing the written word provided the opportunity for individual recall without the emotional associations of song, rhyme, or rhythm of speech. Not recalling, but problem solving was what mattered; not repetition, but seeing and creating anew. (1989: 110)

Thompson (1991: 387) documents the more general role schools played in the process of inculcating "time-thrift": "Industry, Frugality, Order and Regularity" were taught through enforcing a chronological time sense. Celia Haig-Brown quotes a residential school survivor:

> In the morning, we had to get up at six o'clock, perfect silence. We all took turns going into the bathroom: we'd fill our basin full of water and we'd take it to our bedside. We'd wash, take that basin, empty it, clean it out, put it back, fix our bed, get dressed and as soon as your finished— you only had half an hour to do all this—brush your teeth, get in a line and stand in line in perfect silence. (1988: 54)

According to Gunn Allen, chronological time structuring is useful in promoting and supporting a sense of time required for "efficient" industrial production. "The idea that everything has a starting point and an ending point reflects accurately the process by which industry produced goods" (Gunn Allen 1986: 149).

Keeshig-Tobias makes visible the more subtle Eurocentric and linear biases of the educators, which devalued Ancestral Traditions, making them into historical artifacts, things of the past:

> All through school, remember, our growing up, remember, the holy sisters, the priests and the lay teachers they all told us such things did not and could not exist in the modern world, their world, the white man's world. That's why our culture faded away like worn out clothes and useless things cast away, and locked them deep inside, so deep that some of us couldn't even find them. It's no wonder we were so crazy mixed-up. It was like being chased by the wind. (1992: 109)

Eurocentrism predisposed the colonizers to believe that separation of children from their family and communities would best serve the longer-term interests of assimilation into the colonizer's "superior" culture. "There, attendance would be ensured, and all aspects of life, from dress to use of English language to behaviour, would be carefully regulated" (Barman, Hebert and McCaskill 1986: 6). Curriculum was limited to basic education combined with institutional maintenance (agriculture/household) "in order to prepare pupils for their expected future existence in the lower fringes of the dominant society" (Barman, Hebert and McCaskill 1986: 6).

Throughout the generations, the education of Aboriginal peoples has been an effort to transform our culture and worldview. As Dr. Marie Battiste, Mi'kmaq scholar, summarizes:

> Through ill-conceived government policies and plans, Aboriginal youths were subjected to a combination of powerful but profoundly distracting forces of cognitive imperialism and colonization . . . . In effect, education did little except equip Aboriginal youth with resentment and cynicism and erode human consciousness in Aboriginal communities. (Battiste and Barman 1995: vii)

Appropriating Voice

Aboriginal people in the schools were very aware of the "civilizing functions," including standard practices of "physical punishment for speaking their own language even when they knew no English" (Barman, Hebert and McCaskill 1986: 10). The colonization process, and in particular education, targeted oral Tradition—our voice. The decimation of our tribal languages is mourned by many. This process, aided by colonial education, is understood as one fundamental aspect of cultural genocide. Johnston eloquently expresses the Traditional view of the connections among transmission of an Aboriginal worldview, language and language loss:

> They lose not only the ability to express the simplest of daily sentiments and needs but they can no longer understand the ideas, concepts, insights, attitudes, rituals, ceremonies, institutions brought into being by their ancestors; and, having lost the power to understand, cannot sustain, enrich, or pass on their heritage. No longer will they think Indian or feel Indian. (1992: 10)

Language as a symbol system is always challenged as part of the power structure in an ecological revolution. Johnston asks: "[W]hat is it that has undermined the validity of some of the 'Indian' languages and deprived this generation and this society of the promise and the benefit of the wisdom and the knowledge embodied in tribal literature?" (1992: 15). He notes:

> In the case of the Beothuk and their language, the means used were simple and direct: it was the blade, the bludgeon, and the bullet. The speakers were annihilated . . . . In other instances, other means were used to put an end to the speaking of an "Indian" language . . . . If a boot or a fist were not administered, then a lash or a yardstick was plied until the "Indian" language was beaten out. To boot and fist and lash was added ridicule. (1992: 14, 16)

Ridicule was an effective tool against Aboriginal children who had been Traditionally exposed to Elders who used humour to challenge their conduct towards others. When combined with physical assault, the impacts were strongly felt. Johnston continues:

> Both speaker and his language were assailed. "What's the use of that language? It isn't polite to speak another language in the presence of other people. Learn English! That's the only way you're going to get ahead. How can you learn two languages at the same time? . . . How can you get your tongue around those sounds?" On and on the comments were made, disparaging, until in too many the language was shamed into silence and disuse. (1992: 15)

Language is an expression, a shaping force, and the transmitter of the culture; when it is lost the culture is crippled. York (1990) estimates that fifty of Canada's fifty-three Aboriginal languages are in danger of extinction. Thirteen languages are considered extremely endangered because there are fewer than a hundred speakers. "Once they disappear, they will be gone forever. There are no foreign countries where the language will be preserved" (York 1990: 36).

Today, appropriation of our voice is visible in the publishing industry: those who control whose voice gets heard. The book *I Am Woman*, by Lee Maracle (1988), is self-published, a choice she made to overcome the coercive powers of the dominant literary institution, which would make her "speak it right"/ "speak white." They would do this either by refusing to publish her text or by shaping it through the editorial process to fit the conventions of Native life-writing, as happened to Maria Campbell's *Halfbreed* (Lutz 1991). Maracle "will not keep silent about the oppression she has suffered. Nor, however, will she collude in the norms of the dominant discourse which values struggle negatively and privileges narratives which work toward unity and harmony in resolution" (Godard 1992: 213). McMaster and Martin discuss this perception:

> The stories which we would have liked to tell were largely appropriated and retold by non-Aboriginal "experts" in such fields as anthropology, art and history and especially in the political realm. Not surprisingly, the appropriated stories distort the realities of our histories, cultures and traditions. Underlying this paternalistic and damaging practice is the supposition that these "experts" have the right to retell these stories because of their superior status within the cultural and political constructs of our society. (1992: 17)

This "superior status" is now being challenged by many voices. McMaster and Martin aptly question:

> I want to say my own things to the world, and so, of course, given history, part of "my own things" is that you don't let me say anything. The question now is, will Euro-Americans want to hear the Aboriginal stories and come to accept them? (1992: 17)

Authenticity: Who Is the Real Indian?

The chronic history of appropriation of voice through the colonial process, as well as government appropriation of our right to define our own identities through the Indian Act, provides the context for the issue of authenticity. The search is on for the "real" Indian, someone who is authentic enough to be *the* authoritative voice on what an "Indian" is. Alfred Young Man, a Plains Cree artist and educator, explores authenticity:

> Are North American Indians "real"? Can a non-Indian do Native American art? . . . Does the loss of language necessarily imply cultural loss and if so why does this raise questions of whether or not an artist is still culturally a Native American? Who finally decides when an Indian is something other than an Indian? And when this "someone"

decides, why must it always be a "specialist"—someone who is mysteriously given authority by society at large—who decides rather than an Indian? (1992: 82)

The definition of authenticity is culturally biased by the Western mechanistic linear view of culture. The Western notion carries with it an expectation of geographical "roots," "a stable territorialized existence" (Clifford 1988: 338). Clifford challenges: "How rooted or settled should one expect 'tribal' Native Americans to be—aboriginally, in specific contact periods, and now in highly mobile twentieth century America?" (1988: 338). The Western mindset views cultures as "dying" rather than accounting for "complex historical processes of appropriation, compromise, subversion, masking, invention, and revival" (Clifford 1988: 339). Clifford observes: "Native American societies could not by definition be dynamic, inventive, or expansive. Indians were lovingly remembered in Edward Curtis' sepia photographs as proud, beautiful, and 'vanishing'" (1988: 284). A linear time sense allows some people to distance themselves from the Ancestors who so brutally colonized the Americas in our early history. As Gunn Allen states: "Having perceived us as belonging to history, they are free to emote over us, to re-create us in their history-based understanding, and dismiss our present lives as archaic and irrelevant to the times" (1986: 151).

The current battles over "cultural appropriation" and "authenticity" are arguments challenging the dominant interpretations of reality. While it is understood that the dominant group holds the power to "reward, punish, and control" (Blaut 1993: 39), and thereby may succeed in convincing most people that its interests—social, economic and political agendas—are the interests of everyone, this is not always the case.

Hegemony

The Eurocentric colonial worldview has highly influenced what is considered "theory" in today's educational settings. Said explored the "main fields of scientific, social, and cultural inquiry" and his findings were clear: "[W]ithout exceptions I know of, the paradigms for this topic have been drawn from what are considered exclusively Western sources" (1993: 41). Knowledge, critical theorists argue, is inextricably tied to power; "[W]hen [knowledge] becomes institutionalized, culturally accumulated, overly restrictive in its definitions, it must be actively opposed by a counter knowledge" (Clifford 1988: 56). Many who are acculturated to the dominant worldview assume that theirs is the most accurate and presumably adaptive worldview in the history of humanity. But Eurocentrism is at best an approximation of reality rather than an accurate image of it.

According to Said, "being on the inside shuts out the full experience of imperialism, edits it and subordinates it to the dominance of one Eurocentric and totalizing view" (1993: 28). The irony is that

> the imperial European would not or could not see that he or she was an
> imperialist, while the non-European in the same circumstances saw the
> European *only* as imperial. . . . Can one speak of imperialism as being
> so ingrained in nineteenth century Europe as to have become indistin-
> guishable from the culture as a whole? (Said 1993: 162)

Blaut informs us that

> the elite groupings of European countries together, in spite of their
> cultural (and national) differences, are a basic and permanent belief-
> holding group, and their beliefs form, to a large extent, a single
> ethnogeography and ethnoscience . . . . [T]hey have together under-
> written the production of a coherent belief system about the European
> world, the non-European world, and the interaction between the two.
> (1993: 33)

Said confirms that the British, French and American imperial experience has a
"unique coherence and a special cultural centrality" (1993: xxii).

To openly acknowledge the hegemony of Eurocentrism as a belief system
is controversial. Challenging Western cultural hegemony means acknowledging that for centuries Westerners have studied and spoken "on behalf of" the rest
of the world; the reverse has not been the case. Now I join with others in the
"immense wave of anti-colonial and ultimately anti-imperial activity, thought,
and revision" that has challenged and begun to overtake "the massive edifice of
Western empire" (Said 1993: 195). As Said tells it, it is the first time Westerners
have been required to confront themselves "as representatives of a culture and
even of races accused of crimes—crimes of violence, crimes of suppression,
crimes of conscience" (1993: 195). Such opposition confronts the deeply-rooted
denial embedded in the psyches of Westerners regarding their own cultural
hegemony.

According to Said, "[T]here is no minimizing the discrepant power established by imperialism and prolonged in the colonial encounter" (1993: 166). It
is important to not discount the intensity and depth of the impact of enforced
colonial practices on Aboriginal consciousness. The imposition of colonial
consciousness was understandably traumatic, especially given that it was European custom to make the Indigenous people change by either controlling us or
killing us! What would history have been like if the colonizers had simply
accepted their difference from the cultures they encountered and not criticized
Traditional customs and teachings? What might have happened if the colonizers
had respected geographical and ecological boundaries of various tribal societies
and had not tried to take over all the Native lands (Beck and Walters 1977)?

Resistance Retheorized:
The Native Perspective

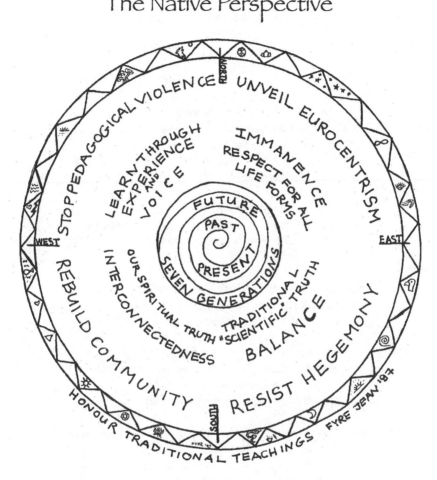

Eurocentrism
Colonial practices . . . Genocide
Delivered through Military, Missionaries, Politicians , Educators
Tried to make our Peoples . . . our Cultures . . . our Languages
Endangered species.
Render our stories of Resistance Invisible
In His-Story.

Our peoples have Resisted.
Do currently . . . and will continue to Resist
Acculturation . . . Assimilation . . . Extinction

In whatever the forms.
Honour is owed to the Ancestors
Keeping the Traditions Strong
Throughout the Persecutions.

Be Aware of the complexity
Authority and Resistance.
Multiple forms of both . . . Creating . . . Interacting
Sustaining each other.
All acts of Resistance
Are In-Relation to Authority . . . Force . . . Domination
An effort to break the Spirit . . . the Will.
Be aware
For every act of Authority . . . is Resistance . . . in some form
Embodied . . . Enacted
Our daily lived experience.
How we Resist is cultural . . . is context bound
As is how we exert Authority.

To heal we must Resist
Rather than embrace Authority . . . Authoritarian measures
Recognize Resistance as Strength . . . as a Survival skill.
Learn to nurture it, rather than squash it
Under increased Authority.
The White way is Not the Right way.
Control of Aboriginal people's lives by the State
Is disempowering
Spirals into apathy . . . continued Dependence.

Our peoples are moving beyond apathy . . . victimization
Embracing Resistance . . . Cultural Renaissance . . . Self-determination
Revitalizing . . . Reclaiming . . . the Gifts of our Ancestors.
Our-Story is being told in Circle form
Hear us speak Stories of Survival . . . Resistance
What fuels our fires? . . . What keeps us strong?

Theoretically and politically, the ground of Aboriginality as a discourse has not been established. Weedon observes that "in order to be effective and powerful a discourse needs a material base in established social institutions and practices" (1987: 100). She continues:

Not all discourses have the social power and authority which comes from a secure institutional location. Yet, in order to have a social effect,

> a discourse must at least be in circulation . . . . [It] can offer the
> discursive space from which the individual can resist dominant subject
> positions. (Weedon 1987: 111)

Aboriginal teachers/learners, looking towards the texts used in Western Schools, confront Eurocentrism, objectification, idealization and silence. The absence of Aboriginal consciousness, the silences and the negations offer clues to the suppression/oppression of the Aboriginal worldview. "A hegemonic culture relies as much upon negation as upon positive affirmation for its binding force. The more negation can be inscribed in silence, the more binding it will be" (Fox-Genovese 1991: 237).

The rearticulation of the experiences of oppression and acculturation in a White-dominated System can teach us many things, including the reality that the Western beliefs, versions of history and solutions to life's challenges are not necessarily ours. Those who are unaware of the stories of resistance and cultural renaissance assume that Aboriginal people must eventually yield to acculturation (Kahn 1991). Fox-Genovese discusses a similar theme in teaching feminism:

> The students worry that if power and its attendant violence have always
> been monopolized by men, there may be grounds for believing that
> they always will be. How can women identify with a record of our
> collective life that is only a record of their collective suppression and
> frequent brutalization? (1991: 227)

This text is an effort to resist hegemonic discourse, both by critiquing Western Eurocentric practices and by offering a revitalized version of Traditional Aboriginality.

I wish, as an "outsider within," to unveil and challenge the Eurocentric philosophies and pedagogies that currently define and confine my practice as an Aboriginal educator. This text is part of the countercurrent of resistance to dominant hegemonic forces in the world and, more specifically, in Schools. Following Said (1993), this work is a narrative of emancipation and enlightenment. In its strongest form, it is a narrative of *integration,* not separation. It can be read as a story of Aboriginal people/models who have been excluded from the main group, but who are now fighting for a place in it.

At this historical juncture, the voices of Aboriginal Elders, artists and scholars can no longer be effectively dismissed or silenced. Our interventions are an integral part of an existing political movement, and in many ways are "the movement's *successfully* guiding imagination" (Said 1993: 212). We are using our intellectual and figurative energy to resee and rethink our now shared but contested geographic and ideological terrain. According to Said, "For natives to want to lay claim to that terrain is, for many Westerners, an intolerable effrontery, for them to actually repossess it unthinkable" (1993: 212).

Aboriginal people have developed many forms of resistance, as varied as the attempts to change our ways of life. The impacts of colonization on Aboriginal consciousness have been far reaching. But the imposition of continuous colonial authority has been answered with multiple acts of resistance. This resistance has provided the foundation for the current renaissance movement. Clearly, one cannot argue for the revitalization of Aboriginal Tradition in the modern era if one believes that colonization as a force was successful in entirely "eliminating" the consciousness of Aboriginal Nations. Rather, it is argued that colonization as a force produces a counterforce of resistance; this is played out in the everyday expressions of consciousness and the material conditions of our lives. Said confirms:

> [I]t was the case nearly everywhere in the non-European world that the coming of the white man brought forth some sort of resistance . . . . Never was it the case that the imperial encounter pitted an active Western intruder against a supine or inert non-Western native; there was *always* some form of active resistance, and in the overwhelming majority of cases, the resistance finally won out. (1993: xii)

Freire also names resistance as universal: "The colonial process brings with it an incredible and dialectical counteraction. That is, there is no colonial intervention that does not provoke a reaction from the people about to be colonized" (1985: 183). One form of resisting is to insist that Aboriginal culture is not "vanishing;" our culture is not dead. To an anthropologist or archaeologist, trained in linear progression, cultures do die. To Native American Traditionalists, they do not. According to Young Man, "[F]ar from being a static entity, cosmology is dynamic, changing and moving through time as ritual moves through space . . . . All things exist in Wah'kon-tah and Wah'kon-tah exists in all things" (1992: 88). Our Traditions are not static, only functional in the past; they are forever changing to the new demands of our environments. Aboriginal cultures are "continuously in construction, deconstruction, and reconstruction as specifically ecological, political-economic and ideological processes impact on them" (Young Man 1992: 98).

To view Aboriginal Tradition as "lost" is ahistoric. The conditions of life colonially imposed upon Aboriginal people have involved the worst of treatments and have stimulated a crisis of large proportions today. Many authors document the efforts that have been made historically and are continuing to be made at every level to erase Aborginality, to eliminate or assimilate us, but we resist and survive.[1] I wish to reinforce the Traditional belief that the Elders, their stories and our Traditions still inform the construction of our identities, and so continue as a discourse. As Weedon states, "[N]ot all discourses in a given field carry equal weight or power, in any society one set of discourses is dominant, and it reflects particular values, and class, gender and racial interests" (1987: 36). While Aboriginality no longer is the shared worldview of all inhabitants of North America, it does continue to exist.

Decolonization

The process of decolonization, as articulated by Blaut, involves two parts. First, it is necessary to resurrect one's own history and to find out how it has contributed to the history of the world. Second, it is necessary to rewrite colonial history to show how it has led to poverty rather than progress. Trin Minh-ha poetically expresses this challenge: "You who understand the dehumanization of forced removal—relocation—reeducation—redefinition, the humiliation of having to falsify your own reality, your voice—you know" (1989: 80). The representation of the "Native perspective" defies what the Eurocentric popula-tion has known and has historically enshrined as "fact," namely the natural benefits accruing to the colonized from their encounters with a "superior" European state. We are challenging the complex system of denial that allows people to still believe that the exploitation of colonies and colonial peoples is morally justified because "[n]othing can fully compensate the Europeans for their gift of civilization to the colonies" (Blaut 1993: 16).

McMaster and Martin provide an apt summary of the Native perspective regarding the relationship between European and Aboriginal peoples: "In their ignorance of the cultural practices that had enabled Aboriginal people to flourish for centuries, the colonists introduced to the continent a legacy of conquest, conversion, cumulation and control" (1992: 12–13). These practices still continue today, disguised in the language of "modernization," a process by which now "decolonized" countries gain prosperity by accepting the continuous and increasing diffusion of economic and technological advancements from the "formerly" colonial countries.

Rewriting History

George Longfish, a Seneca/Tuscarora artist and educator, speaks his view of the "facts" of the colonial project:

> Change had a great effect on indigenous people who have gone from a culture closely in tune with nature and the environment to participa-tion in the industrial revolution, not to mention the spiritual revolution. Five hundred years later the non-Indians, who have had little respect for human rights, animal rights, or the earth's environment, are having to overcome their own ignorance and come to terms with the alterna-tive concept of making change that doesn't destroy the elements of this planet and its people. (1992: 150)

Aboriginal writers across tribal affiliation share a common and universal critique: the history of "Indian" and White relations, commonly referred to as "fact" in the textbooks, is socially constructed as an act of colonial privilege and power and must be challenged and reconstructed in the voices of Aboriginal peoples. In Fanon's words, "[B]y a kind of perverted logic it [colonialism] turns to the past of the oppressed group and distorts, disfigures and destroys it" (in Godard 1992: 199). Ortiz claims that "historical documents enshrine the worst images ever visited on Indian peoples . . . . Conventional history is so at odds with the facts that Indians often simply ignore it . . . . History is so distorted it is irrelevant" (in Sioui 1992: 59).

Decolonizing "subjects" insist on the right to see their community's history whole, coherently, integrally. They work to restore "the imprisoned nation to itself" (Said 1993: 215). Said asks, "How does a culture seeking to become independent of imperialism imagine its own past?" (1993: 214). We must recognize and resist our colonial identity

> as a willing servant [and discover our] essential, pre-colonial self . . . . To become aware of one's self as belonging to a subject people is the founding insight . . . . We must not minimize the shattering importance of that initial insight—peoples being conscious of themselves as prisoners in their own land . . . that sense of beleaguered imprisonment infused with a passion for community that grounds anti-imperial resistance in cultural effort. (Said 1993: 214)

Resistance itself needs to be retheorized and reformulated as "an alternative way of conceiving human history" (Said 1993: 216).

Rewriting history from the Native perspective requires highlighting the many acts of resistance engaged in by our Ancestors. Although the colonial powers enacted a belief-set based on their own cultural superiority, acculturation was not willingly accepted by Aboriginal peoples. Said documents how people around the globe have "banded together in asserting their resistance to what they perceived was an unjust practice against them, mainly for being what they were, i.e. non-Western" (1993: 218). "Opposition to a dominant structure arises out of a perceived, perhaps militant awareness on the part of individuals and groups outside and inside it that, for example, certain of its policies are wrong" (Said 1993: 240).

Resisting Schooling

Many recognized the efforts to colonize through pedagogical violence as wrong, and they individually and collectively resisted the enforcement of schooling. They failed to attend institutionalized educational settings. This prompted further authority measures, such as the passing of an act in 1920 to make attendance compulsory. Even with legal penalties and state imposed rights to take children to the schools, many families continued to resist. As a consequence, as late as 1951, eight out of every twenty Indians in Canada over the age of five possessed no formal schooling (Barman, Hebert and McCaskill 1986).

As Longfish acknowledges, "[W]hen we came to the new system to learn the wisdom of the dominant race, to our surprise we found that this wisdom involved little or limited information about or acknowledgment of Spirit" (1992: 150). Isabelle Knockwood (1992), a Mi'kmaq Elder, reinforces in her narrative of how our Ancestors withstood the strapping and other "spirit-stripping" measures enacted by the mission nuns. Fiske argues that while subordination of females was at least one agenda of residential schools, for some Carrier women at least, it was subverted. She states:

> Women resisted efforts to undermine their social position and to restrict their personal autonomy. Women and men selectively utilized novel skills and knowledge beneficial to themselves; in so doing, they effectively subverted the missionaries' intentions by broadening their economic strategies and by developing sophisticated political responses, which to a large measure were spearheaded by schooled female leadership. (Fiske 1991: 145)

The recent efforts to reveal acts of resistance to dominant educational processes is supported by Freirean theorizing. According to Freire, "[W]hen the dominated culture perceives the need to liberate itself, it discovers that it has to take the initiative and develop its own strategies as well as use those of the dominant culture. The dominated culture does this . . . to better fight against oppression" (1985: 193).

In order to put forward the Traditional worldview, we need to continue to challenge the Western paradigms that guide today's educational Systems. Continued resistance needs to be mounted, as Western educational models are still playing a large role in reinforcing altered forms of consciousness. Thinking with the head (cognition) as separable from the heart (feelings) is expected and continuously reinforced in Western schooling. Vine Deloria Jr., Lakota scholar, points out that education itself is a barrier to the revival of Tradition and community:

> As more Indians fight their way through the education system in search of job skills, their education will increasingly concentrate on the tangible and technical aspects of contemporary society and away from the sense of wonder and mystery that has traditionally characterized religious experiences. In almost the same way that young whites have rejected religion once they have made strides in education, young Indians who have received solid educations have rejected traditional religious experiences. Education and religion apparently do not mix. (1994: 247)

Reclaiming Subjectivity

We have had our immanent value as individuals and as a group devalued through colonial processes. The decolonizing process requires Native people to reclaim their own voices and subjectivities. "After all the academic discussion is over . . . in the end it is subjectivity that matters: our world views as they proclaim us, in images from our lives" (Todd 1992: 78). Subjectivity, according to Weedon, is "the conscious and unconscious thoughts and emotions of the individual, her sense of her self and her ways of understanding her relation to the world" (1987: 32). The subjectivity of individuals has recently been acknowledged as a contested terrain. The revitalization of the "Native perspective" can be articulated as "subjectivity in process" (Weedon 1987). When we resist a particular subject position and the mode of subjectivity it brings with it, we are doing so from the position of an alternative definition. Everything we do signifies compliance or resistance to dominant norms, so potential forms of resistance are "wide ranging encompassing all areas of social meaning . . . not all resistance is conscious" (Weedon 1987: 87).

Decolonization requires that we challenge the internalization of the structurally imposed reality of being victims and being inferior. Longfish asks:

> How do we rid ourselves of these ideas and concepts that result in low self-esteem? How do we better ourselves? The learning process revolves around identification. "Who are we?" We have a long history to review—we have been survivors. (1992: 150)

He poses the most frequently asked question of today's bicultural Aboriginal: "How can Native people separate themselves and integrate into a white society without losing themselves?" (Longfish 1992: 151). How can we bring our cultural and survival information with us without further victimization? Longfish offers his ideas on decolonization of the subject:

> The more we are able to own our religious, spiritual, and survival information, and even language, the less we can be controlled . . . . The more we get rid of the "stupid" pictures in our space and believe in our own abilities, the more we are able to make change work for ourselves. To rid ourselves of these pictures and own who we are is to take control and not play the game by white rules. (1992: 151)

Longfish's proposal of re-establishing a positive Aboriginal identity, in now Eurocentric America, offers the seeds of radical change. The process of taking control of our lands and our lives was facilitated by many colonial tactics, and it will take a multifaceted approach to achieve decolonization. According to Said, "[D]ecolonization is a very complex battle over the course of different political destinies, different histories and geographies, and it is replete with works of the imagination, scholarship, and counter-scholarship" (1993: 219).

Finding Our Voice

Decolonization requires and allows reclamation of voice. Voice is a complex, multifaceted, multilayered process. Traditionalists believe in the power of expression through voice—words are believed to be sacred. Spoken words/ sounds are one way of expressing our relatedness to each other: "speech is the materialization, externalization, and internalization of the vibration of forces . .. everything in the universe speaks" (Minh-ha 1989: 128). What we know, what we have learned from our lived experiences is embodied in our voices. When spoken and heard, Aboriginal voices pose a challenge to the dominant order of who speaks and who listens in Western society. "The voices of the unheard cannot help be of value," states Métis/Salish author Lee Maracle (1988: 1). Remember the words of McMaster and Martin: "I want to say my own things to the world, and so, of course, given history, part of 'my own things' is that you don't let me say anything" (1992: 23). Feminists articulate this as the "mute symptom of misery"; deprivation and oppression are overcome through the process of "speaking of bitterness" (Hart 1991: 68). We are reclaiming our voices. Through voice we speak/write of our acts of resistance, the healing and empowering values of our Traditions and the role of the European colonizers in the destruction of our communities. Through voice we are gaining our own sense of conscious reality and providing another lens through which Eurocentric educators may view themselves.

> With history being made up of the voices of all nations, all peoples instead of just one European people, the sand will be taken out of the eyes of Europeans showing them what their own history and worldview has been doing all these years. (Charnley 1990: 21)

Once our voices become heard in the struggle, the ground shifts. "There are now two sides, two nations, in combat " (Said 1993: 207).

Culture as Resistance

Cultural knowledge is an essential component of cultural resistance. Language and, in particular, the practice of a "national culture" are central to resisting cultural hegemony. Slogans, pamphlets, newspapers, stories, poetry and drama organize and sustain communal memory. Through acknowledging and revealing Ancestral ways of life, our cultural expressions can enhance emotions of pride as well as defiance. Local narratives, Elder's autobiographies and memoirs "form a counterpoint to the Western powers' monumental histories, official discourses, and panoptic quasi-scientific viewpoint" (Said 1993: 215). Gunn Allen describes our Ancestral oral Tradition as a vital form of resistance:

The oral tradition ... has, since contact with white people, been a major force in Indian resistance. It has kept the people conscious of their tribal identity, their spiritual traditions, and their connection to the land and her creatures. Contemporary poets and writers take their cue from the oral tradition, to which they return continuously for theme, symbol, structure, and motivating impulse as well as for the philosophic bias that animates our work. (1986: 53)

According to Gunn Allen, many have effectively resisted both colonization and genocide through focused attention on the retention of "Traditional ways" in the face of White domination:

American Indians in general have more often than not refused to engage in protest in their politics as in their fiction and poetry. They have chosen rather to focus on their own customs and traditions and to ignore the white man as much as possible. As a result they have been able to resist effectively both colonization and genocide. (1986: 82)

We are resisting by "writing back," by disrupting the European narratives and replacing them with either a more playful or a more powerful new narrative style. "The conscious effort to enter into the discourse of Europe and the West, to mix with it, transform it, to make it acknowledge marginalized or suppressed or forgotten histories is of particular importance . . ." (Said 1993: 216). Joe David, a Mohawk artist, provides a contemporary role model:

The catalyst for strong expression, logically, is direct involvement. I would not be compelled to make a strong statement, whether it be in print, paint or spoken word, had there not been this outrage, this anger engendered by an attack on my people. Strong emotions came with the realization that in Canada, the "colonial attitude" is alive and well, that "Might is Right" is still the doctrine practiced. Freedom, equality and justice are still relative as long as you are rich, white or subservient . . . . That is my perception: As Native people, that is our reality . . . . Part of the artist's role should be to jump into social issues: see a wrong and try to right it, learn a truth and try to paint it. Jump in with both feet, get dirty and feel the full spectrum of emotions. Take some responsibility. Use the tools of our trade to challenge the government's sanctioned version of the truth. (1992: 141)

Resistance as a Survival Strategy

Resistance for Aboriginal people has always been necessary for our survival, and activists' voices "in the thick of the battle" have "an understandable tendency to[wards] . . . combative, often strident assertiveness" (Said 1993:

274). Russel Means, a modern-day Lakota orator, inspires us to rearticulate the idea of resistance. He questions whether solutions posed by the White world can offer us answers to our present dilemmas, as it is "a culture which regularly confuses revolution with continuation, which confuses science and religion, which confuses revolt with resistance" (Means 1980: 38). Means expresses a sweeping challenge to the construction of "resistance" in Western theorizing when he states: "We resist not to overthrow a government or to take political power, but because it is natural to resist extermination, to survive. We don't want power over white institutions; we want white institutions to disappear. That's revolution" (1980: 31).

It is a revolutionary, utopian dream to envision a world in which Aboriginal people are free of colonial domination. We, as Aboriginal people, need to use our own cultural belief-set to inform the strategies used to battle against the colonial reality. Following Means, we need to critically analyze the notion of resistance as "essential" to our survival. We also need to critically interrogate the concept of "agency" as it applies to our quest for decolonization. Many Aboriginal Ancestors did resist actively with agency. This is evidenced historically in our acts of resistance and rebellion in the Red River areas and all across the country (Miller 1991). In many ways our people have resisted the imposed violence by the state, including brutalization by the RCMP and ongoing victimization in the "justice" system. We have taken collective stands against the continued military intervention brought to bear against our communities across this Nation; Oka, in Quebec, the Innu of Davis Inlet and the Haida at Clayquot Sound are some recent examples. We are informed by Said that "the slow and often bitterly disputed recovery of geographical territory which is at the heart of decolonization is preceded—as empire had been—by the charting of cultural territory" (1993: 209).

Politically, tribal communities—recently united as "First Nations"—have only now begun to see some success arising from their generations of struggle as a nation-wide resistance movement (Erasmus 1989). The shared cultural identity as Aboriginal, and political identity as "First Nations" of Canada, is strategic, just as the shared identity as "women" made possible the contemporary feminist movement (Spelman 1988). Today, the political arena is still governed by numbers, and collectivity is a precondition for voice. Politically, the agenda of self-determination requires a position of unity, evident in the language of "First Nations." Said asserts that nationalism, defined as "restoration of community, assertion of identity, emergence of new cultural practices" (1993: 218), has been mobilized as a political force in the struggle against Western domination everywhere in the non-European world. "Natives banded together in independence and nationalistic groupings that were based on a sense of identity which was ethnic, religious, or communal, and was opposed to further Western encroachment" (Said 1993: 218). Teaching nationalism is an expression of the need to find an "ideological basis for a wider unity than any known before" (Said 1993: 210). The basis of this unity is often found in the rediscovery and repatriation of suppressed cultural and spiritual practices. This process is inherently contradictory; to a certain degree we must work to recover forms already influenced and infiltrated by the culture of the colonizer.

Spiritual Resistance

In order to declare a "Native perspective," we must resist hegemonic Western perspectives and embrace our subjectivities as rooted in pre-colonial Traditional worldviews. According to Young Man:

> The Native perspective would prefer to state that Native art is, in fact, part of a continuum of Native American culture and metaphysical existence that has persisted for thousands of years with no loss of authenticity. Indian activism, as a concept for continuity, has been around for centuries and certainly was in existence at the time of Columbus. Though this fact has many detractors, it needs no further proof than the walking, Native Americans themselves, wherever they may be found on the American continent. (1992: 81)

To rediscover and repatriate a revitalized "Native perspective," we must first be able to acknowledge our Ancestors' multiple forms of resistance to colonization. We must honour the fact that, throughout the ordeals of five centuries of colonization, some Elders remained certain of the strength of their Traditional worldview. They were able to pass these values and practices to their children and grandchildren through stories and ceremony. Harold Goodsky, an Anishnabe, tells us that his grandmother counselled him to resist the acculturation policies:

> One thing that scared me is when I was young my grandmother told me never to speak English, never to go to church. "Because," she said, "if you do, you'll become half animal, half snake, and half man, and you'll be swimming in water all your life." (in Beck and Walters 1977: 165)

Many have resisted silently, inwardly, with their spirit, by refusing to change. Merchant acknowledges that, although Aboriginal discourse was losing ground as the dominant form as more and more colonizers arrived, with arms and diseases which resulted in a vast reduction of their numbers, "the surviving Indians maintained much of their tribal heritage, mythology, customs, and spirit" (1989: 98). Aboriginal forms of consciousness continue to survive today within the wider constraints of the now dominant Eurocentric consciousness.

Spiritual resistance can be manifested through ignoring—by continuing to practice your culture when you are told not to. Silence—the guarding of Ancestral secrets—has long been embraced by our Elders as a successful tool of resistance. As Clifford insightfully realizes:

> Accounts of conversion as a process of "giving up old ways" or "choosing a new path" usually reflect a wishful evangelism rather than the more complex realities of cultural change, resistance, and translation. Recent ethnohistorical scholarship has tended to show that Native Americans' response to Christianity was syncretic over the long run, almost never a radical either-or choice. Moreover, in situations of drastically unequal power . . . one should expect the familiar response of colonized persons: outward agreement and inner resistance. (1988: 303)

Vine Deloria Jr. records this pattern in some depth:

> The record of Indian resistance is admirable. When people saw that they could no longer practice their ceremonies in peace, they sought subterfuge in performing certain of the ceremonies. Choosing an American holiday or Christian religious day when the whites would themselves be celebrating, traditional Indians often performed their ceremonies "in honor of" George Washington or Memorial Day, thus fulfilling their own religious obligations while white bystanders glowed proudly to see a war dance or rain dance done on their behalf. (1994: 240)

Vietnamese Buddhist monk, Thich Nhat Hahn, captures the way resistance has had to become a daily-lived spiritual form:

> So perhaps, resistance means opposition to being invaded, occupied, assaulted and destroyed by the system. The purpose of resistance, here, is to seek the healing of yourself in order to be able to see clearly . . . . I think that communities of resistance should be places where people can return to themselves more easily, where the conditions are such that they can heal themselves and recover their wholeness. (in hooks 1990: 43)

Spiritual resistance flourishes through treasuring our children and honouring the visions and words of our Ancestors. We resist by recognizing our grandmothers' and mothers' political role in the "homeplace as a site of resistance" (hooks 1987) and by embracing the politicization of love as a powerful force that challenges and resists domination. The revitalization of our role as mother (Armstrong 1990a; Fiske 1992), the reaffirmation of the extended family and development of harmony in our sex roles (Battiste 1986) are all known means of sustaining spiritual resistance to encroaching, enforced European ways. Slash, a central character in Jeannette Armstrong's novel by the same name, encapsulates the heart of the spiritual renaissance: "All the questions that were unanswered for years suddenly seemed so simple . . . it wasn't a matter of belief. It was more, it was knowing for sure" (Armstrong 1988: 201).

This text explores the revitalization of Traditional Aboriginal spirituality as embedded in contemporary cultural forms and as translatable to a Western School context. It is part of the larger communal effort to continue to speak of an "Indian way" despite the systematic efforts to make us "vanish." While Westerners are "unaccustomed to viewing life as a totality," and therefore "cannot understand the persistence of the tribal peoples in preserving their communities, lands, and religions" (Deloria 1994: 292), we are resisting, surviving and thriving. Traditional Aboriginality is a current discourse. It is not only alive and well, but it is achieving a vital renaissance. This becomes more recognizable when it is acknowledged that Traditional worldviews can be located in both current factual analysis and fictionalized accounts. Republication of Deloria's text *God Is Red,* along with the recent increase in publication of Aboriginal material by Aboriginal people, attests to the spread of the "Native perspective."

According to Said, "[C]hanges cannot occur without the willingness of men and women to resist the pressures of colonial rule, to take up arms, to project ideas of liberation, and to imagine a new national community, to take the final plunge" (1993: 200). The ideas and the costs of colonial domination have to be challenged publicly until "representations of imperialism begin to lose their justification and legitimacy" (Said 1993: 200). To gain freedom from colonial oppression, we need to impress upon the hegemonic culture the independence and integrity of our own Traditional culture. We are cautioned by Said: "[T]he empire never gives anything out of goodwill. It cannot *give* Indians their freedom, but must be forced to yield it as the result of a protracted political, cultural, and sometimes military struggle that becomes more, not less adversarial as time goes on" (1993: 207).

Backlash

Aboriginal people have come through the "darkest era" of colonization and are now moving towards a more hopeful vision of the future through embracing and politicizing the Traditional forms of consciousness which were denied our Ancestors. The Eurocentric belief system is currently being challenged for its obliteration of the non-European role in history. The emergence of a critical body of thought, including the rewriting of history and reformulating all forms of discourse about "us," is a challenge that is occuring on the cultural terrain.

Notions of White superiority are deeply ingrained. According to Blaut, when one attempts to challenge Eurocentric beliefs, either from the inside or the outside, no matter how persuasive these arguments may be, they cannot be placed, so to speak, on one arm of a balance and be expected to outweigh all of the accumulated writings of generations of European scholars, textbook writers, journalists, publicists, and the rest, heaped up on the other arm of the balance. (1993: 9)

Said expresses a similar sentiment:

Whereas we write and speak as members of a small minority of marginal voices, our journalistic and academic critics belong to a wealthy system of interlocking informational and academic resources with newspapers, television networks, journals of opinion, and institutes at its disposal. (1993: 28)

Challenging Eurocentrism in the face of overwhelming denial is dangerous. According to Blaut, "[I]t has long been a truism that existing scientific beliefs tend to be defended in the face of new hypotheses that question them, and the defense is often fierce, bitter and dogmatic" (1993: 37). Efforts to represent other than the "reasonable," linear, "rational" and decidedly Eurocentric view of the history of our cultures' interrelatedness is a necessary resistance strategy. While declaring the "Native perspective" can feel empowering for the speaker, the reversal may be true for the non-Native audience. Young Man observes:

To an American Indian artist, Native perspective texts may seem all too true and absolute vindication. However, a Euro-Canadian who reads them may begin to feel uneasy and ultimately culpable in a very nasty historical drama indeed . . . . The Native perspective may not be easy to accept, particularly by those who feel adversely implicated by its conclusions. There is no escaping the dynamic theme once the wheels are set in motion. (1992: 83)

The message can be viewed negatively and the speakers labelled ungrateful: "Why don't they appreciate us, after all we did for them?" (Said 1993: 22).

I concur with Said: "And if the old and habitual ideas of the main group were not flexible or generous enough to admit new groups, then these ideas need changing, a far better thing to do than reject the emerging groups" (1993: xxvi). Unfortunately, rejection is all too often the result. Those putting forward alternative visions of the world are often marginalized and personally assassinated as "unreasonable," "irrational" or "over-emotional." As Blaut states, "[I]t is most unusual for a new hypothesis or theory to become accepted as a belief if it contradicts the corpus of accepted beliefs in its field" (1993: 40). But there is also an important countercurrent: "New hypotheses that display a touch of the novel and hold some possibility of solving an already recognized problem are encouraged, indeed rewarded" (Blaut 1993: 40).

While there are dangers inherent in proposing a "Native perspective" of history, culture and pedagogy, I recognize that the issue of cross cultural relations—locally, nationally and globally— is highly sensitive for educators, many of whom are reaching for alternatives. This produces a necessary countercurrent to the backlash reaped from challenging the status quo. I direct this Model to those who are ready to hear the message because they have recognized that their educative philosophies and pedagogies are not suitable or culturally sensitive to all peoples.

I agree with McLaren, as educators "we need to stare boldly and unflinchingly into the historical present and assume a narrative space where conditions may be created where students can tell their own stories, listen closely to the stories of others, and dream the dream of liberation" (1994: 217). Acknowledging and recognizing that, although our lives, our lessons and our students are seeped in colonial mentality, we still must accept responsibility to teach, and we can rely on Traditional forms to do so. I stand strong in my ability and my willingness to accept personal responsibility for understanding power and relationships and to share what I have learned through my own experience and voice. The remainder of this text will explore more specifically those philosophies believed to have Traditionally guided Aboriginal Ancestors and my attempts to introduce them to the Eurocentric classroom context.

Note
1.   See, for example, Miller 1991, Richardson 1989 and Knockwood 1992.

Revitalizing a Traditional Worldview

We as humans
Require plants and animals to Survive
They do Not require us.
We are dependent on Them
Yet we use them recklessly.
Mother Earth is raped of resources
Forests clear-cut . . . Fish and fowl mercury poisoned
Animals slaughtered . . . people starve to death
All to sustain material wealth.
Aboriginal people Traditionally have responsibility as Keepers of Earth.
Respect for all life must be taught to All people
Survival of Earth Mother depends on it.

Elders Teach:
Immanence . . . Respect for all life forms.
Balance . . . Our Traditional "scientific" truth.
Interconnectedness . . . Our spiritual truth.
Self-In-Relation . . . Our identity statement.
We learn by Doing . . . Ceremony . . . Stories of our Ancestors.

Elders say we Know, that is, we learn
Through direct experience . . . Observation
Face-to-face with the event . . . person . . . life force
We experience its Essence.
We learn what we Need to Know
What we Each need to know
What we are Open to . . . depending on Our life path.

Culture is our Collective Consciousness.
Embedded in the everyday lived experiences of a people.
How we challenge . . . Change . . . Survive in particular circumstances.
Culture is subject to the influence of domination.
A tool of resistance.

According to Aboriginal scholars, challenging the colonial order of things requires a dual approach. Jeanette Armstrong, an Okanagan educator, says that it will include

> the dispelling of lies and the telling of what really happened until *everyone*, including our own people understands that this condition did not happen through choice or some cultural defect on our part is important. Equally important is the affirmation of the true beauty of our people whose fundamental cooperative values resonated pacifism and predispositioned our cultures as vulnerable to the reprehensible value systems which promote domination and aggression. (1990b: 144)

Charnley also acknowledges that Traditional philosophies, which are distinguishable from colonial beliefs, must provide the basis for survival strategies, even in contemporary times:

> We must use our own understandings of wholeness and balance and not bend to the violent means of domination and separation that history has proven are the European's goals: "divide and conquer" as the old adage goes. "Unite and nurture" would be more to the First Nations person's way of thinking. (1990: 20)

Aboriginal authors in this era are beginning to reclaim their history and rearticulate the belief systems that we understand to be underlying the "lifeworlds" of our Ancestors prior to colonization. These efforts, as documented by modern-day artists, shamans, Elders, anthropologists, historians and educators from diverse Aboriginal tribal affiliations, will provide an articulation of an understanding of the foundations of a Traditional worldview.

Spiritual practices are understood by Traditionalists to have allowed the Ancestors to live cooperatively prior to colonization, and to survive the processes inflicted on them since. This is an effort to construct a web of understanding, to weave together a pattern of thoughts—beliefs articulated into words—acknowledging what this generation of Aboriginal people has to say about the gifts of our Ancestral heritage. While the environmental context has shifted incredibly over the last 500 years—the Ancestral forms of understanding and relating to our Earth Mother, necessary for subsistence and harmonious existence prior to industrialization, are now being applied to a different set of survival challenges. Given the history of appropriation, the prescriptions of the English language and the politics of publishing, all of which have distorted written transmission, efforts have been made to base this section on examples from the oral Traditions of Aboriginal people. Traditional knowledge has been "constructed" for use within this analysis through excerpts from interviews, speeches, prayers, songs, conversations and other documented sources. I am conscious of the debates of cultural "authenticity" and recognize that any move from oral Tradition to the written word requires an act of translation and participation in a cultural practice that is not of the Ancestors' making. Words and the oral Tradition have long been our teaching tools; the written word, "paper stories" (Cruikshank 1992) are only recently being embraced as avenues for cultural revitalization.

The Traditional Worldview

The philosophical foundations underlying our Ancestral cultural practices are the "common sense" of our Traditional societies and are perceived as inseparable from the "ordinary" daily lived experiences of Traditionalists today. As Aua, an Iglulik shaman, says, "[I]n our ordinary, everyday life we do not think much about all these things, and it is only now you ask that so many thoughts arise in my head of long-known things; old thoughts, but as it were, becoming altogether new when one has put them into words . . ." (in Beck and Walters 1977: 8). Aua expresses a contemporary sentiment that speech acts give meaning to reality, as well as describe it. Raes (1992) notes that speech is not "unmediated" but rather it is influenced by the structure and rules by which speech is determined. It is only within a contemporary context that Aboriginal Traditional foundations are being articulated in this way. Prior to colonization, Aboriginal systems of thought were incorporated into our daily lives. It was the dominant mode of consciousness. Patterned into our unconscious through stories, rituals and humour and enacted in everyday experiences, Aboriginality was common to all members of North American society. Today, we represent a numerical minority: our worldview has been ravaged by colonialism. We now revitalize our Traditions under pressure from a hostile environment. As Harding notes, "After all, why would anyone bother to articulate a theory of knowledge of her beliefs if the ground for those beliefs were not challenged?" (1990: 87).

I wish to articulate the "commonsense" foundations of early tribal "lifeworlds" in order to apply them. In this case, I am working in a School, a context that has been constructed as part of Aboriginal existence only since colonial invasion. This is part of the effort to reconstruct and revitalize a Traditional "belief set," which can act as a unifying force among diverse tribal groups. Several constructs—immanence, balance, interconnectedness, Self-In-Relation and learning through doing—have been developed and will be explored.

Immanence: Respect for All Life Forms

Aboriginal Traditionalists respect "immanence," that is, we share a *belief in, knowledge of and respect for unseen powers*. These unseen powers are non-material energy, "something loose about the world and contained in a more or less condensed degree by every object" (de Angulo in Beck and Walters 1977: 2). These mysterious powers are found in all Earth's creatures: rocks and crystals, birds and feathers, trees and wood, plants, animals and humans, and are visible especially in dreams and visions and through ceremony. In our world all things have inherent value, because all things are beings.

Georges Sioui, a Wendayette artist, expresses a similar view: "Amerindians lived in integral democracy that included not only human beings (or certain categories of them), but all beings of all orders" (1992: 67). "We do not have to earn value. Immanent value cannot be rated or compared. No one, nothing, can have more of it than another. Nor can we lose it. For we are, ourselves, the living body of the sacred" (Starhawk 1987: 15).

These mysterious powers are manifested and observable in the way the seasons change, the way the day follows night, the way the sun moves across the sky. All the physical changes throughout the day—from the colours and sounds of dawn through the afternoon to the stillness of nighttime—all these changes have personalities, are forms of energy shape-shifting. Ongoing cyclical changes affect each one of us and we learn to read the signs they show us, to learn from Mother Earth herself how to change and adapt to ongoing demands. Growth itself, the germination of seeds and the stages of the life cycle are all part of the great mystery of life (Beck and Walters 1977). Eva McKay, a Cree Elder, expresses a Traditional sense of reality:

> Native People are very close to nature. When we come into buildings such as this we feel closed in, like budgies in a cage. The evening sunset

indicates the end of the day, the early dawn when the birds start chirping tells us there's a new day, there's new life. The sunset and early morning give us a spiritual feeling. The world is a spiritual creation of the Great Spirit who has also given us breath . . . . Should you become weak, strengthen yourself by looking at the world around you, and see that you are not alone in the sacredness of life which was, and is and always will be. (1992: 346)

Cycles of growth and change are often marked by collective rituals and ceremonies to recognize the spirits of the seasons, to honour and thank them for the good they bring and to ward off the negative aspects: dread, fear, disease and disaster (Beck and Walters 1977). Power is understood as all-pervasive and consistent. Through knowledge of it, we can come to understand it and thus utilize it to advantage. Knowledge in this sense is "virtually synonymous with power" (Kearney 1984: 148).

According to Deloria, the world that the Traditional person experiences is dominated by the presence of power, which manifests itself as life energies—"the whole life-flow of a creation" (1994: 88).

Recognition that the human beings hold an important place in such a creation is tempered by the thought that they are dependent on everything in creation for their existence . . . the awareness of the meaning of life comes from observing how the various living things appear to mesh to provide a whole tapestry. (Deloria 1994: 88)

Sacred oral Tradition deals with all these aspects of life and power and teaches us how to find our place within the world around us. Our universe is based on an understanding of "dynamic self-esteem"; the "ability of all creatures to share in the process of ongoing creation makes all things sacred" (Gunn Allen 1986: 57). To Cree Medicine woman, Twyla, "[U]nity is the great spiritual law . . . the law of nature . . . . Everything had its place, and everything works in unison . . . equality to the Indian meant that everything in this universe had a place" (in Steiger 1984: 110). Malcolm Saulis, a Maliseet educator, concurs with Twyla:

A universal sense among native people exists in regard to spirituality and that it coexists in all aspects of life. It is not separate but integral, it is not immutable, it is not replaceable, it resides in the essence of the person, and it is not always definable. It is in the community and among the people, it needs to be expressed among the people. (1994: 15)

Balance: Traditional Scientific "Truth"

Our Aboriginal Ancestors relied on Mother Earth as our metaphor for all of life. The complexity of daily subsistence required a shared vision, a clear understanding of and respect for the interconnectedness of all life. Understanding and describing the balancing of various forms of energy is a foundation of Traditional "science."

Donawaak, a Tlinget Elder, gives advice that reflects a Traditional relationship to our sister, the tree:

> The foundation, you have to know your roots, where you are coming from .... You see a tree that is weak, about to give up. Sometimes you find people like that. Why is that tree just barely making it. Because the roots are not strong. If the roots are solid and strong, then you see the tree is strong and pretty. It can withstand cold, hot weather and winds. The human has to have those roots because we are growing too .... We are put here with them. We are also part of the plant life. We are always growing, we have to have strong roots. (in Colorado 1988: 601)

Seeking the roots, their functions and the relationships and connections between things forms the basis of Aboriginal scientific methodology. As Deloria says, "[T]he universe is alive" (1986: 6). To see a Native speaking with a tree or a crow does not carry the message of mental imbalance, but rather is a "scientist" engaged in "research." Barney Mitchell, a Navajo teacher, says that "the greatest sacred thing is knowing the *order and structure of things*" (emphasis added; in Beck and Walters 1977: 11). The knowledge necessary to achieve balance is represented in the Medicine Wheel.

Medicine people, shamans, who studied Mother Earth and her mysteries found that everything is made up of four elements: air, light (fire), water and earth. Each aspect of creation, all plants, animals, humans and other energy forms, maintain their "shape" by a balance of these elements in their structures. Learning and teaching in the Traditional way embraces the mental, spiritual, emotional and physical aspects of the individual, the family, the community and Mother Earth as a whole. According to Deloria, "[T]he task or role of the tribal religions is to relate the community of people to each and every facet of creation as they have experienced it" (1994: 85). Tribal religions function "to determine the proper relationship that people of the tribe must have with other living things and to develop the self-discipline within the tribal community so that [people act] harmoniously with other creatures" (Deloria 1994: 88).

Interconnectedness: Our Spiritual Truth

We are taught a common understanding of interconnectedness: that all things are dependent on each other. All things and all people, though we have our own individual gifts and special place, are dependent on and share in the growth and work of everything and everyone else. We believe that beings thrive when there is a web of interconnectedness between the individual and the community and between the community and nature.

Our community prospers when the work that each member performs is in alignment with the Earth and is a direct and sacred expression of Spirit. In Aboriginal Traditional forms, the spiritual infuses a person's entire existence within the world. A spiritual connection helps not only to integrate our self as a unified entity, but also to integrate the individual into the world as a whole. Spirituality is experienced as an ongoing process, allowing the individual to move towards experiencing connection—to family, community, society and Mother Earth.

Traditionalists believe that a healthy and prosperous culture is one that lives within the fundamental laws of reciprocity, where no more is taken than will be returned. According to Maggie Hodgson, a Cree healer, Aboriginal culture's greatest strength is our community-mindedness: "In keeping with the Native way, what they receive is given back to the community as their spirits touch the community in a healing way" (1990: 38). "It is spiritual connectedness between and within all that exists that has been one of our greatest weapons, healers, liberators in our battles against genocide" (Charnley 1990: 18). Our Elders teach us that to be without relations is to be really poor.

To recognize interconnectedness is to know oneself as part of a vast circle in which all expressions of life—the birds, animals, trees, insects, rocks—are our brothers and sisters, are all equally beloved and vital to our Mother Earth (Medicine Eagle 1991). "The American Indian sees all creatures as relatives (and in tribal systems relationship is central), as offspring of the Great Mystery, as co-creators, as children of other mother, and as necessary parts of an ordered, balanced, and living whole" (Gunn Allen 1986: 59). The idea of kinship is based upon the concrete observation that each of us is totally dependent upon the same things. All of nature is in us, all of us is in nature.

> We can stop very quickly and think about what this means. If we lose our hands, we can still live. If we lose our arms, we can still live. If we lose our legs, our noses, our hair—all kinds of other things—we can still live. But if we lose the air, we will die immediately. If we lose the water, the plants, the earth, the animals we will die. We are more dependent upon those things than we are upon what we call the body. As a matter of fact, we don't really have a body separate from these other things. (Forbes 1979: 3)

We are like one big family with "all our relations." Nothing we do, we do by ourselves; together we form a circle. That which the trees exhale, I inhale. That which I exhale, the trees inhale. We live in a world of many circles; these circles go out into the universe and constitute our identity, our kinship, our relations. As George Manuel, a Plains historian, suggests, "[O]ur ideologies and religions respect all life . . . even as [hu]man has life, air and sun have life, deer, moose have life. Our religions teach us that Mother Earth is the giver of all life including our own life" (1974: 40).

Our images of relationship are a part of past collective experience and shape our strategies for interacting with social and physical aspects of others in the present. Traditionalists view self as intimately interconnected with others, well-being as dependent on the well-being of other life forms. "Ecological conscious-ness" (Kearney 1984: 74), common in Traditional societies, predisposes the self to be more altruistic. Acting in the best interest of others, and in the interest of the world in general, becomes consistent with self-interest. Rather than a concern with "power over," there is a need to balance and harmonize the multiple and ongoing relationships between self and other. According to Gunn Allen, "[T]hose reared in traditional Indian societies are inclined to relate events and experiences to one another. They do not organize perceptions or external events in terms of dualities or priorities" (1986: 58). Throughout the remainder of this text, I will refer to this worldview as Self-In-Relation.

Self-In-Relation: Our Identity Statement

Aboriginal Traditionalists have long recognized the link between individual responsibility and community well-being. The knowledge that each person is responsible for his or her actions In-Relation to the larger community is a fundamental shared belief. Self-In-Relation is linked to a tribal worldview and is very important in the formation of an Aboriginal identity. A person must first know him- or herself and his or her family line, tribal nation and responsibilities to all relations if he or she is to function within an Aboriginal identity (McCaskill 1987). According to Paula Gunn Allen, "An American Indian woman is primarily defined by her tribal identity. In her eyes, her destiny is necessarily that of her people, and her sense of herself as a woman is first and foremost prescribed by her tribe" (1986: 43). According to the Traditional view, an Aboriginal identity provides a framework of values upon which one views life, the natural world and one's place in it.

Madeleine Dion Stout, a Cree educator, works to conceptualize an Indigenous model of human relations, which is both "multigenerational" and "transdirectional." She reveals several key components related to the construction of Aboriginal identity:

1. discovering the centrality of *self*, especially individual will and ability or "medicine";
2. transmitting individual power to *family* through values, attitudes, behaviour and institutions;
3. extending the family to the broader end of *community* and developing *agency* to connect diverse groups of people;
4. challenging the existing imbalances between the cultural/structural divide of all peoples of the *world;* and;
5. recreating *self* in solidarity with those who are, those who have been and those who are yet to be. (Dion Stout 1994: 14–5)

To the Traditionalist, the individual is only knowable as a member of a specified community, and communities are only recognizable through their constituents. As Madeline Dion Stout instructs us, "[M]orality and the duty and obligation found in community, is at once the domain of the individual and the collective. By merely tracing the spiral from its periphery to its center and vice versa, a unique and free individual is revealed" (1994: 15–16).

Figure 1: All My Relations: The main characteristics of a multigenerational and transdirectional model of Self-In-Relation to Others

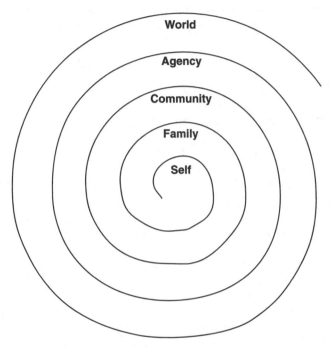

Source: Maggie Hodgson, personal communications; Madeleine Dion Stout (1994: 15)

We are able to see ourselves and our immanent value as related to and interconnected with others—family, community, the world, those behind and those yet to come. Through embracing this worldview, each individual becomes intensely aware of personal accountability for the welfare of others. We are taught that we must, each in our own way and according to the dictates of our own conscience, attend to communal responsibilities. Personal awareness of intergenerational responsibility and "proper conduct" are still expected throughout the life cycle. Although we exist together in community, we are all taught to understand that

> in the end you are alone—that is, you have to make decisions for yourself, decisions that will effect the community and the natural world. Therefore personal awareness is at the heart of responsibility: to be aware of what is going on around you and what life holds in store for you—all of life's possibilities throughout your life to Old Age. (Beck and Walters 1977: 63)

The poem "Creation" by Lee Maracle expresses a contemporary translation of personal responsibility:

> I know nothing
> of great mysteries
> know less of creation
> I do know
> that the farther backward
> in time that I travel
> the more grandmothers
> and the farther forward
> the more grandchildren
> I am obligated to both.
> (in Grant 1992: 338)

The individual was taught to be responsible for his- or herself, but not in isolation from the community or the natural world. Forbes expresses a Traditional view:

> A person who has developed his [or her] character to its highest degree, and who is on that path, will also be able to master specific skills. But if they don't have that spiritual core, they will use those skills to hurt other people . . . . They have the skills, but they have no morals. They will do whatever they are paid to do. So knowledge without the spiritual core is a very dangerous thing. (1979: 11)

According to Gunn Allen, the perception of humanity collectively rather than individually as "cocreator" discourages people from "setting themselves up as potentates, tyrants, dictators, or leaders of any other kind" (1986: 67). She clarifies the link between our understanding of relationship and other aspects of worldview. She illustrates how our beliefs about interconnectedness are integral to our sense of time and space. Native Americans view "space as spherical and time as cyclical . . . the circular concept requires all 'points' that make up the sphere of being to have a significant identity and function, while the linear model assumes that some 'points' are more significant than others" (Gunn Allen 1986: 59). She argues against the linear notion of time and posits an essential Aboriginal sense of time, which has persisted throughout time and is based on a ceremonial and circular understanding of order and harmony.

> For an Indian, if being on time means being out of harmony with self and ritual, the Indian will be "late." The right timing for a tribal Indian is the time when he or she is in balance with the flow of the four rivers of life. That is, Indian time rests on a perception of individuals as part

of an entire gestalt in which fittingness is not a matter of how gear teeth mesh with each other but rather how the person meshes with the revolving of the seasons, the land, and the mythic reality that shapes all life into significance. (Gunn Allen 1986: 154)

Traditional Pedagogies: Learning through Experience and Voice

In the Traditional worldview, high value is placed on communal/family responsibility, particularly the obligation to educate children in a holistic way. The Traditional way encompassed all aspects of the person's life, In-Relation to the world around her or him. "Learning emphasized such values as respect for all living things, sharing, self-reliance, individual responsibility, and 'proper conduct.' Children also had to learn how to utilize the environment most effectively for economic survival" (Barman, Hebert and McCaskill 1986: 3).

Recognizing immanence as the essential spirit and energy of all creation, we show respect and learn from all of our teachers. As Brooke Medicine Eagle, Métis shaman, asks:

> Do you recognize your teachers in All Our Relations—in all their surprising forms? Do you take to heart the profound wisdom voiced from time to time by the little children in your life? Are you willing to learn from the simple grasses of the Earth about the importance of flexibility and tenaciousness? What have you learned from your family pets? (1991: 32)

Part of enacting our responsibility has to do with seeking knowledge in experience and stories ourselves, using our own bodies and senses to learn. Learning the way means going directly to the source. The people experienced life with their entire bodies, with all their senses including language and thought, to find the answers to these questions and to aid in their understanding of themselves and their world. Knowledge was integrated with experience and wisdom with divinity. To focus us on our own learning process, the Elders stressed listening and waiting and not asking why. "You don't ask questions when you grow up. You watch and listen and wait, and the answer will come to you. It is yours then, not like learning in school" (Larry Bird, quoted in Beck and Walters 1977: 51).

Methods of learning shamanism involve meeting spirit guides who will accompany us through life as teachers, special guardians and helpers. We find spirit helpers in our solitude, out in nature, usually while fasting and sometimes during a vision quest. We find them "by watching patiently and without expectation, by exercising instinctual perception sensitized to be able to recognize the many vibrations and currents of the earth and finally to be able to see the invisible world and its entities" (Lorler 1989: 28).

For this reason, silence is sacred. The origin of language and the power to speak with plants and animals is a mysterious thing, learned and known by only a few people. The only way a person can learn the language of the wind, trees and streams is to be silent for a long time, making silence an important part of sacred language, prayer and song (Beck and Walters 1977). A great part of our beliefs is grounded in respect for the immanent powers and listening silently to learn from them. This is reflected in Aboriginal "mimetic" consciousness, "an integration of all the senses with the body in sustaining life" (Merchant 1989: 20).

Traditionally, no special educational institutes existed. Everyday lived experience and the sacred, as manifested within the social group as a whole, was the "school" of our Ancestors. "The practical and the religious, the manual and the intellectual, the individual and the social flowed as one complex integrated function" (Gresko 1986: 89). A central theme within this informal educational model was learner initiation and direction of the process; instruction was provided upon request, after observation and reflection by the learner (Sterling and Hebert 1984: 295). Mead argues that conversion, "purposefully attempting to alter the ideas and attitudes of other persons," did not occur in tribal societies (1942: 634) .

My Elders cautioned, "Too much thought only leads to trouble"; "keep your eyes open and your mouth shut"; and "there is more to life than meets the eye." By this they meant to educate me as to the foundations of truth in Aboriginal society: accept as knowledge only what can be fully assimilated into daily experience. "True knowledge is considered to be that which is derived from experience. Events are viewed personally and knowledge must enable the individual to survive in the bush" (Bowers 1983: 939).

The Ancestral Traditional beliefs provided a strong code of morals and ethics, which set the limits and boundaries for the way in which individuals ordered their behaviour with each other. Beliefs reinforced by our Ancestors are being revitalized today through Traditional methods of healing and teaching, ceremony and storytelling.

Ceremony as Pedagogy

Through Traditional use of ceremony, each community member enacts a personal commitment to the "sources of life." This is intended to make us aware of the effects of our actions on ourselves, the community and Mother Earth. Our beliefs are evident and reinforced when we recognize the powers of the unseen and begin by calling in the powers of the Directions. "This is done to invite the archetypical qualities of the cardinal points, that they might bear witness, lend support, and impart wisdom to our endeavors. This acknowledges that we human beings need help" (Cahill and Halpern 1992: 37). Speeches, stories and songs recall our personal responsibility to continually reestablish our links to each other and to all of creation. These basic principles are acted out so that they can be well understood by everyone. However, not all aspects of the ritual will be understood by everyone, as some knowledge is "learned and rehearsed in secret, under the supervision of specialists" (Beck and Walters 1977: 37). The community shares a physical experience, marking important changes in the Earth (seasons and moons) and in the lives of individuals (birth, naming, puberty and death) to make the person aware of the meaning of life and his or her contribution to the community. Ceremonies are physical enactments, performed collectively; "they appeal to the emotions, to the imagination, and to the intensity of feelings in each individual and in the group as a whole" (Beck and Walters 1977: 38).

Gunn Allen defines ritual as "a procedure whose purpose is to transform someone or something from one condition or state to another" (1986: 80). The purpose of ceremony is to integrate, to connect the individual with his or her fellow humans and to link the community of people with that of the other life forms. We are to understand that this larger communal group, what we know and experience as our world, is interconnected with the worlds beyond this one. "A raising or expansion of individual consciousness naturally accompanies this process. The person sheds the isolated, individual personality and is restored to conscious harmony with the universe" (Gunn Allen 1986: 62).

Ceremony is the physical embodiment of Self-In-Relation. It provides the unconscious and conscious foundations for the everyday practice of respect for the immanence of all other aspects of creation. This respect includes other humans who share our context, those who have gone before and those yet unborn. Reinforcing the fundamental law of reciprocity uplifts community mindedness, which is one of the central survival mechanisms in our struggles for maintenance of a collective identity in the face of encroaching individualism. Elder Xaye t'an, a Tewa, explains:

> [T]he purpose of our ceremonies is not entertainment but attainment; namely, the attainment of a good life. Our dramas, our songs, and our dances are not performed for fun as they might be in the white man's world; no, they are more than that; they are the very essence of our lives; they are sacred .... [In Traditional practices,] during the time of a ceremony, a drama, a dance, the entire atmosphere of the community is charged with excitement and many special activities go on. Special foods are prepared, special decorations are made for costumes and homes, special prayer-sticks constructed, special songs composed—in short, a circle is drawn around the community and everything within that circle is sacred and taken out of the ordinary. (Beck and Walters 1977: 39)

Prior to ceremony, "certain procedures are followed in order to prepare the mind and the body to be receptive, to be aware . . . you want to make yourself receptive to knowledge and divinity" (Beck and Walters 1977: 23).

> Our Native Elders have taught us that before a person can be healed or heal another, they must be cleansed of any bad feelings, negative thoughts, bad spirits, or negative energy—cleansed both physically and spiritually. This helps the healing come through in a clear way, without being distorted or sidetracked by negative "stuff" in either the healer or the patient. (Broden and Coyote 1991: 1)

Spiritual fasting is conducted with the guidance of an Elder or respected healer and is done in a natural setting. By surrendering our physical needs for water and food and engaging in ceremony while out on the land, we can open up our senses and our spirits to our Earth Mother. Fasting helps to cleanse the body of "toxins that are stored from keeping old anger and fear in [the] body" (Phyllis in Hodgson 1990: 44). Another common procedure for purifying the mind and body is "smudging," in which we burn certain herbs, take the smoke in our hands and rub or brush it over the body. It is a process that helps us to cleanse our mind, spirit, heart and body; to make ourselves empty" of negativity and receptive to healing. According to Broden and Coyote, two Anishinabe, "[T]he Elders say that all ceremonies, tribal or private, must be entered into with a good heart, so that we can pray, sing and walk in a sacred manner and be helped by the spirits to enter the sacred realm" (1991: 3). To be able to pay proper attention and to honour Ancestral Traditions, our Elders advise, the space should be prepared carefully. It should be clean and orderly. Lighting, air and overall atmosphere are very important. Tom Ration, a Navajo teacher, tells this story:

> Our parents would say to us, "Arise, wake up. What are you sleeping for? Take the ashes out. Clean around the outside, we do not want trash around the hogan!" This is done so the Dawn People do not see all the trash. They will know they are welcomed to this place. "There is no wealth here, let's go in an give them some," they will say (by wealth they meant trash). Where the place is dirty and trashy, they will ignore the place and say, "too much wealth here, let's go to another place." (in Beck and Walters 1977: 54)

Storytelling Is a Form of Teaching

Our Ancestors taught us that those with knowledge have a responsibility to pass it on. Teachers are individuals who have taken upon themselves to become especially knowledgeable about the world and its fundamental relationships, a knowledge they then must pass on to others. In cultures in which experience is particularly valued, Elders are expected to pass their knowledge on to younger people by both word and example. The special regard for Elders as teachers, historians and sources of authority underlies ethnographic accounts by "outsid-

ers" (Cruikshank 1992), as well as contemporary discussion by "insiders"—
Aboriginal people concerned with incorporating Traditional values into present-
day life (Armstrong 1987; Medicine Eagle 1991; Buffalo 1990).

According to Smith, an Athapaskan Elder, until recently, every Athapaskan
learned from either direct experience or verbal descriptions or instruction. "An
ultimate value of oral tradition was to recreate a situation for someone who had
not lived through it so that the listener could benefit directly from the narrator's
experience" (Cruikshank 1992: 339). Traditional people retain the value for the
ear, and they believe that an accepting, subjective stance is essential to full
understanding. The strong oral Traditions that are common to all tribes predis-
pose Aboriginal people to listen intently and respectfully to Elders and teachers
in a non-demonstrative, introspective way, experiencing fully what they hear.
This reflects a respect for self, "a respect for the world outside the self and a
recognition of the potential for knowledge and insight to come from anywhere"
(Macias 1989: 48). Gunn Allen recognizes the importance of stories in maintaining Aboriginal identity:

> Since the coming of the Anglo-Europeans beginning in the fifteenth
> century, the fragile web of identity that long held tribal people secure
> has gradually been weakened and torn. But the oral tradition has
> prevented the complete destruction of the web, the ultimate disruption
> of tribal ways. Oral tradition is vital; it heals itself and the tribal web
> by adapting to the flow of the present while never relinquishing its
> connection to the past. Its adaptability has always been required, as
> many generations have experienced. (1986: 45)

The persistence of stories and storytelling suggests that it is central to an
Aboriginal intellectual Tradition and provides the core of an educational Model.
Tom Ration reinforces the responsibility of the "keepers" to teach in the modern
age:

> The stories that are told can be repeated . . . to make them last. If we keep
> them to ourselves, in about fifteen or twenty more years we will not
> have them. It will all be gone. There will not be any songs or prayers
> because the legends go along with all this. One cannot exist without the
> other. (in Beck and Walters 1977: 30)

The Elders' stories are our identity statements. Elders' oral testimonies
have been called "statements of cultural identity," in which "memory continuously adapts received traditions to present circumstances" (Cruikshank 1992:
12). Elders continue today to take shared cultural Traditions, use them to
interpret events from their own experience and then pass them on to succeeding
generations. Traditional narrative is used to explain life experiences with an

emphasis on common themes: "landscape, mythology, everyday events, and continuity between generations" (Cruikshank 1992: 2). Elder women's stories differ from both Native men's accounts and those of non-Native women. For Traditional women the recurring theme is one of connection—to other people and to nature. "Connections with people are explored through ties of kinship; connections with land emphasize sense of place. But kinship and landscape provide more than just a setting for an account, for they actually frame the story" (Cruikshank 1992: 3).

Gunn Allen elaborates on how our Ancestral notions of time are still captured in our Traditional stories:

> The structure of the stories out of the oral tradition, when left to themselves and not recast by Indian or white collectors, tend to meander gracefully from event to event; the major unifying device, besides the presence of certain characters in a series of tales, is the relationship of the tale to the ritual life of the tribe. (1986: 152)

In Traditional stories, "dream, event, myth, tale, history, and internal dialogue are run together . . . . The structure reflects the point that particles move in moving time and space and that individuals move in a moving field" (Gunn Allen 1986: 153).

Annie Ned, a Tlingit Elder, speaks: "Long time ago, when they know, what they see, that's the one they talk about, I guess. Tell stories—which way you learn things. You think about that one your grandma tells you. You've got to believe it, what Grandma said . . . . Old-style words are just like school!" (in Cruikshank 1992: 267). Relying on "old-style words," she answers questions about her youth with speeches, probably learned from those orated in ceremony, as a demonstration of how she actually learned as a child. She uses this form to discuss "what kids should know," reaffirming familiar themes: the power of words, the skills needed to survive and the importance of learning from one's grandmother (in Cruikshank 1992: 267).

Those who were "keepers" of Traditional knowledge "help pass knowledge and sacred practices from generation to generation, storing what they know in their memories" (Beck and Walters 1977: 27). Because the information was delivered orally, there was a special regard for speech and for the truth. Elder Ned insists that the correct way to tell stories involves reliable repetition: "[Y]ou don't put it yourself and tell a little more" (in Cruikshank 1992: 268), because you are not actually the person telling the story. You are only a transmitter from the original narrator, whose experience it was. A recurring theme of Kitty Smith, an Athapaskan Elder, is that authority to speak about the past comes not from originality but from accurate repetition. In all her teaching, she insists on naming her source, and she differentiates between two kinds of authority: the received wisdom from Elders—"I know what I tell. This is not just my story—lots of people tell that story. Just like now they go to school, old time we come to our grandpa. Whoever is old tells the same way" (in Cruikshank 1992: 268); and direct experience, from having witnessed a particular event: "That one story my grandpa tells me. But this time, myself, this time I'm telling you the story" (in Cruikshank 1992: 268). She is careful not to speculate when asked questions outside her experience: "I don't know that one. That's what they say, but I don't see it. Whoever tells you this, ask him" (in Cruikshank 1992: 268). She challenges the authority of anyone younger than herself. Referring to someone ten years younger, she comments: "[That person] is too young. [That person] didn't see it. Just a kid. Old people, that's the one's I'll tell you" (in Cruikshank 1992: 268). Authenticity is a critical issue in the minds of Elders. As the translator to the "paper world," most of Elder Smith's focus is directed at ensuring that the listener learns to "get the words right" (in Cruikshank 1992: 268). This is amusing, considering the number of Aboriginal authors who have trouble getting their work published because they are not saying it right/white (Lutz 1991).

The Elders' concern for accuracy and "truth" allows us to see that validity claims for Traditional minds are embedded in the actual experience. But, simultaneously, experience is understood as particular, subjective and contextual. What, then, is a true story? To an Elder, it is one narrated by a person who either participated directly, observed first hand or heard it from someone who did. Many "truths," multiple interpretations of the same story or experience, are permissible because each storyteller understands the "facts" from their own location and adds each new experience or story to their repertoire as one adds beads to the string. Ruth Whitehead illustrates how the personal, the community and the tribal are interwoven in Mi'kmaq stories:

> Within the framework of the traditionally long story cycles, individual storytellers often transferred elements from one cycle into another. The intent or whim of the teller was the string onto which episodes, actions, characters and messages were threaded like beads. Such "beads" could change their color and forms as well, so each retelling of a story, even by the same person, might be different. The structure was fluid, accommodating itself to the teller's will. All its elements could change their shapes, their content. (1988: 2)

The story is a living thing, an organic process, a way of life. Stories are fragments of life, "fragments that never stop interacting while being complete in themselves" (Minh-ha 1989: 143). In a similar way, truth is fluid and changing. Vine Deloria Jr. reinforces the construction of a Traditional truth claim:

> In tribal religions no effort is made to define religion as a system of

doctrinal truths about the nature of the world. It cannot, therefore, be verified . . . . Over a long period of time, however, the cumulative experiences of the community become a truth that has been manifested for the people. (1994: 291)

Stories have always been accepted by Traditionalists as a way of teaching and learning from others' experience. Angela Sidney, a Tagish and Tlingit Elder, is an excellent role model as a keeper and teacher. As the eldest daughter, she looked after her mother, using their time together to listen to her talk about family and clan histories, Traditions, songs and stories. Through this process she absorbed normative rules about social behaviour for potlatching, puberty, marriage and childbirth. As times were changing, many stories tell of Elder Sidney's disappointment when her own experience never precisely matched the "old ways." She gained an ability to recognize contradictions between what people said "should" happen and what actually did happen, and she developed a preoccupation with evaluating and balancing old customs with new ideas. Elder Sidney uses narrative to discuss all these issues, showing an

uncommon ability to step back from her experience when she explains her culture or her language . . . mak[ing] her life history an exceptional cultural document. Part of her talent lies in her capacity to understand the kind of context a cultural outsider needs to be taught before that person can actually begin to hear what she is saying. (Cruikshank 1992: 21)

Elder Sidney subscribes to a modern-day Aboriginal worldview when, through her stories, place names and genealogies, she builds a framework for constructing her life story in the context of her tribe. As the Elder becomes more confident that the listener is grasping the building blocks she is providing, more and more of the stories begin to place her own experience within that context. "I was relying on the scaffolding of narratives and names she [Elder Sidney] had already provided" (Cruikshank 1992: 26). This is a description of the Traditional pedagogical practice of reinforcing Self-In-Relation, the interweaving of the individual in the community, in the tribal history and in the geographic context.

The knowledge base of the Yukon Elders, along with many other tribal Elders, is expressed in Traditional story form. This challenges the view that language loss equivocally means culture loss. Annie Ned sees herself as one of the last Elders and, therefore, a particularly important teacher. In her own childhood, instruction came directly from "long-time people" (in Cruikshank 1992: 268) who taught with stories. She brings Ancestral responsibility to teach, still active for today's Elders, together with insight into modern-day pedagogical process. Elder Ned's primary concern is that "school kids learn from paper" (in Cruikshank 1992: 268). Her continuing objective has been to prepare a book they can read: "Kids used to do jobs for old people—get wood, water. They paid us with stories! We bring wood: now! Time like school! We stayed there—we listened" (in Cruikshank 1992: 268).

Elder Smith's motives for recording her stories are also related to her intergenerational responsibility. With reference to a great-grandchild she said: "Well, she's six years old now. She's going to start school now. Pretty soon paper's going to talk to her!" (in Cruikshank 1992: 16). Most schools teach things that are totally outside the experience of Elders and rarely call on them for assistance. "Paper stories" can be a connection between the world of Tradition and the schools' "paper world." The Elders feel that once legiti-mized—i.e., on paper—the stories should be able to be a part of the school curriculum.

Moving our oral stories to paper has mixed results. Reading and hearing the stories can bring us closer to our culture but can also create more distance as we no longer have to visit the Elders for the stories. Basil Johnston, an Ojibway author, reflects a Traditional view of "paper stories": "Ever since words and sounds were reduced to written symbols and have been stripped of their mystery and magic, the regard for them have diminished in tribal life" (1992: 10). The following comment by Elder Ned emphasizes parallels between narrative explanation and academic storytelling. After a long day of hearing archaeolo-gists present their findings to the community, she stood up and asked:

> Where do these people come from, outside?
> You tell different stories from us people.
> You people talk from paper—
> Me, I want to talk from Grandpa. (in Cruikshank 1992: 356)

In a very real sense, her oppositional stance has helped me identify what seems to be the central issue: storytelling is a form of teaching, and teaching a form of storytelling. Our cultural locatedness influences the way we tell stories and largely determines who will hear them and what meaning they will take from them. Translating these ideas and this teaching Model to paper has risks, but it is also a responsibility.

Living our lives as Traditional Aboriginal peoples has become, through the imposition of colonial consciousness, a much more highly complex function. We can and do reflect on the Ancestral gifts of immanence, balance and interconnectedness as they are pedagogically expressed in "experience" and "voice." As Traditionalists, we must continue to acknowledge the Ancestral responsibility to teach the values and ethics that once sustained, and are now required, to revitalize Self-In-Relation. We can continue to rely on the Ancestral pedagogical forms to do so. The consequences of separating the learning of skills and facts from the Traditional worldviews that guide our making of "meaning," our understanding of "proper conduct" In-Relation to other life forms, is visible globally. "The spiral towards genocide in most indigenous cultures, as well as humanity as a whole, should convince us that in having removed these safeguards from learning we may have removed the sole means for our continuance" (Armstrong 1987: 19). Our Ancestral ethics call on us to recognize that Aboriginal people "stand at a pivot point at this time in history," where we each have the responsibility of "deciding for our descendants how their world shall be affected and what shall be their heritage" (Armstrong 1988: 13).

In the contemporary era, our lives—experiences and voices—are contextualized by the immediate and daily interface with "colonial mentality." To move wisely towards visioning for the future, we require a clear understanding of Traditional Aboriginal identity, philosophy and pedagogy as they are continuously revealed in the modern context. Colonialism disrupted the epistemologies and pedagogies guiding our Ancestors' daily lives and continues to play a large role in separating Aboriginal people from a positive identity construction. It is necessary to continue to unveil the philosophies and pedagogies that were/are used to dominate us in order to better challenge them. As Armstrong reminds us, the lies need to be dispelled—the current conditions of our people "did not happen through choice or some cultural defect on our part" (1990b: 144). A combination of critical analysis and cultural renaissance are necessary strategies in the struggle to advance a Traditional Aboriginal worldview in the contemporary age of Eurocentric domination. We turn now to a detailed description and analysis of my efforts to enact a teaching Model based on both Traditional culture and a critique of Eurocentric ideologies.

The Model-In-Use

The Sacred Circle
Honoured by most Tribal peoples of the Earth
On the Plains named the Medicine Wheel.
Symbolic of Wholeness and Completion
Mother Earth in her Roundness . . . Fullness . . . Abundance.
Four is the Sacred number
Four seasons in the cycle . . . Four elemental powers
Four races of humanity . . . Four laws of living in community
Four Directions of the Medicine Wheel.
Weaves the Web of Interconnectedness with all of Creation
Between those who have gone before . . . those who will come after.
Circle is a container for energy . . . we Share together

The Model-In-Use

Strengthening . . . Healing each of us . . . Together.
Helps us continue with our struggles
As we "walk our talk" each day
Honouring our selves . . . All others
The Ancestors . . . Mother Earth.

What lessons did we learn
Applying the Medicine Wheel in this Model-In-Use?

In Aboriginal Traditional practice, healing and learning begins with efforts to make our own levels of consciousness knowable. How do I know what I know? What theories or philosophies do I espouse? What have I learned through my experience? To begin with myself is a conscious, political choice. Once we accept our "selves" as the ever present "subjective I," "like a garment that cannot be removed" (Peshkin 1988: 17), we call into question one foundation of Western intellectual tradition: objectivity. I understand myself to be In-Relation to my research subject: myself, my students, my teaching, our journey together through cross-cultural terrain. Following Raymond, I espouse "passionate teaching": "We are deeply involved in the things that we study. We cannot pretend that we do not care. We look at our subject with passion because we are our subject" (1985: 58).

Following Weil and McGill (1989), I will speak about theory and practice related to teaching and learning from my own position, in the first person, in a specific rather than generalized context. "One of the strengths of experiential learning in practice is the meaning that we give our actions and therefore our thinking. They are not separate entities. Meaning is not 'out there'; we are part of that meaning and we can therefore convey it personally" (Weil and McGill 1989: xx).

I agree with Devault (1990) that we need to analyze more carefully the specific ways in which we use personal experience as a resource. My personal history and my collective identity has provided impetus and direction for the research. The embodied experience of myself and others is used both as a teaching/learning tool and to develop "content" for this work. I am aware of articulating my personal and collective consciousness throughout this analysis. To declare "what I know to be true" is a complex undertaking, particularly as my own consciousness is influenced in part by my Aboriginal Ancestors' mimetic consciousness and our interactions with Western colonial consciousness. While the pedagogical tools articulated in this Model arise, for me, out of my Aboriginal Ancestral Traditions, several have supports in feminist, anti-racist and other critical theory bases. Through a weaving of Traditional and critical, I endeavour to illustrate the usefulness of Ancestral forms for resolving modern problems. During this time of "decolonization" of previously suppressed voices and of renaissance of our Ancestral gifts, we need to use more time and energy to address our own worldviews and less to summarize and reconfirm Eurocentric thought forms.

I am working to uncover and acknowledge prior theoretical assumptions, grounded in my own experience and worldview. I refer specifically to how I have applied these understandings to a complex modern problem—teaching respect for diversity in a moderately diverse classroom in a dominantly White, Eurocentric institution. I reflect on my classroom experience, as I perceive it to be. As well, I invite participants—students and community members—to express their understanding of the process and content of the learning/teaching interaction as it was enacted within the Model-In-Use.

The Project: A Grounded Approach

While I feel it necessary to reflect on my role in this educational endeavour, I have been taught that teaching and learning are always done In-Relation. I trace my own teachings and learnings through the Model, and also give voice to others who were an integral part. The following description and analysis of the Model-In-Use relies on the insights of students and Community members, who contributed their voices through journals and Talking Circles. I want to understand more deeply what aspects/combinations of the classroom content and practices contribute to what kinds of transformational learning, and for whom. I pursue a "grounded" approach to data collection (Acker, Barry and Esseveld 1983), using participants' contributions to guide the unfolding of the story. My students in the Cross Cultural Issues (CCI) courses are asked to keep weekly journals to air feelings; to record thoughts, insights, observations and experiences; and to report on actions. I invite students to specify what has impacted on them with respect to their development as more culturally aware people. They can elaborate on: a piece of in-class information, one of the readings, a gut feeling, a memory from their past, a racist incident or a taste of power or powerlessness. They are to discuss the details in depth and end by answering the question "what do you now know or do differently?" (see course outline in Appendix).

In making this request, I am asking students to observe their own lived experience. To do so, they must "perform a reflective act of intention" (Schutz 1967: 102). We are not visibly present to ourselves, so I cannot observe myself In-Relation to the others in my environment. For this reason, I must rely on self-talk, with the language available to me, to create meanings for myself. Many times I have had the experience of being caught in a difficult encounter and living through it in confusion, only to discover with utmost clarity the oppressive nature of it minutes/hours/days later. Sometimes clarity is achieved through self-reflection; often it requires sharing the experience with others. Hearing myself saying it out loud always helps contextualize it, so I encourage sharing experiences and feelings. This can be done in class, in the journal and through Talking Circles. I have experienced and witnessed the power of finding and sharing voice in the Talking Circle, so it has become a central process in my classroom and a vital method of data collection for this project.

Following activists like Armstrong (1990b), Charnley (1990) and hooks (1990), I have adopted writing as a tool for clarity and expression, for assisting myself and students in releasing feelings and transforming personal pain into structural change. I teach that stories are a form of Traditional pedagogy and that we must all locate ourselves in our own narrative. According to Benhabib, "[W]e tell of who we are, of the 'I' that we are, by means of a narrative" (1992: 214). Our personal narratives are "deeply coloured and structured by the code of expectable and understandable biographies and identities in our cultures" (Benhabib 1992: 214). Our stories are never merely personal, nor are we the "mere extensions of our histories" (Benhabib 1992: 214). Our current daily lived experience takes place within the "meaning-contexts developed out of [our] previous lived experience" (Schutz 1967: 105).

In this Model-In-Use, participants are encouraged to present their classroom and life experiences and learnings in the form of a "story," making connections between their personal experiences and the cultural and structural realities that frame our individual/family/community lives. Students are specifically asked to use the journal to tell stories of current or past cross-cultural encounters. Sometimes they share the deep-rooted feelings that have been harboured for years. They are encouraged to demonstrate their structural insights, and they often express a newfound conviction to do better in the future.

Many students reflect on how journalling helps them articulate and reflect on their experiences and feelings in a manner previously unavailable to them. Several found that "there was definitely not a lack of issues to write about" (Tia 93-j). The following excerpts will illustrate the usefulness of journalling as a learning tool and as a source of data about feelings and experiences regarding the course.

> It's hard to pinpoint my most important learnings because I feel that everything I have written presents an idea or a feeling I would not have normally thought about. I'm just beginning to become culturally aware, therefore everything I learn is of value to me . . . .
>
> I wrote my journals on a weekly basis and although there were times I didn't always know how to express my ideas, I was never hard pressed to find a topic . . . . The ease with which I found topics signifies something in itself—oppression and racism are everywhere and many people feel the impact on a daily basis.
>
> Attending class and writing journals have provided me with the opportunity to unlearn certain things and to express my ideas and feelings. I have also developed new ways of thinking aside from my white middle class perspectives. Most of all I have gained an understanding about my white privileges and how I can use my own voice to help change society's racist attitudes and actions. (Gela Apr 93-jsum)

> I feel the journal was difficult to write. I am not used to putting my feelings on paper. However, I think that what I have written is a good reflection of how I have felt over the course. I see some changes in myself and in my outlook that has caused me to reconsider some feelings and opinions. I was unsure of what to write, sometimes, but I avoided getting caught up in things like, "How long should it be?" I wrote from the heart and only put down what I truly felt. In this sense I feel that I have achieved the spirit of what I wanted—which was to reflect my inner struggle with these issues and to convey it honestly. (Mac 92-j)

Once they complete the course, students are invited to resubmit their journals and assignments or "tasks." My analysis of others' journal writing of their own lived experience/perceptions of the teaching/learning encounter was a rich source of material for exploration of the Model-In-Use. In this way, I embrace myself as teacher and my relations with students as a subject of this narrative.

Along with data collection from journals,[1] ten Talking Circles[2] were held so that students who had experienced the Model and community members[3] who had participated in the class could contribute their voices to the description and analysis. Circles were taped and transcribed. Many people contributed to Circle Talk on CCI, several from the Aboriginal, African Canadian and Asian Communities, balancing the journal contributors who were primarily White. Several categories of data were constructed and deconstructed and what remained in the analysis were the following themes: reviews of the Model/course overall; reflection on the critical themes; discussion of the Talking Circle process; community-building as seen by community participants; specific lessons for professionals in building community relations; change—how to make it happen, what are the costs and blocks; and visions—where do we go from here. Many of these themes were integrated with data from journals and added to information already available.[4] Many contributors review the Model and the overall experience very positively.

Randi expresses sadness at the closing of the class: "As class ended tonight, I had a sense of sadness, the most wonderful educational experience in my life thus far is over!" (Apr 7 93-j). Unicorn recalls the ways in which she found the Model "extremely empowering":

> Your method of teaching was refreshing to me. I have learned ways of assessing myself and the affects racism has on me. I felt good about who I am and my history and hopefully for the future because I was able to express my learning and processing in non-traditional (white) ways. Extremely empowering. (Dec 2 93-j)

Cal notes his observations of the last class:

> This class was a bit different as several students were absent. The atmosphere was a little different as fellow students were legitimately

feeling as though they were going to lose something from their lives. The circles, with the groups each week was an opportunity to try to deal with the immediate frustrations and the racism of the day or week, for me . . . . The class despite my frustrations and expectations turned out to be very good to a great extent this had more to do with the model that was being used. (Apr 7 94-j)

Some White participants were also openly appreciative of the Model. According to Van, "The Native culture and the Circle and this class is invaluable. Even if people are uncomfortable, that's learning! And that's good, that's great, you need to be uncomfortable in your life (TC3:36).

The most interesting and challenging Circle Talk data analyzed the contradictory and often paradoxical aspects inherent in using this Model in a Eurocentric School context and with a culturally diverse group. Contradictions do not exist separate from the experience—they are embedded in and contextualized by it. For clarity and integrity in conveying a rich and flowing description of the Model, I have left the critical analysis to the end.

I will begin now with a discussion of the underpinnings of the Model-In-Use itself. I will focus on holism and my position as the "teacher as healer," which is fundamental to an understanding of the Model. I will then take you on a journey around the Medicine Wheel, describing the Model-In-Use as it relates to each of the Directions. As Eber Hampton points out, "This way of thinking is sacred in the sense that it is bigger than anything I might say. It helps me to understand in that it stimulates my thoughts and feelings rather than being contained in my words" (1995: 16). The Medicine Wheel is an organizing principle; it is dynamic and developmental, and it expresses movement.

Holism

Traditional understandings are embodied in the Plains tribe's "sacred centre": the Medicine Wheel or Sacred Hoop. Medicine Wheels are actually ancient rock formations used for contact with Ancestral spirit forms during ceremony. However the metaphor is also used by modern-day Traditionalists to illustrate/invoke/reinspire understandings of Ancestral beliefs in this contemporary world of separation and abstraction. Through use of the Medicine Wheel, people are taught to acknowledge the essential immanence and interconnectedness of all things, and challenge "the opposition, dualism, and isolation that characterizes non-Indian thought" (Gunn Allen 1986: 56). This paradigm challenges us to shift from the linear, mechanistic cause-effect models of thinking now dominant in the Western industrial world, and to embrace the circular, ever-evolving dynamic captured in a single phrase: all life is a Circle.

My understandings about the Medicine Wheel began with early teachings by my parents, especially my father, who was himself a practitioner of Traditional "medicine." I have also been influenced by my work and life with several Aboriginal groups and in different institutional contexts since leaving my

Ancestral roots in the northern prairies. We are taught that each of us must take from our lives the teachings as we are able to know them, given our path, and we must grow and share with others for the continued revitalization of Aboriginal culture. As Kathy Absolon, a Cree educator, reminds us, "When we speak about the teachings of the Medicine Wheel there is always the danger of those words becoming rhetoric unless our talk is accompanied by an action that reflects the nature of the talk" (1994: 29). This description and analysis of the Model-In-Use is the story of my efforts to "walk the talk," to bring the Medicine Wheel to life in my teaching, to embody it and to teach it so that students can learn to embrace the gifts of Aboriginal culture.

According to Absolon, the word "heal" has the same roots as the word "whole" and "holiness." The interdependence of holiness and wholeness are integral to healing and teaching in Aboriginal Tradition: "[t]he holiness, or sacredness, of healing is manifested as a striving towards wholeness of spirit and an attempt to incorporate this wholeness of spirit into ourselves, our families, our communities, and the environment" (Absolon 1994: 5). In the Traditional worldview, wholeness or holism is equated with balance. "Healing is a therapeutic process, an evolution toward balance; the process accesses essential healing dynamics which are spiritual in quality and power" (Absolon 1994: 7).

Accumulated anthropological evidence indicates that Aboriginal people, prior to contact with Europeans, had a sophisticated and effective system of healing that was based on a holistic worldview (Weatherford 1988). According to Ed Conners, a Mohawk educator, "The healing system accepted that maintaining health and effecting healing required a knowledge of the interaction between the physical, mental, emotional and spiritual" (1994: 2). A healthy lifestyle rests upon the ability to maintain a balanced commitment to growth and maintenance in all four areas of the Medicine Wheel. As applied to transformational pedagogy, all four areas are relevant to the growth and maintenance of an alternative consciousness. As Conners warns, "Failure to attend to growth in any one aspect of self can throw the entire organism into a state of imbalance, resulting in deterioration within the other realms of experience" (1994: 2). The holistic perspective promoted by use of the Medicine Wheel permits one to see the entire educational process as a complex, integrated whole; psychological, spiritual, emotional and physical are all part of the human consciousness and are inseparable. Using Traditional methods, "one would never think of, nor attempt to practice healing in any one of these areas separate from the others" (Conners 1994: 2). Nor should Traditional educators fall prey to the division of these domains, which is currently required in Eurocentric pedagogical paradigms. Imbalance is the overall diagnosis Traditionalists have of current Western processes. An Aboriginal worldview, represented by the holism of the Medicine Wheel, highlights the narrowness of Eurocentric thought, and calls into question the high value that is placed on intellectual analysis and reflected in the exclusive focus on cognition in transformative pedagogies. Hart and Holton seek to develop a more comprehensive concept of emancipatory education, asserting that "an inclusive focus on critique, on the power of reason in isolation from other human powers can lead people to pessimism and a feeling of helplessness rather than to social action" (1993: 2).

A Traditional Aboriginal perspective pays attention to learning and teaching as an embodied experience. Our Ancestral consciousness was mimetic (Merchant 1989) and participatory. Traditionalists continue to believe that the more of our senses—sight, hearing, smell, taste and touch—that we use in learning/teaching something, the more likely we are to understand and remember it. As Minh-ha poetically expresses it: "We write—think and feel—[with] our entire bodies rather than only [with] our minds or hearts. It is a perversion to consider thought the product of one specialized organ, the brain, and feelings, that of the heart" (1989: 36). Ancestral sources of knowledge incorporated and added to the rational, logical data. According to a local Mi'kmaq source, the Elders have always taught that there are five physical senses and six non-physical senses: thinking, memory, imagination, dreaming, visioning and spirit-travelling (Pictou 1993). Mi'kmaq people recognize that these are all gifts from the Creator and they use them as other people use their sight. Using dreams, visions and spirit-travelling is important to help people heal and to give people insight into what needs to be done. They do not see the "spirit" as trapped in the body but interconnected with it (Pictou 1993). Storytelling, metaphor, myth, ritual, meditation and art are ways to tap into "right brain" energies essential for more holistic learning. According to Griffin, "[T]he role of metaphoric thinking is to invent, to create, and to challenge conformity, by extending what is known into new meadows of knowing" (1988: 11). Our Elders teach that this capacity is only released by quieting the rational mind, relaxing and moving into another state of consciousness Through this process we are able to find our own personal meaning from any educational experience.

Teacher as Healer:
A "Personal" Challenge to Eurocentric Hegemony

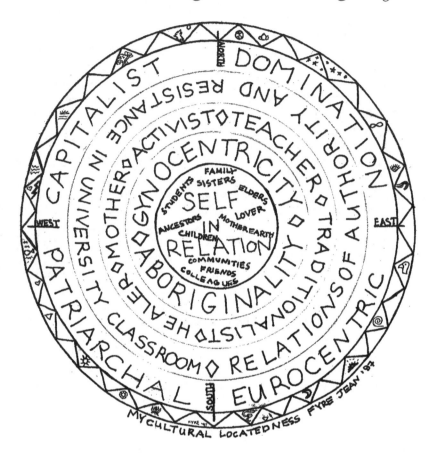

Part of the learning loop for Traditionalists is encouragement to learn from our experiences, our successes and our mistakes. We observe, then we do, and then after we might ask an Elder or someone with more experience to help us interpret what happened.

> The course has been like that for me. My vision of the Model is that I'm going to continue to learn that way, and I'm hoping that I'm going to keep moving forward with it and learn from what I've been doing. (Fyre VC3:23)

I constructed the Model, enacted it and asked others, including Elders, to reflect on it. I am learning, in an applied form by developing this Model-In-Use, how to take a culturally specific, anti-racist approach in an educational institution. Absolon provides guidance in this area, reminding us of the Traditional epistemology—walk your talk, heal the healer:

> We cannot begin to help other people deal with their imbalances unless we first begin to heal ourselves and deal with our own imbalances . . . . We can only facilitate a healing journey to the degree that we as healers have had the courage to journey on our own. If you have not dealt with your own traumas of racism then how can you help another deal with their internalized inferiority? . . . The healer's openness to change is a key element in the healing process. (1994: 14)

Katz and St. Denis draw upon studies of Traditional teachers—Elders and Medicine people—to elaborate upon the notion of "teacher as healer":

> The "teacher as healer" is one who, infused with spiritual understanding, seeks to make things whole . . . seeks to respect and foster interconnections—between herself, her students, and the subject matter, between the school, the community and the universe at large—while respecting each part of these interconnected webs. (1991: 24)

Traditional teachers must display qualities of the "heart": "courage, commitment, belief, and intuitive understanding" (Katz and St. Denis 1991: 28). Heart is not limited to feelings, rather it "involves the total person as he or she operates in her deepest essence" (Katz and St. Denis 1991: 28).

This Model-In-Use is an expression of a change process, a vision enacted of my own deep desire to be both a Traditionalist and an activist in my daily lived experience as a teacher. I "walk my talk" in my multiple environments when I consistently endeavour to take actions that I perceive to be congruent with Aboriginal/anti-racist/feminist/decolonial/environmentalist social change agendas. As a Traditional teacher, I recognize that I am on my own healing/learning journey. As I tell my own stories and follow the path of the Wheel in each teaching section, I pay attention to my own process so that I relearn and re-experience the Model each time it is produced. I do not approach teaching as an exercise in pedagogical transmission; rather, I embody and transmit my experience as a guide—as one familiar with the process, having previously undertaken it. As teacher, I do not stand apart from but am an integral part of the process. This style is also described in Alaskan Native culture as the "carrier role" (Carroll 1986). The helper/teacher/carrier helps bring a person to a place (mentally, spiritually, emotionally or physically) where that person may, in turn, become a helper/teacher to others. As Jock tells it, "Each person is a teacher and a healer with a strength to offer and a weakness or pain to heal" (in Absolon 1994: 13).

Sarah, a Mi'kmaq Elder, acknowledges the relationship between the teaching Model and the healing effect it produced for her:

> Just the idea of coming here and introducing part of my culture—this made me proud. And it empowered me and I feel when things are not going right or I feel powerless or helpless, coming to a session like this really empowers me because I firmly believe in it. I didn't before. But as time went on I felt refreshed and new ideas began to surface. And I felt a power because I'm becoming a believer in the ancestral way. And I'm very thankful for that. Introducing some of this concept . . . it was really challenging. It's just real nice to come here and get revived and charged up again. (VC2:4)

Teacher as healer is a strong message asserted by many Aboriginal educators today. When we follow the Medicine Wheel path of teaching, we can look to the work of shamans who were/are Traditional teachers and healers. A shaman's functions are concerned with making whole, finding balance. The starting point of each shamanic action is discovery of the root cause of the problem and, through a transformational act, reconnecting the individual to the whole, to the cosmic laws. Shamans have a duty to decipher the existing imbalance so that the person can again live in harmony with his or her body and soul, a state that is described as "health." This takes place primarily on the spiritual plane, but includes the mind, heart and body as well. The real transformational work is done by the persons themselves, as the shaman awakens their own "inner healer" to help them learn the message of the "illness" and allow transformation into "health" (Lorler 1989). Medicine Eagle reinforces this view: "The function of the healer is to embody and manifest that wholeness of Spirit in such a way that he or she can guide those who have fallen out of rhythm, who have stumbled into dis-ease, and help them to reestablish their balance and rhythm" (1991: 60). The teacher as shaman may help to awaken the inspiration of each learner to be open to what they each need to know to achieve balance and interconnectedness in their own lives and work.

Following Traditional processes requires a component of mutuality in the teaching/learning relationship. There is an emphasis on honesty, openness and authenticity, with efforts to minimize social and power differences. The Aboriginal worldview, Self-In-Relation, reminds us that as educators we must remember to consider ourselves In-Relation to our students. According to Kleinfeld, "The intensity of the emotional relationships that characterized the most effective teachers of Indian and Eskimo students could be judged inappropriate according to the usual Western professional orientations" (1975: 305). She notes that when teachers had been socialized in Western university education programs, "they sometimes felt a conflict between the professionalism they had been taught and the personalism that they say 'worked' in the classroom" (Kleinfeld 1975: 305).

Being unfamiliar with the specialized, impersonal relationships characteristic of large Western institutions, Native persons may interpret impersonality as dislike or disrespect. We are acculturated to be In-Relation and to expect others, whether educator or student, to care about us as total persons, not as learners or teachers of a particular subject matter. In the Traditional way, "[y]ou've got to be personal . . . . What you have to do is shed the barrier of formality that you put up between you and the class. Approach them like people you know . . . . The classroom should be like a little family" (Kleinfeld 1975: 318). While it is unexpected and can be considered "inappropriate" in Western Schools, I challenge "impersonalization" as a form of Eurocentrism by maintaining a "personal" approach. The Model is built on my own identity and my experience of the world as an Aboriginal, feminist and anti-racist educator. As I teach, I rely on my embodied experience of the world and of the evolving educational process as dynamic content for teaching/learning about race relations. In this quote from Circle Talk on CCI, I address the complex issue of my identity/subjectivity and how it evolves through/into teaching in the classroom:

> When I come to the heart of why I'm teaching this way, it really comes down to feeling alienated, and isolated, and voiceless in my own experience as a student. And I'm trying to find now, a place for myself as a Native teacher, in a location [where] I still feel isolated, alienated and voiceless. I'm trying to use what little teeny bit of voice I have . . . designing the course outline and building the curriculum. (Fyre CC2:31)

Hampton (1995) notes that Aboriginal education models generally are now arising as creative solutions to the tensions we feel personally as we attempt to fit ourselves and our practice into non-Native structures. I continue to explore this reality on a daily basis.

> I see this Model as a piece of my own resistance, in trying to work in a Native way in a White organization . . . . But it is hard to embrace your own background, your own identity, as a cultural identity. It's really hard in a White place . . . . I had to come around to being myself first. To really deciding that's who I am and that's what my heart is, and that's where I am in the world, that's who I am in the world. Then if I can embrace that, why is it that I'm trying to embrace that? What is it about that, that is good for me that I want to share with other people? Then how can I bring more people in to that and then how can I use that to create change? So to me, the Model is really my own process, the way that I've learned to make sense of the world. The way that I've learned to make sense of my own identity position in the world, which is really conflictual. Now I'm trying to teach from that same position. Sometimes it's really personal and terrifying; and I leave class and I ask: Why did I ever say those things to that group of people? I don't even hardly know them! (laughs) Here I am saying some of the most personal things that ever happened to me in my life. I'm trying to model that . . . . It's ok to say

about the mistakes you've made. It's ok to say about your struggles, if you've had an identity struggle . . . . Sometimes it's a big, painful experience to come around to embracing that. Now, having embraced it, speak out about it. That's what I'm trying to model . . . . It really does feel very personal to me, it's a very personal teaching model. It's a very personal experience to be in the class. I've certainly had that feedback from students and from the community participants. It's been a very personal experience to them. (Fyre CC2:31)

The following journal excerpts serve to illustrate that participants do see me as a "person," this Model as "personal" and the process as one in which we are engaged together.

The first breakthrough was in meeting Jean who instantly proved to be non-authoritarian with a very warm humane personality and then seeing how the class was conducted, so informally. (Lola Sept 14 92-j)

Thank you, Jean, for guiding us so sensitively in an emotional and delicate topic. It was a wonderful experience. (Char Apr 6 93-jsum)

I would like to note that as powerful as the content of the course was it would not have been as powerful without the strong life force and commitment that you, as a Métis, a woman and a teacher, brought to class. (Van Dec 93-jsum)

Students' journalled responses to the personal stories I tell in class reinforced my own analysis. Being "personal" helps trigger a personal response from students. Students are encouraged to struggle to see me as a "person" rather than a cultural artifact or authority figure. Van's response to a "teaching" story I tell captures the effect that I intend "personal" story work to have: "[W]hat touched me was you and your presentation of your story and your spirit. You allowed the class to see your pain and vulnerability, yet maintained your strength and presence as a teacher" (Van Sept 22 93-j).

I was pleased to hear an Elder from the Aboriginal community give me a very Traditional form of praise.

It was really nice to get to know Jean . . . . I was really glad I did because I found out that she has such a special way of giving. Giving back to the people. She's got such a giving and sharing and concern for the people. I appreciate the message that it has to give to other people. (Sarah VC 2:24)

What is always "personally" gratifying to me is to be able to provide a role model to others who are struggling to survive in their lives and/or in School:

I have been most impressed with the aura and spirit of the . . . [teacher] who has demonstrated a courage in and out of class unlike any other person that I have encountered. She has spurred me on to take greater control of my life to bring about more balance. It becomes so important to balance family, work, and community. It is obvious that my consciousness and my person have grown a great deal. (Cal Apr 7 94-jsum)

I wanted to thank you personally for the inspiration that you have given me to pursue my career along aboriginal thinking. You've given me the direction I was looking for, when I was lost. (Randi Apr 7 93-j)

As I have helped and am helping other women heal, I feel Jean may help restore my strength in grass-roots feminism and women's up-front real support of each other . . . a spark of hope. (Gracie Sept 29 92-j)

The spontaneous praise offered by participants at Circle confirms my will to continue this work. I found these disclosures heartwarming, and they help balance and reenergize me:

The Cross Cultural Course and the Circle work were one of the . . . only things that gave me the strength to continue at the . . . [School]. (two second pause) And then when times are tough, it gives me the courage or continued strength to want to remain to try and do my part. (Unicorn VC2:2)

I was in a course with . . . [a teacher] who validated me as a person, as an equal, not as an inferior. And it . . . was the first program or course I'd taken in the university setting that I was finally a person. . . for the first time in my life was I was allowed to be me. And . . . when I thought about that, that in itself brings me much pain . . . . As a Black person, an indigenous person from Nova Scotia, and not able to be yourself because you're Black and you're different. And . . . finally I was allowed to . . . be me, and I thank Jean for that opportunity to . . . be able to express my thoughts, my pain on racism. How I was able to feel that from a young child and . . . through all the institutions, and especially . . . at the [School], which caused me much pain for the very fact that it's supposed to be a helping profession, a profession that is colorless and painless. (Hattie TC2:19)

I feel good that I took this course in the second term because in September I just came here, I don't feel I settled down, and after I take all the courses that are taught by the white . . . [teachers], then suddenly I go to this course and I have a very big conscience, when I'm in the class. (Cindy TC2:3)

In the School context, efforts must be consistently made in the learning process to equalize and humanize teacher-student relations rather than consciously or unconsciously accepting and using strategies informed by "power over" (Starhawk 1987). Participants have acknowledged that I strive to be "personal." I have struggled to consistently treat all participants with respect, as living beings with spirits, feelings and thoughts, not as inanimate objects—"the empty vessel." I follow Kleinfeld's (1975) advice, and I use early sessions to combine clarifying objectives and terminology with establishing the foundations for classroom relationships. "In contrast to other teachers who plunge . . . immediately into academic work," Kleinfeld advises teachers to spend "a substantial amount of time at the beginning of the year establishing positive interpersonal relationships, not only between teacher and students, but also within the student group" (1975: 336).

Establishing social relationships is a task prerequisite in Aboriginal culture. This is revealed in many ceremonies, including the Greeting Circle. The Greeting Circle, introduced every first class, is customary at the beginning or end of a Traditional gathering. A Circle is formed and each participant is greeted verbally or physically or both, by every other member in turn. After their initial hesitation, which is an expected response to anything "new," students often really enjoy the experience. It is an excellent method for getting a feel for the energy of the group and a non-threatening way to introduce students to the more participatory learning approach exemplified by this Model-In-Use. A Native participant, new to this Tradition, expresses her enthusiasm: "The greeting circle was my first experience with a different Native tradition, it was a wonderful opportunity to get to know people, what a powerful feeling to be such a part of a wonderful tradition!" (Randi Jan 6 93-j). Gracie gives a thorough analysis of the process and how it may contribute to developing human "connectedness":

> Three things I liked about this: 1) the sense of physical connection connotes a sense of "joining" with another human. 2) The sense of greeting from another, listening to their voice—tone and delivery—and eye contact combined with your own greeting gave a sense of give and take, listening and being listened to—equal participation, and 3) the idea of slowly warming up to possible negotiations and differences by way of human "connectedness" versus separation. (Sept 17 92-j)

The experience of Traditional teaching definitely has provided many lessons for me and for students, both direct and "inside-out."[5] As an Aboriginal woman I teach from my own lived experience, I tell my own stories, I speak from the heart and I practice listening respectfully. It is ongoing work to continuously re-establish my Self-In-Relation to members of the Communities in and outside of the classroom/School. Along with the rigours of teaching, I expend my time and energy on "social" functioning of the class and the Circles, including cooking, singing, dancing and attending to the needs of the participants. I take up issues as they offer themselves in my day-to-day life as a mother, partner, teacher, healer, scholar, advocate and concerned community member. I teach from these forms of daily lived activism, which simultaneously keeps me challenged to remain in the activist role while incurring high personal and professional costs.

As I learn and teach through my own life and experience, I reweave the web of interconnectedness of our Ancestral ways. I help to revitalize our connection to each other and to Mother Earth, begin to heal and to vision our path through these challenging times. The Elders teach us that in order to receive what we truly need and want in the world we must Giveaway what we have. The Giveaway, enacted personally or in ceremony, is an integral component of the Aboriginal Traditional worldview. I now Giveaway to you, educators and students, to those who are open to learn and share our Gifts respectfully and honestly, in the spirit of caring and sharing—this Model-In-Use. It is a method of teaching/learning and healing that was developed through a revisioning of Ancestral Aboriginal philosophy, combined with my daily lived experience as an anti-racist, feminist, experiential educator and activist.

To all my Relations, Taho.

Notes

1. All students who were registered for Cross Cultural Issues from September 1992 to April 1994 (four sections) were invited by letter to participate in the project. The total number of students invited was sixty-one. Twenty-nine students declared interest and signed consent forms. Twenty-one students resubmitted journals, five of these also resubmitted assignments. Others participated in Talking Circles.
2. Ten Talking Circles were held. We began all sessions with coffee and bannock while participants gathered. We began Circle with a smudge and Traditional prayer, and concluded with food and chat. Each Circle followed a three-round process: opening round for introductions, theme round to process issues and response round. All Circles were held in Halifax in the spring and summer of 1994.

Circle	Date	Number of participants
Opening Circle	March 26	14
Theme Circles		
Consciousness	April 26	6
Context	April 30	8
Community	May 14	9
Change	May 28	10
Community Circles		
One	May 7	4
Two	May 11	7
Visions Circles		
One	June 11	10
Two	June 15	7
Three	June 18	9

All Circles were audiotaped. The first two Circles were not audible and it was impossible to recover the data.

3.   Community members directly involved in the Model through attendance at the Cross Cultural Issues classes were all invited to take part in the project. They were encouraged to bring friends/family if that increased comfort level. A total of eighty-five members of Aboriginal, African Canadian, White, Acadian, Asian and Gay and Lesbian Communities were invited by letter to attend one or more of the ten Talking Circles. Thirty-one community members participated. Community participants were asked to sign consent forms at the Circle(s) they attended.

4.   Editing Talking Circles to dissect data from the transcription was a difficult process. Much that was of potential importance in revealing the community-building and healing dynamics of Circle work was eliminated in the effort to confidentialize and categorize the participants' talk. Among those things excluded were personal information; stories that did not directly relate to the Model; supportive talk by some participants to others in Circle; and certain community-building terms, "you know," "right," and "like _____ said." Phrases such as "sort of," "like," "I guess," "of course," "I think," "I'd say," "so to me," "it seems," when edited out, make speakers appear to express more authority than they might feel. I have gained appreciation and the will to examine more carefully which data analysis process would be more reflective and inclusive of the process, as well as the content, of the Talking Circle as a research tool.

5.   Inside-out lessons, or Trickster tales, are those that we teach or learn through reversal. We see or experience something "negative" and learn from it what we do not want to be or do. Our Elders teach us that to heal and grow we must be open to learning from all opportunities.

The Eastern Door: Challenging Eurocentric Consciousness

The East corresponds to the Element Air
Breathe in the Air
A life force Necessary for human existence.
Our breath is our link to All of Creation.
. . . Breathe In. . . Breathe Out
Relax.

Picture Springtime
Crocuses blooming . . . Grass greening
Fresh Growth . . . New beginnings
A Breath of fresh Air

Dawn . . . streaming yellow light
Clarity . . . an awakening
Beginning a new day . . . a new start on life

Call the creatures of the Air
Fly with the Eagle . . . wings spread high in the sky
Closest to the Creator
Respect and honour the high flying ones
They bring us Illumination . . . Vision . . . Clear sight
An "eye opener."

Reach for the power to Know
How do we know?
How do we learn?
Seek the power of the East to face the Dawn
Cut through Untruth . . . Illusion
Eurocentrism presented as objective knowledge
Recognize the power of your Mind
The influence of your thoughts . . . Others' thoughts
On your own Actions . . . for and with others.
The power of your Mind to take in or reject information/ideas
Versions of "Reality" as they are made Visible to you.
How do we learn to See
To shift our Historical . . . Socially-constructed
Culturally-located Consciousness?
If we can be Acculturated to hold dominant views
Then we can also be Unacculturated.
Awareness is the beginning.
Will to Resist . . . to Challenge . . . Change
Structures that Confine us.
Consciousness is noticeable when it shifts
"Seeing the world" through "different lenses."
Experience an "eye-opener" . . . "a light came on"
What triggers these shifts for you?
What words describe the process?

Let us Conscientiously Question Our Consciousness

How Do We Know? Consciousness-Raising Revisited

In the Cree Tradition of transformational practice, awareness is the beginning. "The Plains Cree medicine people heal individuals by bringing unconscious conflict and resistance to a conscious level where they can be worked with" (Buffalo 1990: 118). Awareness is also seen by feminists, and by those targeting racist oppression, as the beginning of the will to resist, to challenge and change the structures that confine us (hooks 1990; Collins 1991). The transformation process begins when we air feelings, perceptions and personal reactions and discover that they are socially constructed. According to Charnley, "In order to really know what is working against us we have to be able to question, reflect on one's own experience and see it in relation to and in dynamic with other people and environs" (1990: 16). What Charnley is advising is often termed by critical educators as "consciousness-raising." Consciousness-raising is an educational and healing model that focuses on the sharing of personal feelings, attitudes and behaviours to gain a deeper understanding of the collective reality produced through societal conditions. Through consciousness-raising, participants learn how to use their own "personal" experience as a starting point for individual and/ or "political" change. To gain political relevance, "personal" experience must be understood as being shaped by the concrete social conditions of our lives. The feminist consciousness-raising model, strong because it begins with lived experience, deals with feelings, works in non-hierarchical groups and uses our own voices, is an avenue for developing cross-cultural understanding. According to Hart, the overall pattern of the process is "one of moving from surface phenomenon related to the immediate present; then to the depths of pain, anger, or bitterness related to past experiences; and outwards again toward utopian outlooks for the future" (1991: 68). This view respects Aboriginal philosophy, as we are taught to always consider the past, the present and the future. It also resonates in this teaching Model and this text, as we move continuously back and forth from historical relations and through current daily lived experiences to people's hopes, dreams and visions for their children's future.

In feminist consciousness-raising models it is voice that is emphasized— the regaining of women's voice, in spite of the patriarchy's attempts to silence us. Consciousness-raising has been described by Gould as a process of "going from a discussion of feelings and experiences, to analysis, and then to political action" (1987: 9). Voice is a central pedagogical tool in this Model, for Traditionalists know that learning occurs through both the rearticulation of our own experience and through hearing the stories of others.

Hart (1991) explores enabling conditions for the use of feminist consciousness-raising as a tool for transformative learning. These include: the acknowledgment of oppression, which provides the basis of commonality of experience; the importance of personal experience, which goes against the norm of objectivity; the need for homogeneity in the learning group to establish an atmosphere of self-disclosure rather than self-protection; a consideration of the issue of equality, particularly considering the unequal power relation of teacher and student; and the recognition of the value of gaining and sustaining theoretical distance, which helps us look more clearly at and generalize our experiences. This list, rather than providing indicators that consciousness-raising will be successful, reminds me of the opposite—exactly what a large undertaking it is, given the contextual conditions of work. Many students do not understand or acknowledge oppression and there is ongoing resistance to sharing personal experience in a School setting. While homogeneity may encourage self-disclosure, heterogeneity in the group allows the experience of difference necessary to challenge hegemony. The unequal power relations between student and teacher and among students continue to exist regardless of efforts to equalize them. While theoretical distance can help generalize our experience, it can be counterproductive in this learning situation, which requires affect and connection to heart. In spite of the potential and actual contradictions, I support the use of consciousness-raising in the classroom, to engage in struggle within Schools, to change them and society through the personal transformation of students. I wish to reappropriate, adapt and adjust the consciousness-raising process and to expand its conceptualization.

If one can be acculturated to hold dominant views, they can also be unacculturated. The altering of consciousness, theorized by many feminist, anti-racist and critical educators, is one of the central aims of this work. I ask: how can students, steeped primarily in hegemonic Eurocentric consciousness, become aware of the nature of their cultural conditioning? I consider this to be a necessary beginning on the journey of change in attitudes and behaviours towards peoples from our Communities. The Western foundations, upon which modern-day society rests, must not stand unchallenged. Students, many of whom are White and middle-class, need to explore the legacy of their Eurocentric culture and recognize its impacts on their lives and our lives—personally and politically.

What Do We Need to Know? The Content

Accept the Gift of the East
Be aware of Self . . . Who Am I?
How do I identify?
How do I locate myself in the Structures of Society?

Consciousness is Personal
We all interpret reality through our own "lens."
Our individual reality is also Collective.
Our "cultural locatedness" . . . Our identity(s)
Influence our perceptions.

How am I the oppressor?
How am I oppressed?
Can I connect Personal experiences to Structural realities?
Can I locate myself in the overt and subtle "Wires"
Of the "cage of oppression"?

Fernwood Books — Sample Requests

acct # 2101

3/24/99

R Luther
Social Work
Carleton University
1125 Colonel By Dr.
Ottawa   Ontario K1S 5B6

Pub	ISBN	Title	List	Course name	Adop date	Enroll
FER	1 895686 97 0	Journeying Forward	16.95	Race, culture, and Soc Work	4/99	30
	1 895686 30 x	Circle Works	24.95	"	4/99	30

Examination Copy: To help us keep our costs down we request $5 per shipment. Thank you for your help. We will accept a cheque or visa payment. Fernwood Books Ltd., P O Box 9409, Stn A, Halifax B3K 5S3

There is nothing simple about Oppression.
We experience it as individuals
It is embedded in our society.
Complex barriers have been Internalized
Enacted on us . . . by us
Daily.
Racism . . . Sexism . . . Classism . . . Heterosexism
Do exist.
All are oppressive forms.
Hierarchical power-over must be Examined . . . Challenged.
All are linked . . . All depend on others for their Survival.
Eurocentric Domination . . . White Privilege
Must be Unveiled.
When some Lose . . . some Gain.

Gain Consciousness
Question your Past and Present perceptions
What did you know . . . Do you know now?

Certain theoretical and process conceptualizations are necessary to provide clarity and common language from which to proceed; a shared vocabulary is essential to developing anti-racist literacy (hooks 1988). Teaching shared concepts provides a language for discussion and can aid students in adjusting to being "culturally located." Locatedness helps them to recognize that the privileges or oppressions they have received are based on racial/cultural group membership, not necessarily on individual merit or choice (McIntosh 1990). Oppression, racism, white privilege, and culture, the ongoing critical themes of the Model, are all theoretically produced in current writings by feminists and other critical educators.

The Subtle and Overt Cage of Oppression

I begin with Marilyn Frye's (1983) early metaphorical work on the "cage" of oppression. I theorize and enact it through psychodrama and Talking Circle. Students learn that oppression is many layered and societally constructed while it specifically impacts on us as individuals.

> The experience of oppressed people is that the living of one's life is confined and shaped by forces and barriers which are not accidental or occasional and hence unavoidable, but are systematically related to each other in such a way as to catch one between and among them and restrict or penalize motion in any direction. It is the experience of being caged in: all avenues, in every direction, are blocked and booby trapped. (Frye 1983: 4)

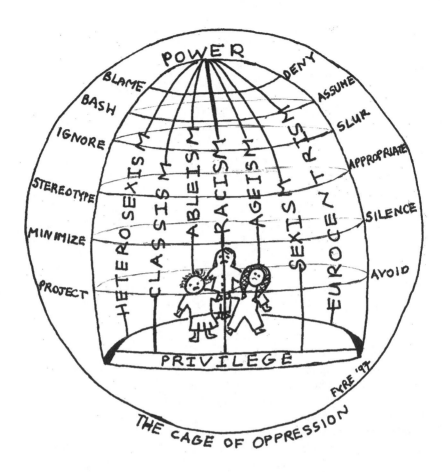

As Frye makes very clear, it is not a singular experience of discomfort that can be classified as "oppression," but rather it is a continuous, ongoing set of relations that have to do specifically with one's membership in a particular group.

> When you question why you are being blocked, why this barrier is in your path, the answer has not to do with individual talent or merit, handicap or failure; it has to do with your membership in some category understood as a "natural" or "physical" category. (1983: 8)

To name oneself or to be named as oppressed, the person identifies or is identified as belonging to a group—racial, gender, cultural, etc. This can immediately serve to collectivize an individual's consciousness, heightening awareness of their structural location. Participants from the African and Aboriginal Communities are able to give an "insider's" viewpoint. Their voices illustrate how oppression is lived with and resisted on a daily basis. Unicorn, an African Nova Scotian participant, shares her insights in her journal:

> How am I the oppressed? I am oppressed based on my race (Black) and as a woman. I am oppressed when:
> • The floorwalkers in department stores immediately begin watching me and following me around,
> • I am overlooked for promotion, credit because of my race and gender.
> • I am expected to automatically assimilate into the white culture.
> • It is assumed that I provide personal or sexual service work based on my skin color and gender.
> • It is assumed that I am angry and violent.
> • I am not portrayed in a positive light by the media not included in important positive community news reports.
> • My culture is not acknowledged or respected in the education, political, social, health and legal systems.
> This is just the tip of the iceberg. Need I say more? (Oct 6 93-j)

As many other feminist and critical educators have articulated, knowing one's Self-In-Relation, one's membership in- and outside of certain socially-defined groups, is fundamentally a group process. Groups are central in the process of "discovering" oppression as imposed upon individuals by society and as experienced in common with others. In teaching about oppression, I follow Brandt (1986), who promotes collaborative, group-centered learning in anti-racist pedagogy. Members of the group can learn from each other. Not only the subject matter itself is processed in group, but the "real life" knowledge of diverse group members is shared as knowledge. According to Redwine, the small group experience can motivate participants to take responsibility for their own learning, while at the same time it provides a sense of community, "a social support group with which to feel a shared obligation and help in time of need" (1989: 88). Sharing experiences can be an important way to learn to value ourselves, to build empathy with others and to reclaim the histories of oppressed groups.

The value of group-centered learning is evident in journals written by students from dramatically different cultural locations. For some, the insight comes from a rearticulation of their own stories of oppression. An Aboriginal participant, Randi, expresses her new insights:

> Class tonight was a very powerful experience, as we talked about oppression it became obvious to me that not everyone understands oppression, but if you've lived with it all of your life, it's right in front of you all the time.
> The oppression that I feel as an oppressed Native lesbian woman often astounds me, I feel so isolated from family and friends, there are

few supports for a Native student who feels alone. As a Lesbian not "out" at work, I find work isolating and depressing.

As we discussed the bird cage analogy it became obvious that sometimes it is easier to look at the bars than to come forward and realize that the Space between the bars is clear but the bars still exist. (Jan 13 93-j)

Randi later summarizes her learnings about oppression: "I learned that oppression occurs across all cultural lines, and that each form of oppression is devastating to a particular group" (Apr 93-jsum).

Consciousness of oppression requires recognition of the everyday lived experience, the personal pain and suffering that accompanies oppression. Attention must also be drawn to our survival—resistance and healing. Phil did a thorough analysis of all the forms of oppression she had experienced. She concludes with a comment about the strength she has gained from her life experiences:

These are the ways I have been most oppressed. I didn't plan to get into so much detail, but it poured out. I never really thought about how I had internalized the oppression before. I can see all of the layers that were so thick and hard to break through. But I can also see how it has made me strong, and given me insight and empathy. It made me willing to challenge things that I think are wrong.

Oppression is very complex, everybody has experienced it both as a giver and as a receiver. But some people experience more of it than others. I don't think that it is possible to do away with oppression completely, but it is very important to be aware of it and how you are affecting other people and also how they are affecting you. If you do not realize that you are being oppressed it becomes internalized. This is even more painful to deal with because you become isolated. When you come to terms with oppression, it can give you strength and courage. (Phil Apr 93-t1)

Depending on the choices we make, our behaviours and attitudes can serve to maintain or reduce oppressive forms. This is true in our personal lives as well as our professional lives. In the enactment of oppression, two roles are required: the oppressed (who receive the bulk of critical focus) and the oppressor (who is seen to be someone or somewhere else). In teaching students to develop their understanding of Self-In-Relation to oppression, I emphasize personal responsibility to interrogate our own social/cultural position as we embody it on a day-to-day basis. Task One (see course outline in Appendix) challenges students to describe the ways in which they have been oppressed and to interrogate the social causes for personal traumas as a means to begin the healing process. Simultaneously it requires an unveiling of opportunities for being oppressive. For some, this is an entirely new concept that requires reframing to include the subtle as well as overt acts of oppression. Specific attention to the detail of our daily lives and how we are playing out these roles in large and small ways assists students in reviewing their own location and forming targets for change.

Uncovering one's role as oppressor takes time and patience, as layers of denial are reinforced by existing White privilege.

> When reading the question, "How am I the oppressor?" I couldn't pinpoint a time when I had ever oppressed anyone. However, a closer examination provided me with lots of examples . . . . First, I feel that I am the oppressor because I rarely take action to stop someone from being oppressed. I certainly know it's wrong but I don't usually speak up unless I am with people I know well. Because of my actions, I help to perpetuate unfair treatment of certain people because I'm too weakwilled as an individual. I can participate in someone else's cause or action just as long as I don't have to initiate the action myself. I sometimes see myself as the oppressor because I would much rather follow than lead. In my experience I have learned that to only follow sometimes means that you end up saying or doing something you really don't believe in. I'm slowly learning that beliefs of cultural equality are only of value if acted upon. (Gela Jan 25 93-t1)

It is often noted as essential that oppressed persons become conscious of the structural realities which "cage" them in the journey from self-blame to empowerment. But little attention is paid to the recognition of internalized oppressiveness: how do we recognize the structures of oppression that keep us attached to the oppressor role in subtle and overt ways? I now recognize this lack in the daily consciousness of most students, as well as in Western literature. This topic necessarily becomes the subject of a lecturette, which always generates much response from previously "unaware" students. Two illustrations will be given. Van records her perceptions of that particular class:

> The discussion was very brief but really hit home. You were talking about subtle forms of racism and mentioned something that I did all my life. That is, thinking that everyone was just like me. I knew that this was a naive way to think, but I did not realize it was negating other's existence and/or experiences. Every time I did this I was erasing someone's reality, allowing their oppression to be invisible. This blew me away . . . . This course is going to blow me away!!! (Sept 22 93-j)

Analee, also a White female, self-interrogates her own acts of privilege following that same class. This reinforces the use of specific examples in the daily lived experiences of participants as an "impact-full" teaching tool.

> When you began to speak of "subtle" avoidances that people some-times make I felt myself growing a little uneasy. You spoke of sticking

with things you know and are familiar with, for fear of getting involved in something that is unfamiliar. When we use this type of avoidance we free ourselves of the possibility of *feeling* or being emotionally responsive or involved with a particular person/situation or event.

As you explained this concept to the class I felt myself wander a little as I recalled a few instances in which I feel I was *avoiding* certain things—especially conversations. At the time, I didn't really think about it, but since you have explained what "avoidance" really involves, I am now able to identify instances in which I have done this very thing.

I tried to rationalize my actions by thinking that I would rather not participate in some conversations or discussions because I simply did not know enough about the topic at hand to add anything worthwhile. Looking back, it may very well have been that, but, I think, no matter how subtle, that it was also a hint of avoidance on my part . . . . It was my keeping a safe distance from things that were unfamiliar to me . . . . It was my way of not having to *feel* in those particular instances.

It is helpful for me to be able to see and understand the many facets of oppression—and realize that no matter how subtle or bold, they are still very hurtful.

This was a lesson learned for me . . . . (Analee Sept 22 93-j)

When participants from the Communities are able to express their knowledge about oppression as a daily lived, personal and emotional experience, this promotes a deepening level of awareness among privileged students of their role as "oppressor."

This circle had quite an impact on me tonight. I have had a *lot* of experience as an oppressed person—incest, emotional abuse, being a woman. But for the very first time tonight, as the black, Acadian, and aboriginal members of our groups spoke, I felt like an *oppressor!* I felt guilty, but couldn't even name what I had done—it was sort of a collective guilt, (without knowledge, intention, or desire). I didn't like it and feel a need to change whatever I can about my personal attitudes and behaviours so that I am less oppressive. I hope as we progress, I can define some things to work on. (Char Jan 14 93-j)

Tonight in class we discussed our personal experiences of oppression. Throughout my two years at this school, I have really come to realize that I represent the oppressor as a result of my gender, class, sexual orientation and race. So when we students are provided with the opportunity to discuss our personal experiences of oppression, I usually resort to shutting down, and do not discuss openly my experiences as oppressor. Tonight just for a moment, I felt like opening up to the class about how I perceive oppression. But then I started to realize that I do not even know how to explain my feelings, because I constantly feel guilty and angry. So instead of opening up, I just acknowledged to the class that I cannot begin to fully understand or explain what oppression is like, because I am the oppressor. (Ken Jan 13 93-j)

Through the articulation of concepts, expression of experience and group processes students are taught, metaphorically and practically, that they have a role to play in oppression and that structural oppression is the norm. Char expresses her awakening in a poem describing her new Self-In-Relation to the oppressor role and the feelings that this generates:

Oppressor

As Painful
As it is
To Learn
How I am oppressed
It is even
More painful
To learn
How I am the oppressor.

I am
Beginning to understand
That to be white
Is a privilege
I had never even considered.

But now that
I have begun to consider it,
I can no longer deny it.

I am beginning
To see it everywhere,
And especially
In me:
• being surprised that the "Speak It" director is black;
• not being surprised that hotel chambermaids are black;
• expecting pictures of Jesus to be white;
• not noticing the absence of black and other racial representation in schoolbooks;
• assuming employees in stores, banks, schools . . . will be white;
• discomfort being alone with a black cab driver;

I do not
Like me
In this role. (March 25 93-t1)

Recognizing Racism as an Everyday Reality
Racism is one form of oppression that affects the lives of "visibly racial" members of Communities on a daily/hourly basis. Brandt describes racism as "multi-faceted and dynamic" (1986: 133). It includes not only acts of "preju-

dice, 'race hatred,' bias, and ethnocentricity" (Brandt 1986: 133), but it must be critically analyzed in terms of power and the legacy of imperialism and colonialism. Racism exerts a powerful influence over people's lives that "ranges from the ideological to the material and from the institutional to the interactional. The elements of this racism could be either covert or overt, hidden or blatant, and can operate in very specific ways in specific institutions" (Brandt 1986: 133).

Essed (1991) outlines explicitly the multiple possibilities in which racist practices can unfold, targeting both the micro and macro dimensions. Most literature primarily reflects the African experience of racism, but LaRocque (1991) and others challenge this construction: "Everyday, Natives encounter some form of personal prejudice or institutional violence. This comes not only from the proverbial 'redneck' but from high and influential places in society— from judges, journalists, doctors, businesses, teachers and politicians" (LaRocque 1991: 73). In this Model, participants are challenged to see the specific ways in which racism has been and is operating around them on an everyday basis. The daily encounter is a common journal and Circle theme. A Black participant, Nadine, journals her reality:

> The occasion to be in a racial confrontation can occur daily. Unless you are a racially visible person, you would not understand the impact of such situations. In fact many White people say that you are being too sensitive or you're overreacting when you express your concerns. (Feb 3 93-j)

Recognizing the everyday nature of racism can help retain focus on the topic and restrain the common reaction: "does she always have to bring up racism":

> When I hear people say that they are tired of hearing about racism for example, I always remember that people who are Black, Aboriginal, Indian, etc. have no choice in saying that they don't want to talk about racism. They live racism every day, hour, minute of their lives. In remembering this it puts my reality and the reality of others in perspective. (Tia 93-j)

As Maracle states, "Racism is for us, not an ideology in the abstract, but a very real and practical part of our lives. The pain, the effect, the shame are all real" (1988: 2). hooks (1990) refers to this as "racist trauma." Many voices in Brand and Bhaggiyadatta's collection speak to the pain and address a response pattern known to many:

> It comes up and overwhelms you. You can't even think for a moment ... you are just consumed. It's a kind of blinding rage and humiliation

that's really wearing on a person. I try not to think about it and then, a couple of days down the road, it will just flash back into my memory. For that moment, I would go through the whole pain over again. (1986: 158)

Phil gives a vivid example of how racism happens in daily life and what to do when it does:

This afternoon I was crossing the street with my daughter . . . and a friend's daughter . . . sang [a racist song]. I was so angry that I felt as if I was breathing fire. I stopped on the corner and got down on one knee so that I could look directly into her eyes. I told her never to say racist things like that ever again. I told her it hurts people. I asked if she knew what it meant, and where she learned it. By the time I had finished she was in tears. I felt that I had gone too far, I gave her a hug and told her that I know that she wouldn't deliberately hurt people, that she was a kind girl, but that she has to think about what she says or sings before she opens her mouth because even if she didn't mean to be hurtful she was. I walked them to school and we talked about racism and the things that other children say at school. I told her that if she hears someone saying things that are hurtful to another person, she should always tell them to stop, and help the other person.

I was very concerned because of the intensity of my reaction to her. I didn't want to traumatize her, but at the same time I wanted her to realize how strongly I feel about it. I think that it will be an experience that she will never forget. I hope that she learns from it. (Jan 15 93-j)

Participants from the Communities often tell stories of racism and how it negatively impacts on children and adults. This challenges the listener's commonsense understanding of today's "tolerant" society. One story told by a Mi'kmaq participant, Redbird, will illustrate:

And I walked up to my doctor's office just last week and I was called a [slur] by a total stranger on a street! And it was so early in the morning that it was only him and I on the street and I thought—is he speaking to me? And I looked around, there was no one else there, and he turned back "yes I'm speaking to you." And then about four days later I was on my way to my daughter's to help her out and I got called the exact same name by another man just walking down the street with such a vicious, cruel look on his face! And I thought, you know, do I stand out in a crowd or something? What is it about me or something? (CCI:18)

The ending line—"What is it about me or something?"—is a commonly expressed reaction to racism. It signifies a form of complex denial of the structural aspects that have been internalized in us all. Being systematically trained to internalize racism, and reinforce the internalization in others, victims become labeled and label themselves as the "problem." If we have recognized the pattern, assessed the situation as oppressive and are safe enough to attempt to confront the perpetrators, we are labeled as "over-reacting" or "hostile" "trouble-maker(s)." We learn to ask, "Am I overreacting or too hostile?" We engage in self-interrogation and leave oppressive systems intact. Through complex forms of internalization, we become our own critics and can attach these labels and expectations to ourselves and others like us. This reproduces "anomie" from and within our group and contributes to our own oppression. Vada expresses her own internal dialogue about the link between slurs, personal pain and reaction to others in her journal:

> In our class yesterday you spoke about that people often do not think they are racist at times you feel they are racist towards you. I have been struggling with this issue for some time. Because I am a white immigrant and coming from a wealthy European country, people seem to believe that I do not experience discrimination and do not see me as an immigrant. When they, through racist jokes or statements about immigrants show their dislike for immigrants and our move to Canada, they do not realize they make me feel uncomfortable and targeted. I have often wondered if I am only overreacting to these statements, and should not think of myself as an immigrant. But, when I try to convince myself of this, something in myself tells me, "Yes, I am an immigrant and what people say about immigrants they also say about me." I also feel that I should be allowed to feel that I am discriminated against when the situation makes me feel uncomfortable, silenced and different. These situations make me feel like an outsider and not interested in becoming a Canadian. The class discussion made me feel that maybe I do not overreact when I feel discriminated against. I should probably go with my gut feeling. (Feb 28 93-j)

Recognizing this pattern and refusing to wear the labels is one form of resistance. We need to be able to go with our "gut feeling" and react strongly when we feel discriminated against. As students come to recognize themselves as part of a larger structural dynamic, they begin to recognize more specifically how our daily lives are directly affected. State apparatuses divide us into categories based on physical and other traits and then mold us to fit the assigned, and then internalized, labels. Students can often relate to racial language, slurs and stereotypes, as forms of power. Unicorn gives a vivid illustration of the power of language in shaping the representations of our people and our own identities:

> As a Black Nova Scotian, I have been described and defined by others as "colored, minority, visible minority, target group, you people," etc. This made me feel like a problem . . . . By categorizing oppressed peoples in the above way, it presents an issue having to do with being

in a minority group or problem concerning numbers instead of the real problem stemming from privilege, power and oppression. (Dec 2 93-j)

Many expressed how slurs and stereotypes have been used against them, what feelings are associated with these negative qualifiers and, more essentially, how even our names become contested terrain. Vada has this story to tell:

> People have also told me that I should change my name to a name that is easier to say. While it makes me mad to hear this, I feel that my name is the one thing that I have that tells me and others who I am. (Feb 93-t1)

In many and diverse ways, the state challenges our identities through the construction of categories, labels and codes. This is done in the name of "efficiency," so prized by the mechanistic mentality. This is clearly recognized by Mac in his analysis of "bureaucratization of culture":

> The most humiliating thing I felt this far is how the Federal Government gets to decide who is Native and who isn't. It just seems crazy when you think that there have been cultures here for thousand of years and now one must virtually apply to some faceless bureaucrat to be legitimized in being recognized for one's own identity. The bureaucratization of culture. If you don't fill in the forms correctly then it can't get processed and then nothing is real. Categorization for manipulation. (92-j)

In Joane Cardinal-Schubert's art installation, part of the *Indigena* exhibit, racism is visually discussed through an examination of the labels and stereotypes she experienced growing up in a non-Native society. She metaphorically offers a choice to viewers as to how they wish to look at Aboriginal people:

> Do they wish to look at their skin color and thereby color what knowledge they possess of Native people? Do they wish to look at a different view of history? Do they wish to look at a more personal examination of the individual and the contribution of that person on an individual level? Do they wish to look at the ancestors to prove their theories about Native people are misinformed? Do they believe a fenced-off area is all Native people want out of life? Do they believe Native people are misinformed about the details of history that are not included in the history taught in the schools of this country? . . . [I]t is difficult to see all the facts in just one look. It is uncomfortable to peek through the little holes of this site. You miss some of the picture. What's more, it is an uncomfortable and unsettling experience. Good! Now you know how I have felt for most of my life. (Cardinal-Schubert 1992: 133)

Loretta Todd confirms this as a common theme: "I remember being spied upon, vulnerable and invaded. It reminded me of how public our lives have been-investigated, studied, always subject to inspection" (1992: 78). Nadine, an African Nova Scotian, tells this story in her journal.

> In anticipation of my new job next week, my partner asked me an interesting question. He said ". . . do you think you got the job because of your race or because of your ability?" I hesitated then answered that I felt it was a bit of both. Definitely my ability had a lot to do with it. I wouldn't apply for a job I couldn't do. Yet the Department gains by having their "token" Black in management. This fills their affirmative action policies and takes the onus off them to hire racially visible people in the near future. This puts a lot of pressure on me. I am often plagued with the thoughts that I don't want to become "one" of them. I have known many Black people who achieved professional status only to sell out to their Black community. I have promised myself that I will not allow that to happen. White people don't have these types of worries when they secure employment. They don't have to worry that all eyes are on them and they are not in a position of feeling that they are choosing between their job and their community. (Jan 13 93-j)

While it is clear that some participants may have deep insights into racism and its effects, many students from the hegemonic culture express little or no insight into their own or others' experiences with racial dynamics. This lack of insight becomes an early target, as recognition of racism is a necessary precondition to anti-racist activism. Van captures this well:

> Racism can be obvious when one learns how to see. It can be so simple yet so hidden because we do not know what to look for, or what questions to ask. This takes a conscious effort that requires active thinking and consistent question asking. (Oct 93-t1)

For many White students the most fundamental learning was the uncovering of racial overtones and undertones all around them. As one White participant, Dana, summarizes:

> Now that I have developed an awareness, I see it everywhere . . . . I am now looking for racism and racist remarks in everything that I see, hear, and read. This was an excellent learning experience: A cross-cultural learning experience and awakening!! (Dec 10 92-jsum)

Several students logged their own evolution into critical consciousness. When first beginning to recognize and interrogate racism, the process may feel all-consuming. Gela records in her journal:

I wonder if I am becoming too critical of the environment around me . . . . Am I becoming too extreme in my identification and analysis of racism? I remember when I first began to learn about feminism and the oppression of women. I did not know how to respond to a man who opened or held a door for me. Sometimes I perceived such an action as a simple kind and respectful gesture, whereas other times I wondered if the man thought I was too frail to open the door myself. I guess it's natural for me to be extra sensitive about racism, especially since I am just becoming aware of the many ways racism is expressed by society. (Feb 22 93-j)

Examining oneself for racism is a difficult task for those who have built their identity around being accepting and caring people. It requires personal risk. Mac recognizes and discusses this reality:

How can you if your heart isn't there. If your sense of security is left intact. When there is no risk, there isn't anything at stake. I've never been taken to task about the times that I froze up when a group of young black guys turns onto the same side of the street as I am walking on at night. About those afterthoughts.

There is no line in the sand that, once crossed, means that you are culturally sensitive. You cannot be sure of how you'll act when you only deal with issues on an intellectual level. What about when it hits you in the face. What about when you have to take a stand. What is the point of proclaiming oneself racist but well intentioned. Is that enough? Can I now rest upon my laurels? Am I free to criticize others? Do I have the right? Can one be aware and not act? How do I know which feelings are real? Can I trust the class to give me a break? The last thing that I want is to come off superficially but I don't trust strangers with my innermost feelings. I am worried but I think I may be at the bottom of the issue . . . . The question is, "Do I live up to it?" Do I act racist in spite of myself?

That is the real issue. If we have defined racism as my existence in a white dominated society, then admitting my racism at this point in my awareness is not very meaningful. Some would say that it borders on a truism. And if this is the case, what is the most I can ask of myself? It is time to stop asking questions and start looking at actions. (92-j)

Char provides a continuing dialogue about her racial awakening, traceable through her journal excerpts over the period of the course. At first she records:

I am really confused about racism. I'm not at all sure what it is, what it isn't; I'm not *aware* of being racist, but I'm sure I *must* be. I think I could easily identify blatant racism—aggressive, violent acts. But I certainly can't yet "see" the subtleties and innuendoes that seem so obvious to others. (Char Jan 28 93-j)

She compares her current situation to earlier work uncovering abuse:

> I feel like I'm in the same place I was in 2 years ago regarding my own emotional and psychological abuse . . . . I just couldn't *see* it. But gradually I grew to understand that, so hopefully I will gradually become more aware of racism, both around me and in myself. (Char Jan 28 93-j)

She concludes this entry with a question that illustrates an emerging understanding of the mundane reality of everyday racism:

> I am wondering if racism means that your actions are based on a person's skin color/race? For example, when the little black girl comes selling blueberries. If I buy them *because* she's black, or if I *don't* buy them because she's black—am I being racist? My decision to buy/not buy should be based on my desire for blueberries—not her skin color? (Char Jan 28 93-j)

People often begin with a race awareness that is limited to different treatment based on skin colour. By attending Community-sponsored events, students are often challenged to begin to unveil their own racial constructions. This recognition allows expansion of conscious understanding to include the more subtle forms of racism embedded in us all. Char tells it:

> But it was when they were introducing the director after the show, that I came face-to-face with my own internalized racism: I found myself surprised—expecting her to be *white!!* I can't imagine *why* I would think a film about black people and racism would be white—it didn't make sense when I thought about it. But I guess we *don't think* often enough—it is part of our socialization. This really stunned me—I found it amazing.
> This seems to me like a milestone—in my awareness of my own racism. It's like a light came on—I think I am beginning to understand what racism means. (Feb 7 93-j)

Char began and continued a pattern of interrogating the everyday encounter for subtle and overt racism. This process expanded again when she began to recognize it as being enmeshed with gender:

> An interesting thing happened today. I met a black man coming toward me on the sidewalk. There was so much snow that there was only a very narrow path—wide enough for 1 person. One of us had to move over, and he was the one who did.
> As I went by, I said "Thank you"—but my head was filled with questions.
> Did I expect him to move because I was white? or a woman?
> Did he expect to have to move because he was black? a man?

> In my new assertiveness as a woman, did I decide I wasn't going to move even though the passive-me would have?
> Was it just a simple, courteous gesture on his part, with no deep underlying dynamics of racism or sexism at all?
> I feel confused. (Char Feb 22 93-j)

Confusion is to be expected. Recognizing racism is not as obvious for some as for others, but it is necessary in order to challenge it.

> I feel at the end of this course that I have at least made a beginning of my consciousness and understanding of racism. I recognize I have a lot to learn, and a lot of inner work to do on my own racism.
> I find I "see" incidents of racism much more readily. I am amazed I couldn't see them before. I feel that this new awareness will continue to expand, and gradually I will be able to take more risks to combat racism. (Char Apr 6 93-jsum)

Unveiling White Privilege

Like oppression, racism affects all of us, whether it is because we are victimized by institutions and persons who have been acculturated to believe in White supremacy or because we are reaping the benefits of a racistly organized state. Because White Europeans have come to spacially, politically and culturally dominate through colonialism, some citizens in North America are raised with material privilege and White cultural privilege. This translates into the construct known as *white privilege*. McIntosh (1990) usefully proposes a set of statements by which everyday lived experiences of White privilege are revealed. I use her worksheet for students to prepare for a Talking Circle in which students are asked to reveal personal stories about their own privilege.

> After reading McIntosh's article, I went over the 26 points, and checked off 21 points that reflect my life. This was a really scary realization for me, because it just shows how much I execute my white privilege on a daily basis without even knowing that I am doing it.
> Also another learning experience I gained from this particular exercise, was realizing how each time I am executing my white privilege I am in turn oppressing those who do not have such privileges. This exercise was very educational for me, because it pinpoints exactly where I am being oppressive, and I feel that the first step in fighting oppression, is admitting that I do indeed oppress. (Ken Jan 26 93-j)

White privilege is very much interlocked with racism. As the Model has evolved I have become more and more committed to studying these constructs together. Many Whites have never interrogated race as an issue, and so have never had to see their privilege as related to someone else's pain. Bannerji articulates an understanding of the relationship of racism and White privilege:

And sitting there, hearing claims about sharing "experience," having empathy, a nausea rose in me. Why do they, I thought, only talk about racism, as understanding us, doing good to "us"? Why don't they move from the experience of sharing our pain, to narrating the experience of afflicting it upon us? Why do they not question their own cultures, childhoods, upbringings, and ask how they could live so "naturally" in this "white" environment, never noticing the fact until we brought it home to them? (1991: 10)

Some students unveil their privilege through reversal or "mirror work." When they hear stories about racism, they recognize their own reality as different. White privilege becomes constructed, understood and described by the oppression they do not receive. In particular, Analee notes the absence of the daily recurring pain that is consistently reflected on by Community members:

As [the guest] spoke of his experiences as a Black man, he really said something that has had a big impact on me. He talked about waking up every day and thinking to himself about what type of experiences he will have that day as a result of the color of his skin . . . as a black man, what type of discrimination he will encounter today.
This really made me stop and think . . . . When I wake up in the morning I never think about what type of racist experiences I will encounter today as a result of the color of my skin. This has helped me to see yet another one of the many privileges I have as a white person. Until [the guest] spoke of this, I never thought about it . . . . I am seeing how easy it is not to have to think about things like this when they do not directly affect you . . . . I guess this is something that is a big part of the lives of many people. (Oct 27 93-j)

Gela more generally articulates her privilege as an oppression-free reality:

I cannot readily think of a time when I have ever felt oppressed. Although I am aware of the systematic oppression of women, I have been fortunate not to have experienced the blatant effects of differential treatment on a personal level. I have been fortunate to have been raised in a family that instilled in me the idea that I can do whatever I want if I set my mind to it. So far this has pretty much been my experience. I realize that my life experience has been somewhat sheltered and limited up to this point in time, and that in the future I could experience various forms of oppression in my personal relationships or my work environment etc. However, I never anticipate to experience the kind and degree of oppression that members of minority groups experience on a daily basis, especially women of minority groups. The color of my skin and my middle class status has pretty well ensured my acceptance by larger society. (Jan 25 93-t1)

White privilege is hidden through the complex, multifaceted denial process, which produces individuals who do not recognize their own racial or cultural makeup as White European. Analee's story reinforces the "essential" invisibility of White privilege in the commonsense "lifeworld" of privileged Europeans. She traces her own evolution to a heightened consciousness about her privilege:

> White privilege is something that I never thought about growing up. I lived in a small town that was predominately white and I went to schools where the majority of students and all of the teachers were white. In my home there was never any mention of racism or prejudices but my parents always taught us to treat others as we would like to be treated . . . .
>
> These values were instilled in me as a young child and I have carried them with me to this very day. Something my parents did not teach me about was white privilege. As I have said, it is something that I honestly have not thought about until these last couple of years. I never really gave a second thought to . . . .
>
> Taking many of these things for granted was certainly the case for me. Most of these things seemed so common to me that I never took the time to stop and see what was *really* going on. I am very glad that I am learning about white privilege but you know, sometimes I feel so ignorant for not being able to see things that now are *so* obvious to me. (Analee Nov 17 93-j)

Analee had earlier journalled about the aspects of the class on White privilege that most impacted on her:

> The display that was set up for this presentation was also an eye opener for me. It is sometimes too easy to overlook things that do not directly affect you. For example the magazines, the Hallmark cards, the hair products, etc. . . . all products that have as their focus, the white population. As I was standing there looking at the display I was feeling very stupid as I thought to myself that these are products that we see, and use everyday and too often we do not even realize who these products are geared towards—Why? . . . because that is another privilege we have—it seems so common to us that we do not even question it. (Oct 6, 93-j)

She concludes her entry on White privilege, acknowledging her changed level of consciousness:

> I have definitely had my consciousness raised on a number of occasions in this class—Now, I often find myself asking questions a lot more—both of others, of different situations, and of myself. I am much quicker in identifying things in myself that I say, or do, that are the result

of white privilege. As a result of my learning I am better able to make these connections. In being more capable of identifying white privilege, I am also better able to understand the affects this has on others. It has helped me to see the importance of making changes within myself before I can be effective in fighting for change in the larger society. (Analee Nov 17 93-j)

Being unaware or unconscious of one's cultural location within White-privileged culture can allow individuals to remain distanced from accepting responsibility for the historical abuses of their Ancestors as well as their own and those of their peers in daily life. While many can feel sorry for Aboriginals, Africans or others, they cannot see how they themselves are responsible or what they could do. Some can see that bad actions might have been taken in history, but this does not have relevance for themselves. If they do not and have not blatantly acted in a racist way, either through violence or slurs, they are not racist, and so have no role in the change process personally or politically. Through this convoluted but common rationalization process, the problem of racism belongs to those hurt by it, rather than to those who gain benefits from it.

Embracing Cultural Locatedness
This Model-In-Use follows Young Man in seeing cultures as "continuously in construction, deconstruction, and reconstruction as specifically ecological, political-economic and ideological processes impact on them" (1992: 98). Our cultures are vibrant and help us survive the daily challenges of life under Eurocentric domination. Teaching reverence for the gifts of our cultures is essential to helping people understand how we struggle and thrive as Communities. One way for this to occur is to allow students to actually experience in a sensory way the material gifts of the cultural groups. Char consistently journalled the material aspects of the presentations on culture that were done in her section. These quotations illustrate the kinds of "cultural" experiences that can be orchestrated in the classroom setting. For Char's group, Acadian culture was "experienced" first:

> The Acadian presentation tonight was wonderful. A good history via slides, a video about the Acadian festival in Wolfville, live music by [Acadian entertainer]—very talented and personable. It's easy to tell he loves his craft. The feast—rappie pie.
> It reminded me of the Acadian Song Festival last fall at the Cohen that [my friends] were in. It was so lively and colorful and energetic, just as this presentation was. There is a special quality about the Acadians—it's hard to define, but I came away from both events wishing I were Acadian! (Char Feb 10 93-j)

This was followed by the Mi'kmaq cultural night.

Our presentation on the Mi'kmaq culture was tonight—everyone seemed to enjoy it. I spent the morning making *Lus'knikn,* and *Essawiasikeiwey*—breads much like baking powder biscuits, except the latter had molasses and raisins added. They were baked in oblong pans rather than individual biscuits.

The program included 7 Mi'kmaq children and their leaders from the Friendship Center. They performed several traditional dances with songs and rhythm accompaniment. The class was invited to join in several of them which was fun—but *tiring!* They all wore traditional white leather dresses and moccasins with beaded jewelry and noise.[1] The decorations on the dresses were painted in earth colors—mostly dyes from plants—and the pictures and symbols represented things that were meaningful to the wearer.

This was followed by storytelling—when all the aboriginal class members told of meaningful events in their lives. This is how native history has been passed down from generation to generation—along with song and dance. It is only very recently that the Mi'kmaq language has been written down.

The last part of the evening was the feast—with the bread I had made, a cranberry bread, and stew that [another student] made.

I had picked up a box of Mi'kmaq artifacts from the N.S. Museum and arranged a display on the table, so the class could look at all sorts of samples of hides, bark, paint, grasses, arrowheads, pictures and books. (Char Mar 3 93-j)

The third cultural night that term was on African culture.

Tonight was the Black Culture presentation. There were a *lot* of junior high black young people who sang, rapped, read poems. It was lively and fun.

There was also a good talk given by [Black Elder] who had been to Sierra Leone—lots of pictures, and beautiful carvings.

The third part of the evening was African clothing and designs which were beautiful. They were displayed by [guest] from Nigeria. (Char Mar 10 93-j)

According to Thomas, within an anti-racist approach, culture is "not viewed as a static body of information which can be transmitted easily" (1984: 22). Culture is embedded in the "lived everyday responses of people to the circumstances in which they find themselves... how people have tried to change things which are wrong and unjust... nurturing a respect for the courage and skills it takes to do this .... [and] examining how people develop and adapt cultures to survive in particular circumstances" (Thomas 1984: 23). An African Nova Scotian participant, Cal, notes his reactions to the presentation of Acadian history and culture:

How the Acadians were loaded into boats and shipped away from their homes. This was very much like what happened to Africans. The point that I wanted to make was that Acadians were able, when necessary or possible, they were able to assimilate into the larger society. This was at a great cultural loss. Blacks have not been able to do this because we are seen. (Feb 9 94-j)

Nadine, another African Nova Scotian participant, was accustomed to viewing culture through the lens of visible difference. Her racial construction of culture was challenged and reframed by a presentation on Aboriginal culture.

One point that stood out for me in viewing the Native presentation, was how accustomed and stereotypical we have become, when I found myself looking at the young dancers and saying that they did not look Native. Of the five dancers only one young girl looked what I've conditioned to believe natives should look like. As in the Black race, this could be the result of mixed-relationships today, or as a result of forced sexual behaviour of White Europeans on the women of the earlier generations. Whatever the reason, culture is more than a color or a look. Culture is what a person lives, and passes down to their children. (Mar 10 93-j)

Our cultural locatedness is a strong factor in how we experience the world, informing how we react/act towards others. Culture is often distinguished by physicality, and our bodily reactions are linked to acculturation. We act and feel based on what we have been taught to expect as the "norm." According to Benhabib, culture does not "construct" everything: "The body is an active medium with its own dispositions and 'habits,' which process, channel and deflect the influences that come to it from the outside, in accordance with its own accumulated modality of being toward the world" (1992: 236). Through revisiting the material aspects of culture and acknowledging them as the gifts of each of the Communities, students are engaged in a physical exploration. Feasting, drumming, dancing, singing—tasting, touching, seeing, hearing— invokes embodied learning of cultural difference as challenging and pleasur-able. Culture is experienced as common to groups and distinct for each individual.

This Model-In-Use focuses on the cultural forms expressed in the often ignored "oppositional elements which cause people to resist and challenge those things that hurt and oppress them" (Thomas 1984: 22). For many of us, our survival and sustainability is linked to the Ancestral Traditions of our people, to the stories of resistance told and retold by our Elders, artists and other visionaries. Russell provides one illustration: "When words failed, remember how Aunt Jemima's most famous recipe, ground-glass plantation pancakes, made the masters choke" (1985: 161).

It is embracing our cultural identities to resist acculturation that frames our daily struggles. Simultaneously, we acknowledge oppression and resist these forces. The oppositional struggle is one of the vital and sustainable gifts of our cultures. It has been necessary to engage in continuous acts of resistance since contact with the colonial powers in the modern age. Being a culturally identified African, Aboriginal or Asian today encompasses experiencing both White Eurocentric domination *and* individual and group valuation of independent, longstanding cultural consciousness(es). These more oppositional gifts, gained through resistance efforts necessary for survival, are often disguised rather than taught in multicultural models that simply emphasize material representations (Brandt 1986).

Many cultural groups, targeted in society through racially visible differences, have struggled and learned to embrace their own culture as a gift. Paradoxically, many Whites cannot articulate what their own cultural affiliation is. One White female, Lena, expresses her difficulty in answering the task question, "What is my culture?":

> I have never felt that I have had a culture. I just recognized myself as being white. I am not sure if what has been told to me is specific to Irish/Catholic culture or has been appropriated from other cultures . . . [she states a few ethnic traditions] That is about all I know about my culture. It isn't very much when I see it on the monitor but I haven't given up yet. I am glad I had this opportunity to look at what my culture is and how I relate to it. My partner is Greek and he is always amazed that I didn't know much about being Irish. At least now I have a few pieces of information. Finding out about my culture has given me a certain feeling of . . . identity, I think? I am not sure what this feeling is but it feels O.K. (Feb 21 93-t1)

McLaren proposes "interrogating the culture of whiteness itself" (1994: 214). He believes that "unless we give white students a sense of their own identity as an emergent ethnicity—we naturalize whiteness as a cultural marker against which Otherness is defined" (McLaren 1994: 214). Values cannot be challenged unless they become visible and the learner can find his or her Self-In-Relation to their own cultural identity. The existential categories, adapted by Ibrahim (1985), along with Katz (1985) and others, can be utilized with students to heighten understanding. Eurocentrism means that Whites learn that the world is White. They often only see and relate to White persons and products and are taught White history and culture in the context of their own worldview. According to Katz, because hegemonic White culture is the norm, "it acts as an invisible veil that limits many people from seeing it as a cultural system" (1985: 616). I agree with Katz. It does appear easier for many Whites to identify and acknowledge the different cultures of others than it is to accept their own racial identity. She proposes an understanding based on a logical paradigm: "If we acknowledge that minority group members, in fact, have distinct cultural characteristics, we must logically accept that Whites also share similar cultural dimensions that constitute a separate, unique culture" (Katz 1985: 616). Because "White culture" is omnipresent, it is hard to "see" and accept. In the Western context, Whites are rarely required to step outside of their own dominant norms and see their beliefs, values and behaviours as distinct from other cultural groups. Gregory Jay shares his own process of critically unveiling his Whiteness as a cultural qualifier:

> I found myself puzzling over my own cultural identity. Did I have a race or ethnicity? A gender or a sexual orientation? A class or a nationality? Was my cultural identity singular or plural? And was it something I got by inheritance and imposition, or something I could choose at my own will? Perhaps most important, why hadn't I worried about all of this before? Who was I that I hadn't had a cultural identity crisis? Why had I so suddenly become a white man? (1995: 121)

He theorizes that the notion of cultural identity strikes White people as "strange," because of an ingrained acceptance of individualism: "Identity is supposed to be personal, idiosyncratic, something you don't share with anyone else" (Jay 1995: 122).

> Dominant American culture defines the person as essentially private and thus by definition lacking a cultural identity. A cultural identity would be a restraint on individual freedom, a straightjacket of convention, a prescription of inauthenticity. A cultural identity would limit what the person wore, ate, said, kissed, worshipped, wrote, bought, or sold. (Jay 1995: 122)

To an Aboriginal Traditionalist this is absurd. We are acculturated to realize our Self-In-Relation: "The individual does not form an identity in opposition to the group but recognizes the group as relatives included in his or her identity" (Hampton 1995: 21). How can we inspire an altered consciousness in those immersed in individualism, who are known to actively resist learning either the truth of colonial history or the devastation of modern-day racism? White people are often so blinded by their own language and values that they fail to see the pain of others. These blinders are painful to remove, but recovering the "truth" about historical and modern uses of power is necessary for the healing of people and our Earth Mother. Ingrained dominance, an artifact of a culture steeped in Eurocentric mentality, is evident in every institutional location: schools, churches, politics, the military, the media, the family and the social service state. As Malcolm Saulis, a Maliseet educator, argues:

> [T]he implication is that if you follow the rules, aspire to the same

aspirations, and behave appropriately you will have a place in society and share in its abundance. If you do not then actions will be taken against you to keep you in order. The situation of native people has been that a relationship has been defined over history but now needs to be redefined. (1994: 19)

This redefinition requires the unveiling of White supremacy as common sense in today's society. This understanding is reflected in the words of an African Canadian participant:

> I found the term and use of the word White Supremacy and not Racism to be much more empowering (enabling) expression of how we as Black people should see the world. The statement to explain this was that whites had internalized values and attitudes of their white ancestors . . . . It is how powerful and insidious racism and white supremacy is that makes us forget that we are raised in a capitalist society and what that means in real terms of internalization. (Cal Jan 18 94-j)

People acculturated to the dominant worldview may theorize that "skin colour doesn't matter," "we are all equal," "we all have equal opportunity to succeed." We on the margins of society know by our daily lived experiences, and by the stories of our Ancestors, our Elders, our peers and our children, that this is really the "myth of meritocracy" (McIntosh 1990). When we are working to unveil the complex reality of oppressed and oppressor—the interconnectedness between racism and White privilege—we are expressing our Self-In-Relation. We are all interconnected. Racism exists to feed White privilege—material, political, social and personal benefits are at the expense of those living in poverty with little political, social or personal power. White society—Western-ism—did not rise to prominence because of its inherent superiority, as White historians, philosophers and authors studied by Blaut (1993) and Said (1993) would like us to believe. Their success was built on the backs of Indigenous peoples who have been robbed of their lands, their resources and their labour. Those studying the complex relations of colonialism and imperialism have uncovered that White privilege is maintained at the expense of all others, locally, nationally and globally.

I propose that by applying the philosophy of Self-In-Relation, we can begin a shift from the dichotomous trap that focuses on either individual adjustment or structural change, to embrace simultaneously and ecologically both individual and community change. How can each of us be challenged personally and professionally to take up the structural problems of oppression and racism? We must acknowledge that we are all affected by society and we all participate in those processes. Ask yourself—do you ignore others' pain or do you confront the issues directly? We must all begin by seeing ourselves as In-Relation to racial issues. This relationship can be facilitated by the introduction of relevant content and by processes that re-emphasize and enact in an experiential way the established themes. As Horwitz advises, "One cannot teach something in the complete isolation of the classroom and then hope that a transition will automatically be made to real life" (1989: 86). If learners are going to be able to take their new knowledge out of the classroom and into the Communities, the connections must be made in the classroom.

Encouraging students to adjust their cultural view to embrace the gifts of cultures other than their own, to revision their relationship to the Communities and to accept the responsibility to create anti-racist change requires a "meaning-full" process. I try to encourage each student to process their own subjectivity, to gain insight into their "experience" as formed in relationship to others—their structural location in the complex interweave of oppression and privilege. "Can experience ever be constructed outside of social relations?" ask Brah and Hoy (1989: 71). According to Collins, it is not just experience but collective history that leads to knowledge:

> Black women's concrete experiences as members of specific race, class, and gender groups as well as our concrete historical situations necessarily play significant roles in our perspectives on the world . . . . Knowledge is gained not by solitary individuals but by Black women as socially constituted members of a group . . . . (1991: 33)

By implication, knowledge gained by White individuals is also as socially constituted members of their group, and it shapes their perspectives of the world.

Collins (1991) cautions that collectivity, or being part of an identified group, allows for the possibility but does not guarantee that collective consciousness will develop among all members, or that it will be articulated as such by the group. According to Brah and Hoy, "[T]here is a difficulty in assuming that people have the same understanding of the structural determinants of their experience" (1989: 74). Cal, a student from the African Nova Scotian community, points out that not all Black or Aboriginals identify as group members or can articulate their understanding of culture or oppression:

> One of the other Native guests . . . says that all Natives do not understand their culture or their oppression. This is a point made about Black people as well that this understanding is not innate. This is something that we must struggle toward to develop. (Feb 2 94-j)

The connection between experience, consciousness, voice and collectivity shapes the everyday lives of anti-racist activists and scholars, as well as those whose lives are validated by Eurocentrism. This Model-In-Use is designed to explore and challenge people's beliefs and actions In-Relation to their current socio-cultural positioning. It is an effort to mobilize them to engage in personal and political change. Learning how we are conditioned to be oppressor/oppressed in our daily lives and in our professional roles is critical self-knowledge. This first stage of awareness is necessary to progress further to being an activist/change agent.

> It was in the East that I began to sort some things out in my own mind as I focused on my own ignorance surrounding a number of the issues we would be discussing. I also began an important examination of myself—of my own racist ways, of my privilege as a white woman . . . as well as a recognition of the need for change in myself before I can work with others. (Analee Dec 93-jsum)

Our Ancestors recognized this reality—one must be aware, feel connected and responsible to others, be conscious of being In-Relation. As long as people remain ensnared in material/social/cultural/personal privilege, they will be untouched by the pains and struggles of other peoples. Illusions of equality, democracy, freedom of choice and helpfulness will be maintained. Viewed through the Aboriginal lens of Self-In-Relation, each student must come to find their identity within the complex constructions of the dominant culture. Then they must recognize the necessity of altering their consciousness and their behaviour In-Relation to the diverse Communities.

Note

1. By "noise" this student is referring to the metal jingle cones which are sewn onto dresses to make them tinkle when the powwow dancers move.

First Voice as Critical Pedagogy

The Eurocentric canon has
Locked out . . . Marginalized . . . Discriminated against Some
Does not validate our knowledge or social reality.
Publishing restrictions.
Social Class, Race, Gender and Culture Intersect.
Limit our participation in "Academic" research.
Aboriginal writers turned down by publishing houses.
Not being Native enough . . . too Native.
Whites continue to accrue capital
From Their edited versions of Our lives.
"Don't Talk About
What You Don't Know"
Says Elder Smith.

For many . . . "Experts" tell.
Who are these Experts?
How do They Know?
Who validates their knowledge claims?
I Resist Distanced Objective Rational Knowing.
Resist learning through "experts."
Those who Theorize . . . Generalize their experience
To Define . . . to Identify us All.

Embrace First Voice . . . "the Voice of Experience"
Rooted in Identity.
The Authority of Lived Experience.
Particular . . . Specific . . . Detailed
Embedded . . . Imbued with meaning
Our Personal . . . Structural
Political Cultural Locatedness.
First Voice.
Opportunity for previously spoken for people
To become Included . . . Part of the curriculum.
We First Voices
Embodied Teachers.
The Artifact on display
All eyes on We teach.
With our Experiences . . . with our Voices
Our Heart-felt Voices . . . with our Lives.
Reaching Inside our Everyday Lived Experiences
We Gift to others our "Voice of Experience"
The Pain . . . Loss . . . Anger
Strength to Heal . . . cost of Resistance
In ourselves, our families, our communities
To Earth Mother.
First Voice Cries Out at Me . . . Screams out at Me
Sorrow lodges in my Heart
Anger pumps through my veins
Resistance inspires me . . . tickles my Funny Bone
Awakening my conscience . . . Enlightening my consciousness
I learn . . . learned . . . am learning
From you . . . of you . . . through you
Through me . . . of me . . . from me.
Whether we speak them to your ears or
We enter through your eyes from a page
Our words Echo in your brain.
What can you learn through our stories?

Through your interpretations of our lives?
What links are made Visible
Between Personal realities and Structural processes?

First Voice as a critical pedagogical tool arises out of anti-racist, feminist, experiential and Aboriginal discourse. First Voice is the reliance on the "voice of experience," our own interpretation of experience to guide our knowledge base. As Elder Smith theorizes: "My roots grow in jackpine roots . . . . I grow here. I am the oldest one. If I don't remember more then nobody does. So other people shouldn't talk about what they don't know" (in Cruikshank 1992: 163).

The power of First Voice is rooted in identity and authority through lived experience. Arising out of Aboriginal Ancestral Tradition, First Voice poses a necessary alternative to the truth claims articulated in the voice of the White "expert," who "knows" what we "need." Reliance on the expert is a commonsense and often unchallenged condition for many people:

> As I began to do my education there were all kinds of people and professors telling me these are the problems in the community, these are the things we have to deal with . . . . This was just a continuation of the way life had been for me on the reserve—Indian Affairs Officials, health nurses, social workers, were continuously telling me what I needed or what was missing in my family. (Free CC2:17)

Often articulated and regarded as common sense by members of our Communities, Free speaks the collective consciousness as she questions: "Who defines whose needs? How often and how long do we have to live by having what other people think we need?" (CC2:17). She asserts that more listening is required: "It's time for us to listen to individuals about what they need. So that we can begin to service people and do the things they need as opposed to what we think they need" (Free CC2:18).

The hegemonic, Eurocentric version has become contested terrain in Western Schools. The recording of the past and present conditions of our Communities has not been neutral and has been unveiled as not reflective of the many voices living it. Rather the story (that is, the acceptable, teachable version) has been written/told in the voice of the colonizer/oppressor. One version of reality, Eurocentrism, has been widely accepted as knowledge and underpins the majority of content and methods currently used in Western settings. The commonsense nature of this practice is captured by Lena's entry: "I took social history last semester so I had studied about the Acadian Expulsion but Monday was the first time I've heard an Acadian person talk about it" (Mar 14 93-j).

Hearing the voices of the people whose lives are affected by the history and the daily lived experience challenges the everyday condition of appropriation of voice, both within and surrounding the School setting. Howse and Stalwick propose that the most fundamental question is "[w]ho should speak about Native person's oppression and related social movement experiences?" (1990: 84). They answer: "When such words come only from outsiders it could block a much-needed rereading of history for such a social movement" (Howse and Stalwick 1990: 84). hooks (1988), Sanchez (1988), Godard (1992) and others who discuss this topic agree: we need what I have coined as First Voice. That is, we need to hear each person define/align themselves and speak of their own experiences In-Relation to their own selves/people. We need to move beyond appropriation of our cultural voices, beyond the "we or our" (Harris 1991) expert voice that is heard speaking for us all. "We shall not have our great leap forward . . . until the marginalized and exploited have begun to become the artisans of their own liberation—until their voice makes itself heard directly, without mediation, without interpreters" (Gutierrez, in Howse and Stalwick 1990: 85).

Many students and teachers unquestioningly accept the voice of the White "expert" as speaking the "truth" about Africans, Aboriginals and others. White people who know a very limited amount often see themselves as "experts" because they know more than their colleagues, who know little beyond the recorded version and current media representations. One White participant illustrates this beautifully in his first journal entry for the course:

> Before tonight, I figured I knew a lot about the native culture. In fact I felt so confident that I knew so much that I actually told the class that I would offer my non-native perspective of the native culture throughout this year. . . . When I would get the chance I would dazzle my non-native peers with my new-found knowledge of the Native culture as I see it. I would also quote certain passages of a book I read on the Native culture [name], as supporting what I already observed . . . .
>
> As a result of just tonight's class, I now realize that in order to effectively educate others about a certain culture it is imperative to be a first voice from that particular culture. My working within a Native setting does not constitute me being a first voice of the Native culture. Also even the book I was so proud of quoting as supporting my own experience, was not even written from first voice.
>
> I also realize now as a result of this first class, that I do not know much about Native culture, as I so confidently thought I did . . . . Although I go to work 4 days a week on a Native reserve, I know now my exposure to various aspects of the Native culture have been very limited. (Ken Jan 6 93-j)

Through First Voice, each participant is encouraged to recognize perceptions of reality as socially constructed. Each person's reality is understood as filtered through the lens of collective, cultural consciousness. In this Model-In-Use, one's cultural locatedness is synonymous with one's "authority" to speak about that cultural group. An Acadian Elder reiterates the importance of First Voice, hearing from the people themselves:

I think that the first part of this to know is very, very important when you speak of a different culture or a different language or a different something. Especially with our French language, for example, to know why we spoke French the way we did. To know why we spoke English the way we did. If you want to know about people, I fully agree that the people who are teaching others about themselves, they should be the people who are really those people. I can't tell you, even though I work with the Native or the Black, I can't tell you exactly who they are and what they are. You have to know. Make yourself known that way! (Celi CC2:25)

I often need to caution participants: "Don't talk about what you don't know. If you are not a member of the African, Aboriginal, Acadian, or other Community, you are not in a position to speak about that cultural group or experience." This challenges all participants to keep focused on their Self-In-Relation to the topic. It is difficult, but not impossible, to unlearn White "expertism." As Aboriginal people, for example, are empowered to address the issues of their own identity and community, so too are White people empowered to address issues of privilege and their role In-Relation to racism and oppression.

Representations of ourselves that are outside the already-fixed categories, interrogating the labels of "problem" or "victim" and acknowledging our peoples as co-creators of history and as people who struggle and resist and live incredibly varied and complex lives have become weapons against oppression. Many artists, teachers, visionaries and Elders echo a theme articulated by Rita Joe, a Mi'kmaq Elder, as the "gentle war" (Joe 1989: 28). Through conceptual constructs like First Voice, we express our wish to invoke a society in which we each have opportunity to represent our own selves and our own cultures rather than falling into the appropriation of voice, experience, art and spirituality, which has become the unacknowledged but taken-for-granted basis of "Western" culture.

First Voice for our cultural Communities is almost unheard of in classrooms. What is taught is Eurocentric content (Said 1993; Blaut 1993). The curriculum is not inclusive of the experiences, histories and voices of those on the "margins." Often when "multicultural" courses or content is offered, it is "added on," with one or two "token" representatives included. We are invited to tell our painful stories, to dance, to dress up or to share recipes. We are decontextualized from our Communities, from societal relations and from the body of knowledge being taught as "the" curriculum (Weir 1991). It is necessary to pluralize the singular nature of "the" cultural expert. This strategy serves to challenge widespread tokenistic measures, where one member of a Community is expected to speak for all. First Voice as critical pedagogy challenges Eurocentric styles of curriculum development and targets the ingrained acceptance of the hegemonic voice speaking for us all. This occurs at several levels. Emphasis in this Model-In-Use has been placed on both interrogating textual representations commonly accepted as "truth" in Western life, as well as giving opportunity for members of previously silenced Communities to speak face-to-face, orally transmitting their knowledge.

Interrogating the Text

Given our text-based institutional location, anti-racist theory must be reflected in curriculum content and materials. Acknowledging that materials are not neutral, Brandt suggests several questions: Do materials reflect our society's diversity in a positive light? Do they relate to "oppositional" experience? Do they provide a basis for challenging "stratification and inequitable distribution of society's resources?" (1986: 131). Reviewing syllabus content is essential, as Kalia contends, because "lack of race consciousness, in any 'major work,' even when keeping in mind 'the context in which it was written,' is intolerable in any discipline" (1991: 227). Eurocentric models of education have tended to "lock out, marginalize and discriminate against" (Brandt 1986: 131) culturally located participants by not validating our knowledge or social reality. Using materials that support and validate knowledge and experience outside of "school knowledge" can work to diffuse the power of "hidden curriculum."

As hooks notes, domination is reinforced when the author's "authority is constituted by either the absence of the voices of the individuals whose experiences they seek to address, or the dismissal of those voices as unimportant" (1988: 43). First Voice pedagogy uses the daily lived experiences of the Community members themselves as the starting point. Western publications are notable for a paucity of material that is authored by members of the Communities themselves or that moves beyond the problem-focused orientation prevalent in Eurocentric discourses. Publishing restrictions and social class intersect with gender and culture to keep our participation in academic "research" limited. According to Kalia, "We write short works, because we are generally not supported by a class structure or academia that facilitates our scholarship" (1991: 280). Collins concurs:

> Much of the black women's intellectual tradition has been embedded in the institutional locations other than the academy . . . . Musicians, vocalists, poets, writers, and other artists . . . political activists . . . such women are typically thought of as nonintellectual and non-scholarly, classifications that create a false dichotomy between scholarship and activism, between thinking and doing. (1991: 15)

This dichotomy is predicated upon theories that elevated rationalism above other forms of knowledge. Through healing the artificial split between thinking and doing, we give voice to our experiences as a way of developing heightened consciousness, as a source of knowledge. First Voice as pedagogy is designed to help expand the Western notion of knowledge and, thus, to help students embrace the possibilities of learning from many sources. In particular, this pedagogy emphasizes learning from the words of those who have directly experienced that which is being theorized. Remember the wisdom of Elder Ned when she speaks in the Traditional voice: "Old style words are just like school" (in Cruikshank 1992: 267). The need to relate only in "proper" English interferes with the expression of difference through oral or textual means. The exclusive orientation towards abstract cognition detracts from the "authentic" transmission of culturally-based insights to the "paper world" of School life. Many other Aboriginal authors struggle with this issue and I have come to realize that "correctness is not nearly so important to me as accuracy in feeling as well as in fact" (Hampton 1995: 6).

An emphasis on First Voice necessarily relies on the use of more aesthetic-expressive forms like poetry, stories, speeches, dialogues and fiction to supplement the paucity of "minority"-authored texts. Gordon, Miller and Rollock note that "the meanings of our behaviour are often better explicated in our artistic and fictional work" (1988: 18); they reveal the interiority of our being. Resistance is better revealed in the practice of a "national culture," which includes newspapers, narratives, speeches, poetry, drama and slogans. These form a "counterpoint to the Western monumental histories, official discourses, and quasi-scientific viewpoint" (Said 1993: 215). Poems, stories, songs, speeches and refereed works from Aboriginal, African, Acadian, Lesbian and Gay and other regionally represented Communities form the basis of the readings compiled for use within the Model. When we reveal our political agendas as well as our personal feelings, we offer a new lens through which to view familiar issues, and opportunity for critical reflection is enhanced. One White participant indicates that the interrogation of textual representation has become generalized into her daily life:

> I learned about appropriation and the necessity of first voice literature. I am now training myself to be very careful in selecting reading material; before I would read things without even taking into consideration who wrote it. I do not do this anymore. (Lena 92-jsum)

The Face-to-Face Encounter

Aboriginal people believe in the centrality of "the other" to the individual. We are "born into a social world" and take others' existence "for granted without question" (Schutz 1967: 98). More complex and more compelling in the cross-cultural teaching/learning context is how we come to understand the meaning of others. In acknowledging the primacy of the face-to-face situation, Berger and Luckmann (1967) support an Aboriginal worldview. They propose that "the reality of everyday life contains typificatory schemes in terms of which others are apprehended and 'dealt with' in face to face encounters," and that these typifications become "progressively anonymous the farther they are away from the face-to face situation" (Berger and Luckmann 1967: 31). These typifications "appertain to anyone in the category" (Berger and Luckmann 1967: 31).

Are stereotypes a form of typification? Could cross-cultural understanding, then, best be achieved in the face-to-face, "here and now" exchanges in which "individualization" becomes possible and a person has opportunity to "manifest himself [or herself] as a unique and therefore atypical individual?" (Berger and Luckmann 1967: 32). Many participants express the value of the face-to-face encounter in class, whether it be between me as Aboriginal teacher, and students; among diverse students; or with our guests from the Aboriginal, African, Acadian and other Communities as they visited our classroom and we the Communities. Eileen expresses her insights metaphorically:

> Direct interaction with persons from other cultures have brought me some of my most rewarding experiences in this course. I was able to share issues and interact for a few brief moments without a multitude of racial barriers. It was like we were able to cut through the barb wire and saw hope to keep it open if we worked at it everyday for the rest of our lives. (93-j)

Mac's journal soliloquy speaks the same message. He reinforces the value of the face-to-face encounter as a method to challenge internalized racial stereotypes:

> When someone is invisible it is easy to pretend that they don't exist. It is clear to me that there is so much beneath the surface. You must allow oneself to go beyond the superficial. Into the feelings and fears of another person. To see what they sing and what they cry. To see them as whole human beings. Too busy, too much work, too little time, don't know where to begin, all interfere with this essential truth. Hollywood can't stand up to face to face. It is easier to believe in the myth. It is easier to not take time to find out the truth, it is easier to close your eyes and think, hope, that someone else will take care of it. It is easier to avoid the reality of others when you are swept away by your own. It is easier to rationalize and to put off. It is easier . . . for whom? (Mac 92-j)

When I speak of my experiences as an Aboriginal woman and encourage other members of the Communities to speak of their experiences, the theories and "paper stories" common in educational institutes are brought to life. I invite and encourage students to invite Community members to class to express their own experiences rather than giving voice to White experts. This is a political, consciousness-raising act, part of the larger struggle to resist appropriation. Our Communities have had a specific history with education, which can be a clear model, "an inside-out lesson" (Medicine Eagle 1991) for educators and students about what we do not want to do. I want to use my role as educator to create a model of education that willingly turns its back on the reproduction of hegemony and defends the authentic voice of people previously silenced. I call upon members of the Communities to aid in this struggle.

Insisting on people representing their own voices, their own stories and their own histories has become a central pedagogical tool in my classrooms. Students have come to appreciate the difference between being told *about* someone or something, and being told *by* someone; they experience the difference, see the body behind the words and the feeling in the voice. They can begin to recognize our Traditions and lives as diverse while seeing the cohesion that sharing common oppression can bring. African, Aboriginal, Acadian, Gay and Lesbian and Asian voices represent themselves, individually and collectively, throughout the course, in written materials, in person in the classroom and through "tasks" that require community contact.

Finding First Voice

First Voice as pedagogy challenges why and how certain voices/enunciatory positions are privileged over others. It is "an instance of pedagogic authority used to selectively empower social groups lacking hegemonic authority" (Weir 1991: 25). Empowerment, according to McLaren (1989), is multifaceted. It can refer to "the process through which students learn to critically appropriate knowledge existing outside their immediate experience in order to broaden their understanding of themselves, the world, and the possibilities for transforming the taken-for-granted assumptions about the way we live" (McLaren 1989: 186). Empowerment in this case involves learning to question and selectively appropriate those aspects of the dominant culture that would provide individuals and their Communities with "the basis for defining and transforming, rather than merely serving, the wider social order" (McLaren 1989: 186). The story of Randi's struggle to find her own First Voice in the class will illustrate the process of empowerment through voice as a evolving one. She documents her growth in this area in her first entry:

> As class ended tonight, I reflect on the wonderful experience that it was! I was so happy to finally be able to express my Native identity as part of my being. It was the first time that my Voice was actually being heard, not only by others but by myself. What a wonderful enlightening experience.
>
> It certainly helped tonight, having other first voices present, it allowed for a sense of security at a time when it is hard to be secure when putting one's feelings on the line.
>
> Along with the good feelings came some insecurities about who I am, I have always had trouble speaking in group settings, so hopefully I'll feel more comfortable as time goes on. (Randi Jan 6 93-j)

She highlights key issues, including the necessity of "the ear" or a listening audience, as critical to expression of voice. The necessary "sense of security" is fostered by the presence of other "first voices." This is a crucial factor for anyone who has been chronically silenced. Part of the security of being "voiceful" as a cultural representative is being secure in the knowledge that you are transmitting about your own cultural group. It also requires safety, a belief that you will be listened to respectfully. Given the numerical and attitudinal dominance of Whiteness in the School context, this remains a difficulty. Randi recognizes and reflects on this in a later entry:

> Tonight as I ponder over last class I feel as though some things will never change, I see the looks on people's faces around the room and wonder, do these white middle-class students have any idea what this whole course is about? I shouldn't be so harsh it's hard not to be!
>
> I see anger, dismay, defensiveness, and it makes me angry to think that these people have the nerve to be defensive, we've been defending ourselves all of our lives and we're tired of it!
>
> It's time to give us a break and listen to our stories, songs, tales, we have so much to say if people would listen!
>
> I guess for me I am finally listening to my own songs, stories and tales and realizing that they are a part of me and I'm so proud to be a Native person, I feel so honoured to be me, I feel that I have such a spiritual connection with the earth that it keeps me centered inside even if my life is chaos outside, and heaven knows it's been chaotic this past few months, despite it all I manage to find the strength to attend and feel empowered every time I go. It's wonderful. Thanks again for the wonderful experiences so far. See you next week! (Jan 27 93-j)

When Aboriginal, African, Acadian and other participants have had the opportunity for voice, and are respectfully heard by their peers, empowerment is realized. Randi experienced validation and shares further insights regarding her identity and experience:

> As I presented tonight I was so nervous, will people take me seriously, will they believe my stories, will they listen carefully?
>
> I believe that people did listen and understood what I was saying!
>
> It was one of the most powerful experiences I have ever had in my life, it allowed me to verbalize everything I ever felt about my Aboriginal identity, it made it all seem real, it was as though I had someone to validate my experience and acknowledge that it was real!
>
> You never really realize how oppressed you are until you talk about it! I never realized that until I spoke!
>
> I hope you enjoyed the presentation, thanks for the input during my presentation. (Feb 10 93-j)

The successful voicing of Randi's cultural identity to a listening audience deepened her "sense of security": "I feel a sense of security in class now as I speak, I'm more comfortable and I believe that people truly are listening" (Mar 31 93-j).

As Randi's experience informs us, finding voice is a lengthy process and was a continuous challenge for her throughout the course. Showing external confidence in one's voice can still be accompanied by embodied cues of insecurity. In her final entry she apologizes for her nervousness when she spoke: "I was shaking inside even if you couldn't see it on the outside" (Randi Apr 7 93-j). She concludes her journal by indicating that finding her voice was her most important learning. It is a process that she intends to continue after the course:

> The most important learning for me was that I have a voice, and if I don't begin to use my voice it will get lost! My identity as an aboriginal woman is something to take pride and gather strength in, even though I'm nervous speaking I need to keep doing it until it feels natural, and until I have integrated all the pieces of my identity that I am comprised of. (Randi Apr 93-jsum)

Randi's story continuously expresses a relationship that is accepted as common sense in Traditional minds: every voice needs an ear and every story has impacts on listeners. First Voice pedagogy definitely has multiple impacts on learners. Students in this postmodern age of fragmented identities are reminded that our personal stories are constructed out of the conditions of our lives, and these are dominated by race, class and gender. For personal narration to become part of the process of developing strategies to challenge oppressive structures, the individuals and their stories must be embedded in the power relations in society. "Individuals are enabled to make sense of their personal histories by making links between autobiography, group history and social and political processes" (Brah and Hoy 1989: 73). As participants make these links, they are encouraged to voice their new understandings to the group.

Impacts of First Voice

Voices visibly embodied and persons telling stories of their own lived experiences of exclusion and oppression have an emotional impact on the listeners. Use of First Voice in text and face-to-face reinforces and brings to "life" the curriculum being "taught." The affective impacts of First Voice on students are frequently mentioned in journals. Van emphasizes the role of First Voice in helping shift her learning beyond the intellectual level: "This course will be done in first voice, which will make everything shine in a new light. This first voice approach has already had an effect on me—I'm feeling more of what is being said, rather than intellectualizing it" (Sept 22 93-j). Another student reflects on the insights into the pains of oppression allowed her by First Voice participants. As role models they exhibit ever-present strength and determination.

> Through first voice experiences, I have gained much insight into the pain that culturally diverse individuals live everyday. I can never understand the depth of the pain and frustration but I can empathize

and I can continue to challenge myself and the white culture that thinks it is so superior . . . . I have been inspired by the strength of the guest speakers, and the first voice experiences in class to never give up the fight . . . . (Bejay 93-jsum)

Dana shares her heartfelt reaction to the story of an Aboriginal woman who had relayed her experience of the traumas of residential school:

I felt so much pain for her while she shared her story. I can only imagine how painful the experience was for her. How damaging it would be for her self-esteem, and her pride and cultural identity. After all these years, she still feels pain and this is quite understandable. I feel so angry that any child would have to experience such cruelty and brutality! This school stripped its pupils from their identity, culture, and dignity. Like [name], thousands of other children shall carry the physical and mental scars of this school. How could such a school stay open? Who would allow such education to continue? This institution was very racist and should never have been allowed to educate.

I feel so much anger and rage to think of how many children had to experience this and how it was allowed to operate as an educational facility, or any facility for that matter!!! (Nov 31 92-j)

A recognition of the value of learning through sharing of experience is also expressed:

One of the more important things I realized was the lessons that are to be learned from those of different cultures who speak out and who share their personal experience with us. The lessons we learn from this are often far more valuable than any text book could ever teach. (Analee Dec 93-jsum)

Having described First Voice pedagogy as a "consciousness-raising" tool essential to this Model-In-Use, I will later circle back to discuss in more detail the contradictory aspects of this practice. We will turn now to the South and more specifically explore tools that are grounded in Traditional Aboriginal practice. Of particular relevance is the Talking Circle, the format that produces opportunity for voice both in the classroom and in the data collection process.

The Southern Door:
Introducing Aboriginal Spirituality
into the Classroom

The South corresponds to the Element Fire
The flames of Resistance and Renewal
Burn . . . Burn Behind my eyelids
I muse in the Fire . . .
The Smoke Swirls Up High in the Sky
Sparks fly . . . Flames leap
Intense heat . . . heat that Heals.
Fire that burns up the past.
Picture Summertime
Trees in full leaf . . . bright blue Sky . . . mouthfuls of ripe berries

The Southern Door

Long sandy beaches . . . Aqua marine Waters . . . Warm to swim
Hot . . . Hot Sun beating down.
The Noonday Sun
Bright . . . baking Earth Mother and all her Creatures
Bringing Light . . . Life to all.

Call on the powers of the Crawling Ones
The Spider, the Snake
Learn to shed your skin like the Snake
Layer after layer
Baring . . . Shedding . . . Releasing
Transform your Self with ease.
Be open to change . . . within and without
A change of Heart . . . a change of Form.
Reach for your connection to Spirit . . . to Will
To your own Determination.
Recognize your Gift to change Spirit into matter
Transform through the Direction of Will.

Acknowledge the quality of Will
Energy as it leaps through your body from synapse to synapse
The Spark . . . Energy sparking . . . Firing within you
Your self as a channel of Energy
A link from the Ancestors to the Unborn
Living in connection with other Energy forms on Mother Earth.

Be Aware
What fuels your fire? Keeps you strong?
Whose will guides your life? Guides your work?
Which Culture Dominates your thinking? your view of history?
Culture can spark or dampen our Will.
Fuel or smother the Fires . . . our Desires for Change.
Whose Will Guides this work?
Inspires this teaching Model-In-Use?
Does the Spirit of this pedagogical form
Inspire you to Will for Change?
Together let us Willfully Resist Cultural Hegemony

While First Voice pedagogy begins to raise students' consciousness to the lived experiences of themselves and persons from the various cultural Communities, often the focus remains on oppression and racism in its many faces. Circling now to the South, I will explore how Aboriginal spirituality can be introduced to the classroom context. Spiritual forms challenge students to see the gifts of the cultures. Ceremony can revitalize the will to build community relations and mobilize us to actively resist forms of Eurocentric domination personally and collectively. In this Model-In-Use, Traditional forms of Aboriginal spirituality are combined with anti-racist, feminist consciousness-raising to create a more balanced, holistic Model of practice. Spirit, the "first standard of Indian education" (Hampton 1995: 19), is integrated in the learning process.

To Aboriginal Traditionalists, knowledge/knowing without acknowledgment of the spiritual core, the moral code, is a very dangerous thing (Forbes 1979). Our Elders teach us that "[i]t is the spiritual connectedness between and within all that exists that has been one of our greatest weapons, healers, liberators in our battles against genocide" (Charnley 1990: 18). It is the Traditional philosophies of immanence, balance and interconnectedness that underpin the pedagogies In-Use. The ideas elaborated on in the South resonate with Hart's notion of the "liberatory potential of intuitive, metaphysical and imaginative—playful modes of thinking and knowing" (1992: 213). She believes, and I concur, that "these capacities and modes of knowing are essential prerequisites for engaging in anticipatory, utopian thought and action" (Hart 1992: 213). For Benhabib, "[u]topian thinking is a practical-moral imperative .... [W]ithout such a regulative principle of hope . . . radical transformation is unthinkable" (1992: 229).

These modes of thinking and teaching are also vital for an empathic and imaginative bridging of individual and cultural differences. Pleasure and humour balance fear when one is attempting to develop an appreciation of difference rather than appropriating colonialistically or keeping a "safe" distance. As educators, we all use a number of strategies to assert our authority as conferred by the School. In this Model, Aboriginal strategies are utilized to create conditions of respect, honesty, caring and sharing to assert Aboriginality and to teach Self-In-Relation both inside and outside the classroom. Several forms of spiritual practice widely used by Traditionalists in Aboriginal societies, Ancestrally and in the modern age, have been adapted for use in the classroom context. It is hoped that, through an examination of Traditional educational strategies, "we may identify the changes we must make, not only for our survival as indigenous peoples, but perhaps for our very existence as humans" (Armstrong 1987: 19).

Circle: A Physical Reality

In Ancestral times, the Sacred Circle (Gunn Allen 1986) was central to the teachings of the Elders. The Circle is a form that arises in nature and is imprinted upon our culture as well as our individual cells. Part of the energy of the Circle has to do with the physical structure: a Circle has no head and no tail, no beginning and no end. Everyone is equal in a Circle, the point of reference is the middle, which is both empty and full of everything. Everyone is equidistant from the middle so there is no sense of hierarchy (Cahill and Halpern 1992).

Since the disruption of tribal village life, the transmission of Ancestral wisdom has had to rely upon revisioning of Ancestral methods. Circle work is one form of breathing new life into the spirit of human interchange. Through Circle we are able to gain inspiration, renew personal vision and recreate a cohesive community. Circle is based on a Traditional belief set: the connection between people in a Circle creates the threads that will weave the human species back into the Sacred Hoop of life (Gunn Allen 1986). Traditionalists believe that the Circle contains a recognizable power that defies superficial boundaries. To bring understanding between tribal peoples in times of decision-making, conflict resolution or healing, Circles were formed. Today we face the necessity of bridging differences between the cultures with few processes that are not based on the same individualistic philosophies that have been used to "divide and conquer." The Circle can act to deconstruct the Western dualism of individual/community by allowing us to work individually, in a transpersonal context, while building a community. Establishing a cohesive Circle is an integral part of re-establishing interconnectedness.

Brooke Medicine Eagle (1991) works with ritual action, a therapy method that targets the physical body and, through it, the unconscious in order to teach/heal. She suggests that the embodied metaphor of moving and sitting in a Circle is a learning about interconnectedness that goes to a level that is deeper than that of which people are consciously aware. There is a physical impact on the human system that happens while sitting in Circle.

> The actual physical lesson that it takes to get yourself in a true circle is a part of building the nervous system that it requires to be in the circle of life. Whether it is the circle of your family, or your community, or your larger family of all of Earth's children. (Medicine Eagle in Cahill and Halpern 1992: 127)

Traditional forms of dance, done in a Circle, physically teaches embodied interconnectedness within the greater Circle: "if someone slows down, if someone falls, or gets out of place, it throws the whole circle off" (in Cahill and Halpern 1992: 130). Our Elders teach us that we need to experience that lesson in our lives: "[I]f we knock someone out of the circle and they fall, then the whole circle is affected" (in Cahill and Halpern 1992: 130).

Part of the energy of the Circle has to do with the egalitarian structure, which reflects the Aboriginal philosophy of immanence. In Circle, energy flows from speaker to speaker, creating an opportunity for a different kind of focusing and a different type of awareness about the relationships to self, to one another and to the whole. We experience having more personal authority when we sit in Circle, compared to when energy is focused on one person at the front, the expert, the authority, the one who is imparting to us knowledge—what we "need" to know.

Choqosh Auh-Ho-Oh, a Chumash shaman, says that when we move into a Circle where we can see each other, where the information and the Traditional teachings come through, "we make of ourselves a crucible, like the alchemist's bowl. All the chemistry of all our beings, from our different countries, our Ancestors, our experiences, who we are, the chemistry of our faces and the different looks, creates . . . the circle" (in Cahill and Halpern 1992: 110). Since North America is now a "multicultural" society, one that is the repository of many people's teachings and methods, our Circles will reflect competing cultural influences. This is becoming increasingly true in the classroom context, through measures which are being taken to redress historical inequities in the educational system. I have learned that, even with adaptation to difference in the cultural composition of the group and in the context, the Circle itself, if it is vital, will produce its own healing and message that is appropriate for its time, place and membership.

Ceremony: Setting the Stage

Traditionalists teach that successful teaching and healing depends upon clear intention, but such intention is directly connected to honouring the immanent value of each member. We are taught that it is important to honour all in the Circle and all of life as a part of the Circle. If we are clear about our teachings, we will not be cut off from the real purpose of Circle work, which is to reaffirm our interconnectedness. Facilitating the flow of the Circle's energy is vital to inspiring and maintaining the learning/healing intent of Circle work.

Because inequality, evaluation, separation and individualism are built into the School environment, special efforts have to be made to make the Circle a safe space, a "ceremonial basket" (Gunn Allen 1986) where life-affirming things can happen. To do so, we can return to the ceremonial Traditions of our Elders. If we are going to honour spiritual interconnectedness, a central teaching of Circle work, care must be taken to do more than place ourselves in a circle formation. If our intentions are to revitalize rather than appropriate the powers of the Circle as an Ancestral form, we must invite the Ancestors and the other powers of life into our learning spaces. To do so requires insight into and a thorough understanding and implementation of ceremonial practices. Guidance of or consultation with other Traditionalists is essential prior to undertaking any Circle work. As one Aboriginal participant contributes:

> It's a valuable tool for the most part. I also share that concern that sometimes people do not respect certain things and they end up abusing or not knowing the responsibility that goes with the eagle feather, or sweet grass, or different things like that . . . . I think it's important to try to differentiate that there are different teachings. And that whatever teachings you choose to follow, hopefully you have a spirituality advisor because otherwise you just get lost. (Ray VC2:15)

The Southern Door

The spirituality invoked in ceremonial work is related to the philosophy of Self-In-Relation and recognition of the link between individual responsibility and community well-being. Ceremony reaffirms the knowledge that each person is responsible for his/her actions In-Relation to the larger community. Through ceremony, "[t]he person sheds the isolated, individual personality and is restored to conscious harmony with the universe" (Gunn Allen 1986: 62).

To be able to pay proper attention and honour to our Ancestral Traditions, our Elders advise that the space should be prepared carefully; it should be clean and orderly. Lighting and air, the atmosphere, are very important. Traditionally, special foods, costumes, special prayers and songs are composed—"in short, a circle is drawn around the community and everything within that circle is sacred and taken out of the ordinary" (Beck and Walters 1977: 39). Feasting, drama, art, smudging, singing, dancing and sharing of cultural stories are aspects of ceremony that charge the overall atmosphere, altering the classroom in ways that are more conducive to entering the sense of sacred time and space.

In ceremony we recognize the powers of the unseen and begin by calling in the powers of the Directions, that they might bear witness, lend support and impart wisdom to our efforts. Through the establishment of an "altar," upon which is placed physical manifestations of each element, attention is drawn to the elemental powers. Through an opening meditation on the Medicine Wheel, which invokes the elemental powers of the four Directions, the stage is set to open our learning space to the influences of the seen and unseen powers of the universe.

In most Aboriginal Traditions, prior to ceremony, procedures are followed in order to prepare the mind and the body to be receptive to knowledge and insight, which may come from anywhere. Smudging, the use of burning herbs for purifying space and one another, has many effects on the individual and collective psyche. It serves as a demarcation of time, notifying everyone that "Circle time" is beginning. It is a signal for the mind to be still and in present time; it provides everyone in the group with a shared embodied experience. As the sweet-smelling smoke encircles the area, it is easy to feel the calming presence of our plant sisters, entering and filling all of those present. In the journals students report feeling immediately present and noticeably more relaxed, as I circle the room with the burning herbs.

> It has a very pleasant scent, which in itself is nice, but the circle seemed to draw us all together—to unify the group—which created a sense of purposeful togetherness. (Char Jan 14 93-j)

> As the sweet grass was being held over the candle flame, a silence fell over the room . . . a silence that seemed to intensify with the passing minutes.
> I could feel myself growing very relaxed and comfortable as the sweet grass slowly made its way around the room. I was able to shift

my thoughts away from my worries and concerns of the day and focus solely on the situation at hand. This was especially soothing for me as I often find it more difficult to free myself of my racing thoughts. (Analee Sept 29 93-t1)

I find the smudging a very powerful experience, it helps calm my mind and allows me to feel peace inside myself! (Randi Mar 31 93-j)

The sweet grass and smudging ceremony reminds me of gentleness and the need for community members to be gentle with one another. (Eileen 93-j)

Once sitting in Circle, with our spirit helpers invoked and our minds cleared, we are ready to begin to share ourselves with each other in an effort to learn more through sharing stories. It is important to put in place a style of communicating that will build respect among individuals. In Aboriginal community, a "sacred object" is used in Circle to facilitate communication. Whoever holds the object has the total focus and attention of the group. The object can be any natural energy form, as all have immanent value: a specially carved and decorated stick, a crystal, a feather, a ceremonial artifact or anything upon which the group decides. Some people use a vertically-held stick to represent the unity of earth and sky, some a crystal to amplify whatever anyone is feeling, some a feather to carry the thoughts expressed to the Spirit world. A simple unadorned stick or a rock that is found spontaneously for such an occasion can be used as a reminder to the Circle of the simplicity of speaking and sharing from the heart. Group members can take turns providing "sacred objects," giving individuals an opportunity to share something of themselves with the group.

As many students tend to be very much on the surface of their feelings, crystals can be used as intensifiers: amethyst for clearing and clear quartz for healing. A special gift from my South American sisters, a "rain stick," which when turned vertically makes the sound of the rainforest, is brought to celebrate rainy days and to encourage people to take time to let the rain "wash" their thoughts before they speak. On special occasions when clearing up conflict, I have used the "talking feathers": eagle feathers prepared for the purpose of Circle work (Graveline 1994). During highly ceremonial occasions, a Medicine Pipe is used to remind the participants of the sacredness and importance of the council and our connection to all life forms.

More specifically, he notes the strength-oriented foundations of learning in Circle: our experiences are our teachers. In Circle we learn that we need to uncover and accept lessons from all sorts of experiences and stories. The "reframing" from victim to survivor can produce healing in itself.

I think what I hadn't been able to acknowledge during that period of time was the fact that all those things have happened, but they have shaped who I am right now. I have survived that . . . . I started to look at some of the strengths that came out of that, who were some of the people that gave the support that I needed. (Cal CC2:24)

In this case, the participant parallels Circle directly with therapy.

Because I have not been seeing the therapist, this became my awakening, my consciousness at a personal level, at a political level . . . . Now looking back, I can see things falling into place. Not that my life is a whole lot easier than before, cause it's not! But, I think the way I look at things has changed somewhat. (Cal CC2:24)

*Re*framing one's past history of oppression enables acceptance. When we speak of changing "the way I look at things," we are signifying a change in consciousness. Cal expresses his growth as continuous throughout the CCI course:

As a part of the circle I see myself move through the stages, it was continuous growth. It's transformation . . . . I'm concerned that I can't move further because what I require isn't there. That creates some concern for me because there's . . . this form where I gained conscious-ness; I gained a higher degree of understanding. It has been a real awakening. But there is no platform and there is no support net for me to remain a part of . . . where is my community and where is the circle for me? How do I continue to hold on to that? (CC2:32)

Cal raises a critical issue: to continue to learn and grow as individuals we need a supportive community environment. Sharing and mutuality builds individual and community strength. Through egalitarianism we become more able to recognize our immanence and interconnectedness with each other. These are essential understandings if we are to build community across diversity, inside and outside the classroom. This is the theme of the West—to which we will now turn our attention.

Talking Circle as Pedagogy

Circle as pedagogy
A physical reality . . . a metaphysical experience.
Produces Healing . . . appropriate message
For the Time, Place and Members.
Embraced by many . . . brings closeness
Allows many different opinions to be Voiced
A time to build up confidence of Voice . . . without Interruption
Very easy to express your Feelings and learn from others.

In Talking Circle . . . in "circle time"
We open our Hearts
Speak what we know to be True
Share what we Care deeply about
As Honestly as we can . . . as Respectfully as we are able.
We are able to enter into another's experience through their Words.
A doorway to self-examination . . . a social context for

a "personal" experience.

We Remember a Heart-felt Speak-Out in Circle.
It rings in our Ears.
Pierces our Hearts like an arrow.
The power of Words . . . Magnified . . . Amplified.
Gain energy with repetition . . . Echo . . . Echo . . . to create familiarity.

Learn to speak your own Truth.
Words shoot like flames out of your mouth
Burning your lips like Fire.
A flush covers your body . . . Heat rises up . . . reddens your cheeks.
Your Heart beats fast as the words jump
As if from their own Will . . . out into the Circle.
To amplify . . . Echo . . . Echo . . . in your heart . . . in our ears.
Learn to Listen Respectfully
Know what is Not said
Is as important as what is said.
What do you know about the power of Silence?
See it as a skill . . . an act of relationship
a form of resistance . . . an action.
Through Circle we interpret our Selves
Clarify our Will towards others . . . for ourselves and others
We can each have our own Voice . . . Speak our own Truth.
Speak to me . . . Share from your Heart in Circle.

To instill respect for language and for truth, my Elders counselled, "Don't talk too much," which most often meant "Don't talk too often" or "Don't talk too long" or, especially, "Don't talk about matters that you know nothing about." Elder Ned shares in the Traditional belief that words are sacred and "spoken words are infused with power that increases in value with repetition" (in Cruikshank 1992: 267).

According to Marie Battiste (1986), a Mi'kmaq educator, oral narration was so important to the Ancestors that the most principled and persuasive speakers often became leaders of the tribe because they expressed and lived the ideals of their communities. Deloria concurs: "In the old days leadership depended on the personal prestige of the people whom the community chose as its leaders. Their generosity, service to the community, integrity, and honesty had to be above question" (1994: 248). According to Johnston, an Ojibway author, "So precious did the tribe regard language and speech that it held those who abused language and speech and truth in contempt and ridicule and withheld from them their trust and confidence" (1992: 10).

With regard to the sharing of speech proper conduct was established to build community values of respect, honesty, caring and sharing (Geo 1993). Isabelle Knockwood, a Mi'kmaq Elder, describes the "Talking Stick" process:

> Our Mi'kmaw ancestors used the Talking Stick to guarantee that everyone who wanted to speak would have a chance to be heard and that they would be allowed to take as long as they needed to say what was on their minds without fear of being interrupted with questions, criticisms, lectures or scoldings, or even of being presented with solutions to their problems. An ordinary stick of any kind or size is used. Those seated in the Circle commit themselves to staying to the end, not getting up to leave or walk about because this behaviour is considered an interruption. Anyone who leaves the Circle can return and sit with the latecomers whose only role is to observe and listen. This is because they have missed some information and therefore cannot offer advice or make an informed decision. The person who has a problem or an issue to discuss holds the Talking Stick and relates everything pertaining to it especially everything they have done to solve it. After they are through, they pass the stick to the person on their left, following the sun's direction. The next person, Negem, states everything they know about the problem without repeating anything that was already said. They tell what they or others have done in similar situations. They neither agree nor disagree with what others have said.
>
> The Talking Stick goes around until it returns to the person with the problem or issue, who then acknowledges everyone present and what they have said. Sometimes the solution or answer comes as soon as everyone has spoken. Maybe the person has already thought it out, or it may come as an inspiration on the long trek back home. Or else, it could appear in the form of a vision or a dream. Dreams were a very important part of problem-solving with the First People of the land. Maybe a Spirit Guide will come, or some new information will be brought to light or a series of events will fall into place . . . . (1992: 7–8)

Elder Knockwood's story of the Talking Stick impresses upon us several important Traditions of Talking Circle. One very essential norm of the Circle is that no one is to interrupt the person holding the sacred object. The commitment is the same as in other learning situations—to sit and attentively listen, allowing the wisdom of the teacher/speaker to really be heard. We must each learn to pay each other full attention and to take responsibility for maintaining focus on what each speaker is sharing. This assists people in learning not to project their experience and feelings onto others. The only way to really "know," to really see and hear someone else, is to fully experience and own our emotions and thoughts. Through respectful listening we are better able to enter into another's experience through their words.

Talking in Circle reminds us that to speak is a privilege, that spoken thoughts—words—are sacred. In our Tradition, words are carefully chosen and carefully listened to so that the power of the words and the images behind them "travel between the speaker and the other individuals to become One Thought" (Beck and Walters 1977: 42). This kind of group consciousness—"collective mindfulness"—exists when each individual's thoughts are directed to a collective thought and collective objectives. "Collective mindfulness [is] the concentration brought to an idea or thought by a lot of people at the same time . . . one is mindful when one is aware, respectful, careful" (Beck and Walters 1977: 42). "Mind-full-ness" orchestrates the power of thought, helping to actualize "the ability to create, transform, and vitalize" (Beck and Walters 1977: 43). In many creation stories, the world was thought into existence (Gunn Allen 1986). This reinforces the importance of the revitalization of Traditional beliefs and processes of transmission of the Ancestral worldview.

The Process In-Use

Through use in the classroom as pedagogy, and in the project as a research tool, I learned that clarifying the process and the intent underlying Talking Circle is essential. This is especially true when participants are unacculturated to the Circle. Clarification can simplify the Circle process, which invites participants to join in the experience rather than resist the unfamiliarity of it. It is a good idea to begin each Circle by stating clearly if a specific form or theme is intended. This helps participants to understand what is expected, to collectivize the focus and to keep the process on track.

Circle "rules" In-Use were articulated at the outset of each Circle and became more concise in that evolutionary process. The basic rules of Talking Circle are: one speaker at a time, the person holding the special object is the speaker and all others are to listen respectfully to that person. In Talking Circle you speak your own voice, describe what your own experience has been. You have the opportunity to express what you feel is on your heart to say. The point is to speak "from your heart," of what moves you, of what spirit moves through you when the sacred object reaches your hands. To choose words with care and thoughtfulness is to speak in a sacred manner. This usually takes time and experience; explicit modelling, direction and patience are required. Time, linear Western time, is often an obstacle to using the Circle in Schools. In capitalist society, time itself became commodified. Thompson tells us that "all time must be consumed, marketed, put to use; it is offensive for the labour force merely to 'pass the time'" (1991: 395). An Aboriginal time sense does not support, nor is it supported by, industrial capitalism. Chronological time contrasts sharply with the ceremonial time sense of our Ancestors, expressed poetically by Gunn Allen as: "the individual as a moving event shaped by and shaping human and nonhuman surroundings" (1986: 149).

To the Traditionalist, "time is not a phenomenon that we can waste or spend, but we must learn to patiently move through it" (Absolon 1994: 9). Learning patience, to wait for and to know the time and place when transformation is taking place is considered part of healing and learning cycles. Time, patience and relationships are all required to learn and teach in the Traditional way.

> Honoring the time that is necessary, practising patience through the process and acknowledging one's relationships are all central . . . . Practising these teachings is not easy given the fast paced lifestyle and technologies of contemporary society, yet it is necessary to train and discipline our minds, body and spirit. There are no quick recipes for zapping sacred knowledge into the essences of who we are. (Absolon 1994: 33)

Neither are there quick recipes for curing the ills of individuals, communities and nations today. Malcolm Saulis, a Maliseet educator, gives further depth to the Traditional belief-set regarding time:

> Time and timing are an important consideration since one needs time to learn, to change, to heal and to grow. There is time for things to happen, that spiritual influences destine things to happen in a given way. No one will determine the time for things to happen. Rather a number of elements have to come together in order for events to take place. Time has a physical, emotional and spiritual dimension, which depends on other people to understand the message of each dimension. Some people understand the future, some the present, and others the significance of the past. One must take time in order to listen for messages and to comprehend the significance of what they hear. People become wise only with time and effort. Time is a thing we experience and through experience you see the value of time. Time is an integral part of the whole continuum of culture and tradition, and the heritage gained. (1994: 16)

"Do not rush the council," my Elders counsel. To speak from the depths of the heart can be difficult for those not accustomed to it and it cannot happen if time is being measured. Students need to be cautioned: "Be easy on yourself . . . . If you find your mind rehearsing, just take some deep breaths and focus on the speaker. The speaker, like you, deserves to be heard" (Cahill and Halpern 1992: 47). There is as much energy to be put forward into respectfully listening and really trying to hear what the other speakers are saying as there is in articulating your own voice. It is the balance of that energy that makes a Circle positive or powerful. By attending to others and speaking from your heart, you honour yourself, the speaker, the Circle and the spirit of interconnectedness.

Talking Circle as Pedagogy

As the sacred object is passed from hand to hand and the Circle becomes deeper, emotions are shared more freely. Speaking and listening respectfully in Circle creates an atmosphere of compassion, the building block of community. Circle process can teach us the foundations upon which a proper relationship to oneself and others is developed. The state of conscious awareness contained within a Circle of interconnectedness can generate openness that is rare in Western society today. The energy of a Circle can create a space that can allow for the unorthodox to enter and the unexpected to happen. People, including me, often find themselves exploring issues and making disclosures to themselves and others that surprise them. As modern-day shamans have found, "[w]hen people gather in a circle and their intentions are aligned, it can help them drop the armouring of their personality structures . . . . On the societal level it is also healing because it is a perfect form for joining different groupings of people" (Cahill and Halpern 1992: 2).

The Talking Circle process, kin to Talking Stick (Knockwood 1992), can be useful as a teaching tool when people need to share feelings, experiences or their point of view. Participants from diverse backgrounds can gain insight as they "speak heartfully" and "listen respectfully" while others voice, together reflecting on experiences of racism and cultural difference. The Circle process, as adapted for classroom and research use, is embraced by many students and community participants. As one Aboriginal woman, Dee, exclaims at one of the Circles on CCI: "I think about coming here and being with people again, and feeling the closeness that comes from being in a group . . . it really helps . . . . I'm so grateful to be here!" (TC3:2). Some non-Native students also gave strongly positive reviews of the Circle process overall. As Van declares: "I really yearn to be here, (laughs) which is the only word I can say! I took Jean's course and it really touched me. It made an impact on me, and so I want to participate as much as I can" (TC3:4). Cindy drew parallels between the Circle process and her assessment of Canadian culture:

> The Talking Circle is a nice place because at least there's a place that people can tell what they want to say and it allows different opinions. For me, this Circle reflects the whole environment in Canada. I appreciate some of the culture here. It allows different opinions to be voiced out, though you can't change many things. (TC2:12)

To community participants outside the Aboriginal community, Circle was most often introduced to them in class and through the data collection process. Those newly initiated often had positive reviews: "So I feel like I learned a lot through the process of just seeing how it works, and how effective it can be" (Sis TC3:3). Another community participant expressed how impressed she was, and how the experience strongly impacted on her and her family members who had participated in the class.

I was introduced to the Circles [on] the Acadian night. I came with my grandmother and basically deferred to her in a lot of different areas, but it was quite enlightening for me. What really impressed me was the fact that it is very open and it is very easy to express your feelings. I was quite taken back as a matter of fact. I'm from a corporate background . . . . I was really impressed by it and I was walking around on a cloud for about a week. I felt tingly for about a week. It was really good . . . . The other thing is; I am a lesbian and I found that [names sister] has been really opened up in the last three or four months . . . . Certainly trying to learn more about how I feel and I really appreciate that. And I think that Circle had a lot to do with that as well. (Cat VC3:13)

Voice: Heartfully Speaking

Circle allows for serious reflection and communication regarding deeper issues like the process of identity construction. Those previously silenced are encouraged to find voice and speak up.

And it gives me a chance because I'm not so confident about my part, and I think it takes time for a minority to build up your confidence to confront the dominant culture. As for me, many, many immigrants, when [we] come to the dominant culture, we just try our hardest to integrate or assimilate to the main culture. And then suddenly, I shift my focus and try to maintain my own culture. This needs another kind of mechanism or another kind of strength and confidence to do this. I found that the Talking Circle keeps everybody silenced and I'm the only one to talk. Then I can have time to think and arrange what I'm going to say . . . . It is an entry point for people to find their voice and to speak up. (Cindy TC2:33)

Circle Talk requires all those who do speak to address their own experiences and feelings rather than generalizing or theorizing about others. This, I have found, is a new and sometimes terrifying possibility for those who have been acculturated to be cut off from their hearts. Char expresses this sentiment:

I *was* able to speak my feelings—very briefly tonight. It's never easy for me to do this, but every time I've been able to do it, I have felt better about myself for being honest, open, and following my own integrity. (Feb 10 93-j)

Vina, a student from the African community, journalled her first experience of participating in Circle Talk. She signals the ambivalence that is often felt by speakers unaccustomed to having an opportunity to speak what they know, without criticism or backlash from their classmates:

After smudging we talked in circle. Jean started to pass around a crystal. With this crystal people can tell stories of their experiences or just say whatever they wished to share with the group or decide to pass the crystal along without saying anything. This was very nerve wracking. Knowing my turn was coming, knowing the crystal was getting closer, what would I say? Do I just pass the crystal to the next person? What do I do, what do I say? Oh, no, it's my turn. Then I decided to answer a question someone asked earlier. It was on the term Indian, she wondered where the term had come from. After my answer I thought, hey, that was not bad. (Vina 93-j)

Vina's experience was "not bad" in that she was able to speak when her turn came. But she did not address an issue from First Voice, something close to her heart or her own life experience. This is a more difficult level of involvement in the process, and it happened for Vina in the next round.

However, the crystal went around a second time. Now what do I say? Do I respond to the term mulatto which [another student] had used during the first crystal round. As the crystal went around the circle I must have changed my mind at least five times. Yes I will respond, no I won't, yes, no, yes, no, yes then as the crystal approached me I said no I won't comment because this would mean I would have to share an experience from my life. My mind was made up, no. Suddenly the crystal was passed to me, and I felt compelled to speak. To speak from the heart. I didn't want to speak. I really just wanted to pass the crystal, but I couldn't. All of a sudden my mouth started to speak, these words came out and I could not control them. They were neither anger or judgemental. They were not accusing, they were calm and I began to explain. Mulatto I explained was offensive to me, because I am a light skin black female, I am asked frequently about my cultural background. However the problem does not lie with whites who ask. My only advice to [the student] and anyone else who really don't know was to "JUST ASK." (93-j)

Ambivalence and anxiety are also reported by some White students. The struggle to find voice and to speak heartfully in Circle about topics related to race relations challenges all participants to be self-reflective and culturally located. Analee tells her Circle-talk story:

After the burning of sweet grass, the class prepared to take part in circle talk. That safe, peaceful feeling I had experienced earlier was quickly replaced with feelings of anxiety as circle talk began. As the stone came closer and closer to me I felt a certain churning in my stomach . . . . I had to ask myself why?

As the beautiful stone sat in the palm of my hand I paused for a moment, but was unable to come up with the words to describe how I was feeling, so . . . I passed the stone on and remained very silent.

The stone travelled around the room a second time. This would mean I would have yet another opportunity to speak in circle. Before I knew it I was sitting quietly in my seat staring down at the stone in my hand. I sat for a few moments as the thoughts began racing through my head. Finally, I began to speak. I felt scared as I listened to the tremor in my voice . . . . I had to ask myself, why? (Sept 29 93-t1)

Analee spent a few minutes in an internal dialogue, trying to find answers to these questions. She continues her entry:

As a result of what I have learned recently about oppression, I was able to realize that I was doing the very thing that I have identified in myself as being oppressive— was avoiding talking about anything that made me feel a little uneasy . . . anything that was the least bit unfamiliar to me. As a result, I was able to sit and remain unattached and emotionally distant.

Being able to see this in myself, I began to feel a little saddened. So, as the stone moved around the circle for a second time, I chose to take a risk and try to share with the class what was running through my mind. I was feeling . . . I was feeling scared and overwhelmed . . . but I was feeling. I was glad that I was able to share my fears of unfamiliar— my fears of sharing my thoughts and feelings. (Analee Sept 29 93-t1)

When participants are able to grow throughout the course to be able to speak from their hearts, this enables them to be more in touch with feelings—their own and those of others. Analee concludes her journal with the following entry:

This class did play a very important role in my learning—it provided what I felt was a safe place to speak from the heart. Sometimes this is a difficult task for me because there is so much that I am learning about myself. It can be scary, exciting, and sad all in one. I am learning to *feel* more—to speak from my heart and not my head. Sometimes it is easy to absorb what is being taught and not let it touch you, or touch your heart . . . this is something this class has given me the opportunity to do. (Dec 1 93-j)

Through Circle, students can come to understand the daily lived experience of racism and White privilege as they draw on their own and each others' experiences. Circle Talk helps students gain a sense of trust in their fellow classmates and helps to equalize power between teacher and students as we all sit in the Circle together. Through passing the "sacred object" each in turn, "speaking from the heart" with others present in Circle, we maintain respectful silence and bear "witness" to the experiences of each other. Individuals can come to believe that what they say will be listened to and accepted without criticism.

Silence: Respectfully Listening

Using the Aboriginal Talking Circle reminds us of the relationship between who speaks and who listens. We are taught that we require silence "respectfully listening" to accompany voice "heartfully speaking." When we see silence only as produced through an exercise in domination, we are missing the significance of silence to voice. Aboriginal people are taught to respect silence as a pedagogical tool. In Circle, we listen "as witness," respectfully, to the experience of others. According to Cahill and Halpern:

> Learning how to witness is essential because we live in a time when great numbers of people are beginning to tell their truths. Some of these are hard to hear . . . yet they must be told and heard. When they are not heard properly the telling is undermined and damage, rather than healing, may result. It can take a long time to regain the courage to tell the story again. (1992: 75)

Through having to respectfully listen to each speaker, participants gain an empathic appreciation for points of view other than their own.

> After hearing from first voices thus far from the black culture, the Inuit culture, the Native culture, and now the Acadian culture, I am finally not just experiencing feelings of guilt but now feelings of downright envy, because my white culture pales in comparison to the pride and richness associated with each of the above mentioned cultures. (Ken Feb 17 93-j)

It is a large shift in consciousness to move from pity and guilt to embracing the "pride and richness" of other cultures. Listening to others in Circle does provide an opportunity for self-examination. It can help provide the social context for an experience or viewpoint previously understood as "personal":

> Not until last week have I come to total grips with the fact that the incident two years ago was not a personal attack on me, but indeed a direct product of oppression. I only fully realized this after hearing a class full of students sharing their experiences of oppression last week. It hit me, if I experienced the oppression on a daily basis even half as strong as some of these students said they did, then I would most likely express anger and frustration in not so appropriate ways. (Ken Jan 29 93-j)

Participating in the experience of Circle provided a lens for Van to interrogate herself and her "representations" of Aboriginal culture:

> I have always been interested in Native folklore and the spiritual aspects of the culture. This interest was natural to me and I nourished [it] through reading books, both fact and fiction. As informative as

reading is, it is still second hand knowledge. The reader does not have first hand experience with what they are reading, and is removed from the material.

For me, this distancing allowed me to romanticize some aspects of the native culture. The talking circle is a ritual that I put in a romantic light. I turned this into something "ideal" instead of real. I did not envision it as real people sharing real sorrows and struggles and pain. My vision was more of wise elders telling of spirit quests and native tales of long ago. This to me had nothing to do with the real world and the anger and resentment of the native peoples toward the white culture.

This is where my whiteness shines through, giving me the luxury of not having to think any other way but white. The sharing done by our First Nations guests in circle the other night, certainly helped to put issues into perspective for me. I also realize there are other forms of sharing within the native customs and minimized this with my romantic notions. (Oct 13 93-j)

Altering who speaks and who listens and "reauthorizing" (Schenke 1991) what can and cannot be said is an act of radical transformation. Helping students be empowered to find voice is often an aspect of transformational pedagogy, but requiring silence from those who have been accustomed to voice is not. I reflect on this dilemma in Circle Talk on CCI:

One of our ways of working in Circle is that people are not compelled to speak! If what you get out of Circle is you hear a story that resonates with you, and you never find a voice to say your own story, you're still getting the listening part, you're still taking in the Circle. Maybe not everybody has to be empowered to voice in Circle. That's something I've been really struggling with because, being silenced often myself, when I came to the teaching project, my biggest ambition was to get every student voice-full in class . . . . I have found, really, in my teaching experience . . . trying to figure out what to do when you've got always a few, mostly white students, who are *used* to having voicefulness, and then you've got other students from First Voice who are used to being silenced, and then you've got people all used to having the teacher talk at them, where is the beginning transformational point going to be there? (Fyre TC2:24).

Through teaching the Circle process, I found, quite by accident, that experiencing silence was a profound lesson for White, middle-class students. For many students, a lesson in silence is needed as much as a lesson in speaking, as many have rarely experienced lack of voice and have little respect for the power of words or the act of resistance inherent in claiming lost voice. If we recognize that differences in experience exist due to cultural locatedness, among other factors, then acknowledging these differences in our pedagogies means reflecting critically on the relationship of silence and voice.

While many viewed Circle Talk and First Voice as primary learning and healing aspects, other participants paid more attention to silence and the struggles inherent in learning to listen. While the power of giving voice—speaking heartfully—is an expressed value of Circle Talk, the process itself requires much more listening respectfully than talking. The lesson of respect for silence embedded in the Circle process impacts on participants' voicefulness in sometimes unexpected ways. While respectfully listening is a valued attribute in Aboriginal societies, and "active listening" a highly theorized skill in the helping professions, it is often underutilized in Western styles of communication. As Cindy declares:

> Talking Circle has a good function; they are forced to listen. Though they may not like to listen. (laugh) If for confrontation; sometimes I find that they are so defensive . . . . They may not take our words. But now it's a Talking Circle, they know at this moment they should listen. And I wonder how many times in their lives that they can sit down and listen to what other people say . . . .
> Maybe after awhile we can shift to another Circle that we can confront each other. But when we confront there's a risk that the people will be very defensive and they will not listen to what you say. And it's a win and lose situation for white people. They are very competitive. (laughs). (TC2:33)

One participant reflects on the difficulty of "unlearning" the "activist" mentality. It is a challenge to try to stop competing, analyzing or trying to change or "fix" what the speaker's "problem" is and to learn to really listen to what is being said.

> I like the idea of being able to be a listener and reflect, or especially if you're an activist, you tend to just be proactive and jump in to everything and go crazy and there's times in our lives that it's really important to hear First Voices and learn from that. (Gracie CC2:34)

Cal reflects on learning the Circle process from his own cultural location. He speaks out about the difficulty of learning to listen in Circle Talk:

> The first time I did it, I had a little hard time with it and it's only now that I realize why. We were talking about voices, when someone else is talking, people actually listen, you're not preparing a response like we normally are . . . . You don't have 5 or 6 people talking at the same time. It's also so respectful as well. (Cal CC2:31)

Cal articulates his recognition of what has been previously theorized as "collective mindfulness" (Beck and Walters 1977):

> There's so much that we think, that doesn't have to be said. I can remember being at home and feeling at one in that environment; where we could go for hours, sometimes days, without ever having to ever speak to anyone, and that was ok. There were things that were understood, it's a language unto itself. Thoughts were understood. Anyway, to some extent, it's like being here, there is a union without the words having been expressed. We don't have to respond to everything. There is a degree of understanding. (Cal CC2:31)

This is only possible if the group has acculturated to the norm of respectfully listening. The presence of collective mindfulness is considered by Traditionalists to indicate "successful" Circle work, as communication is occurring without relying on expressed words. Silence in this deeper sense makes possible a form of communication that is less distorted by "representations" or "signifiers." When we are sitting in Circle, telling our stories, sharing our learnings through experience and our feelings, we are establishing relationships among the Circle participants at a depth uncommon in the Western educational context.

The Circle process, while being educational, also emphasizes individual and community healing through sharing stories of pain and strategies for change. The Circles on CCI generated much reflection in the healing aspects of Circle work. This theme is most consistently articulated by Aboriginal participants, many of whom have felt the healing benefits in their own lives and families as a result of Circle work. I reflect on my own early learning about Circle as a healing tool:

> I learned Circle as a healing tool; as something to do, for people to heal with. To heal their conflicts in their families. To heal their conflicts in their communities. To heal feelings from things like sexual abuse or other varied forms of abuse that often get lodged in our bodies, and get lodged in us, and we don't have a lot of ways to bring it out or heal it. And Circle is a very healing forum in community if people can learn to use it. (Fyre TC3:25)

A Mi'kmaq Elder contributes a similar perception:

> Circle is a place of healing. And it's true when they say that Native people need to heal themselves. It's very true because we are the walking wounded. But, little by little Native people are coming to terms with themselves, because they've gone through a lot. (Sarah VC2:18)

Another participant from the Mi'kmaq Nation also expresses a congruent view:

> In some way Circle, Talking Circles, provide that little bit of healing because you're allowed to share in a context that's not necessarily so structured . . . . When you're allowed that opportunity to sit down and

talk in a spiritual context, about spiritual things, but other things as well, it just provides that opportunity to . . . let people see that there are some things that are more important than the knowledge that you get in a book. Our own life experience is a valuable tool. I can really see the value of this. (Ray VC2:16)

Phil shares her experience of the healing force of Circle for her and her family:

I had started healing before I learned all about the Circle . . . . But it's made me so much stronger and it's given me ways of healing my family as well. We've come a long way in the last couple of years by using the Circle. I can see that that's a very important way of healing all families and all people with their worries. It's so powerful to be able to share with other people and to gain strength from everybody else, and that support. To be listened to and respected for what you've got to say. There's really no other place anywhere where that happens. (VC1:16)

A personal narrative of healing through Circle is given by Misel, an Aboriginal community participant. He clearly draws the links between healing and reciprocity in building self-esteem and revitalizing Self-In-Relation to family and community. As is expected in Traditional teaching, Misel begins on a very "personal" note:

Today I know who I am and know what I am, and I know what I don't want. I don't want to bring back that thick, thick wall. I have to work at myself everyday. When people like Jean ask me to come in and do a presentation and a lot of people hear my stories, they think that I am helping them. But it isn't. It's the other way around. You people here are helping me, because everyday I've got to keep healing. And I really like being asked to come out and take part because when I'm in this Circle I am no longer alone! Before, I could be in a room of about 100 people and still be alone. But when I'm in a Circle, I know I'm there, and I'm taking people's strength, and also I'm giving strength. (VC1:8)

He expresses appreciation for the chance to be at Circle, telling his story. This illustrates the reciprocity built into the process. Misel continues:

Jean, I want to thank you for asking us to come back. It really feels nice to be back. Those of you who have heard my story, I hope you've learned or I've shed some light on it . . . . For me, when I get the opportunity to share now—You know maybe what I'm saying ain't going to hit or it ain't going to sink in, take it, put it in your pocket, and if you come across a situation for something like that, take it back out and use it. (VC1:8)

Traditional teachers know that not every story, not every speaker's experience, is going to impact on every listener. Our location in life at the moment of the telling impacts on our ability to take it in. This contributes to producing multiple interpretations of the same reality. Misel reflects on how speaking his voice, sharing heartfully of his experience—staying out of his head—is a healing tool:

> When I went in there I talked from my heart. (4 second pause) And I had something that they didn't have, no matter what diplomas, what courses, what certificates, I had life experiences . . . . And I found by staying out of my head, I don't know what I say, it just comes out. And I believe that this mouth of mine is just a tool because now inside me, there is no more fighting. It is hard but those things we have to grow with, we have to understand it. That's why when we have this Talking Circle it's healing. I can share that a little bit now. (VC1:25)

Sharing in Circle is special because communication in the outside world does not follow the same flow. It does not give the same opportunity for freedom of emotional expression. As Misel tells it:

> It feels good to come in to Circle because out there, once I go through those doors, I can't speak for all of you, but what I got to do is I've got to play the game. I have to turn and go out there and do what I have to do. Then when I come back in; I come in to Circle . . . . Let it go down. And it's nice. It's nice to breathe and say ok, good. I want to get a little bit of that garbage out. Just throw it out. I don't want it. Take it. Somebody else take it. Help me here. (VC1:25)

Misel is a role model; he shows us that healing is possible. Self-love is possible to obtain, but it is a long process that includes reclaiming our own feelings. He concludes his "speak-out" as he began, with a "personal" reflection:

> But I am good . . . . That's took a long time for me to say that! It's ok for me to be me. It's all right. I like that. Because there was a time I wanted everybody to like me so I would forget about me. And I've learned I can't. The most important person in this Circle is me. That's what I have to remember. I used to borrow people's feelings: anger, pain, fear, joy, but it wasn't me. I've learned today it's ok. (6 second pause) How can I say thank you for sharing and caring and letting me be me? But by simply saying thank you. (Misel VC1:27)

Circle as a healing force is also addressed by non-Native participants. One comments:

> This Circle I find is almost an automatic healing space. I didn't know what I expected the first time or the second time . . . it always brings me back to other times when I've healed. Some of it is very comfortable for

me. Very meditative and reflective. But it's together. It's that community thing again. Which is really nice when you hear other peoples' voices and you realize so many other people are dealing with so many things that are the same, part of them different, but similar in many ways. (Bea VC1:22-23)

A powerful testimonial by an African Canadian participant reinforces the Aboriginal perspective of Circle as therapeutic. His contribution validates the heart of the Model. I always hope to create a teaching and learning space that is empowering and healing across cultures, even while being located in a contradictory context. He begins by acknowledging the "personal" impacts of Circle on his own being:

I think it's really important for me to make some statements about the Circle, in terms of the kinds of personal effect it had on me . . . . [reveals personal history]. It's incredible when I start to look back through the circle; the impact that it has had on my life. [reveals personal history] . . . I've learned to grow through the Circle. (Cal CC2:24)

More specifically, he notes the strength-oriented foundations of learning in Circle: our experiences are our teachers. In Circle we learn that we need to uncover and accept lessons from all sorts of experiences and stories. The "reframing" from victim to survivor can produce healing in itself.

I think what I hadn't been able to acknowledge during that period of time was the fact that all those things have happened, but they have shaped who I am right now. I have survived that . . . . I started to look at some of the strengths that came out of that, who were some of the people that gave the support that I needed. (Cal CC2:24)

In this case, the participant parallels Circle directly with therapy:

Because I have not been seeing the therapist, this became my awakening, my consciousness at a personal level, at a political level . . . . Now looking back, I can see things falling into place. Not that my life is a whole lot easier than before, 'cause it's not! But, I think the way I look at things has changed somewhat. (Cal CC2:24)

Reframing one's past history of oppression enables acceptance. When we speak of changing "the way I look at things," we are signifying a change in consciousness. Cal expresses his growth as continuous throughout the CCI course:

As a part of the circle I see myself move through the stages, it was continuous growth. It's transformation . . . . I'm concerned that I can't move further because what I require isn't there. That creates some concern for me because there's . . . this form where I gained consciousness; I gained a higher degree of understanding. It has been a real awakening. But there is no platform and there is no support net for me to remain a part of . . . where is my community and where is the circle for me? How do I continue to hold on to that? (CC2:32)

Cal raises a critical issue: to continue to learn and grow as individuals we need a supportive community environment. Sharing and mutuality builds individual and community strength. Through egalitarianism we become more able to recognize our immanence and interconnectedness. These are essential understandings if we are to build community across diversity, inside and outside the classroom. This is the theme of the West, to which we will now turn our attention.

The Western Door: Building Community Inside and Outside the Classroom

The West corresponds to the element Water
Feel the great waters of Earth Mother
Oceans . . . Lakes . . . Falls . . . Rivers
Streams . . . Brooks . . . Ponds
The Rains . . . Snows.
Recognize the Waters of your body . . . Blood . . . Tears
Our physical need for Water . . . each and every day.
Water to drink . . . Water to wash.
Picture Fall . . .
Brightly coloured Yellows . . . Oranges . . . Reds

Falling leaves . . . Crisp breeze
Fresh vegetables . . . Roots . . . Apples . . . Pumpkins
Bountiful harvest . . . preparation time.
Dusk . . . Light dimming
Red and Purple Sunset on the horizon
Silver and Gold shimmers on the Waters.
Call the creatures of the Waters.
Swim with the Turtle . . . Whale . . . Fish . . . other Sea Creatures.
Feel the ease . . . Fluidity
By which their bodies move through the Water.
Dive deep and accept the Gift of the West
The power to Feel
The Courage to face our deepest Feelings.
Be in touch with the Flow of your own Emotions:
Love . . . Anger . . . Sorrow . . . Joy . . . Ecstasy.
We cannot Feel any of them in their full intensity
unless we are willing to face them All.
Let the strength of your Emotions Flood you.

Deep Feelings need to be exposed
Aired to achieve balance.
How do you Express . . . Repress . . . your Feelings?
Do Tears run down your face?
Tears our link to the great Ocean Waters of our Earth Mother.
Does laughter bubble from your lips?
Does your heart beat with pain . . . yours or another's?
What feelings do you Have . . . Share . . . Voice?
The power to Feel is a Gift.
We need to Feel In-Relation to others
To our Kin . . . our Relations as we know them to be.
Partners . . . Children . . . Friends . . . Community(s)
All of Creation.

Be Aware
How are you Nurtured?
How do you Nurture others?
Learn to understand
The depth of Self-In-Relation
What is the nature of relationships?
The composition of the Family?
Who defines quality quantity of Relations?
Boundaries of the Family Network?
Extension of Kinship through Relational ties

Our Elders teach We are All-In-Relation . . . All of creation.
We believe beings thrive
When there is a web of interrelatedness
Between Individual . . . Community . . . Mother Earth.

"Reach for Your Deepest Feelings"

The West calls us to pay attention to the emotional impact of the educational experience. As critical educators, we are told that we must respect and value the power of pain, of deep feelings, in provoking change. As Galper notes, "[T]he most sophisticated intellectual analysis possible will not lead to a commitment to sustained action until it becomes personally and actively painful to continue in the old way" (1980: 185). hooks says to "remember the pain," because she believes "true resistance begins with people confronting pain, whether it's theirs or somebody else's, and wanting to do something to change it . . . . Pain as a catalyst for change" (1990: 215). Bill Mussell, a Sal'i'shan educator, sees the sharing of emotions as an integral part of the educational project:

> Healing means far more than emoting or discharging feelings. It is a process of experiencing emotions, gaining insight into their source, and identifying and changing negative beliefs and behaviours. It is a holistic process which calls on the powers of the mind, the emotions, the body and the spirit and results in freeing of these powers for positive action in the social and political world. (1994: 8)

The Aboriginal processes In-Use employ various means to help a person accommodate balance and wholeness, to revitalize unity within the self and In-Relation to others. According to Medicine Eagle (1991), this may create a radical discontinuity in the way the person's reality is assembled. Discomfort is produced from the struggle to regain balance. Absolon notes that there may be "feelings of release or relief in exposing, encountering and recognizing the sources of one's problems . . . elated feelings resulting from understanding and working toward ridding oneself of the hidden causes of guilt, shame, anger, jealousy, fear, and other sicknesses" (1994: 10, 11). One Aboriginal participant discloses the depth of feeling, and the cyclical process, related to uncovering, acknowledging and healing emotional imbalance:

> We weren't allowed to show emotions, we weren't allowed to feel and share with others. It's been a real struggle for me, to move from being very physical and very disconnected from myself, to come to a place of being connected. I think it comes in phases. I go from being very connected to very disconnected at times. And I feel like, I am very in touch with myself and I feel good about that. And then there are times, like I said, when I feel very disconnected. And I think that comes from not having had the connections. Because that left a long time ago. So

.... (participant is very emotional and trying to control her crying) So the components of my life I've never received. So it's very hard because I'm physically isolated, to get those pieces. (crying) So I have to use my friends as family to get the pieces of my life and to gain strength among the Native people because the pieces that I need I don't have. So it gets very painful ... but ... I think things are improving. I certainly feel like I've grown over the past two years. (crying openly) Thanks to people like Jean. I have some supports. And it's very hard because the emotional is the component in my life that I've never had. But I am making progress. (Randi VC 1:18)

The release of feelings and re-establishment of community can be an extended process when there is much buried loss and anger. Carniol warns us that "[s]uch explorations with severely oppressed individuals can be fraught with the pain of discovering deep personal and emotional commitments rooted in promises that the system never meant to keep" (1990: 121). Pain, anger and other strong emotions are not exclusive to the Aboriginal and African cultural experience; they are also common expressions of those engaged in the transformational process. According to Culley, a feminist teacher, when students are engaged in a process that "allows them a glimpse, a taste, or a full-face confrontation with the truth that the dominant culture is steeped in the hatred of women" and others, the journey can make them "uncomfortable, anxious, despairing and angry" (1985: 210). Joycechild lists students' reactions to consciousness-raising in a feminist classroom:

[E]xcitement, empowerment, feeling they've been duped/ignorant because they never had this knowledge before, resistance, disbelief, frustration, anger, burn-out, wanting to act but wondering how, feeling as though their worlds have been shaken up, getting hostile/resistant reactions from family and significant others. (in Lather 1991: 128)

There is strong evidence to indicate that emotions and reactions should be aired as part of the educational experience. From the functional perspective, repressed emotions are a block to effective absorption of material. Henry (1989) notes that the determination not to neglect the human side of learning and to acknowledge the role of affect alongside cognition is central to experiential models. Some claim that contemporary culture "offers only one guiding norm about feelings: control" (Heron, in Jarvis 1985: 152). Western Schools restrict emotional content. Education has been dominated by the Eurocentric emphasis on the intellect, which has been regarded as the controller of the emotions. From the critical perspective as a tool of consciousness-raising, there is a close link between emotion and the motivation to act. In Freirian pedagogy, "learning to name the world" starts with identifying issues that the learners speak about with excitement, hope, fear, anxiety or anger (Hope and Timmel 1989). One student,

Vada, expresses her experience in this way: "This is the class which has stirred my feelings the most and the class that has stayed on my mind the most. While it has been a painful learning, it also has been a very rewarding learning" (Apr 4 93-jsum).

Many feelings were generated throughout the experience, including fear and anxiety. For some people feelings were tied to past issues, and resurfacing them was painful. Sometimes tears were shed in class. Moments of sadness, shame, guilt and anger were widely expressed among White participants. Gracie shares the depth of her reactions:

> Yesterday and today I wrote about oppression and I cried all day . . . . As the white race rips through technology with terrifying speed, we certainly have destroyed a great deal of Mother Earth and the essence of ourselves. Large tears from my heart . . . . (Oct 4 92-j)

Most often the feelings expressed are linked to a particular trigger, an exercise, story or speaker. Some participants more than others are able or willing to articulate their emotional reactions. Lena was able to express her reactions vividly in her journal:

> One of the issues which had an impact on me tonight in class was [the African Canadian guest's] statements in the talking circle . . . . Two feelings arose in me while she was speaking. The first was complete shame. Shame for not recognizing the racist practices of the media who covered this issue and shame for being associated with the white dominant society . . . .
> I also felt anger at the media for turning an issue about the oppression of women of all colours into an issue about race. If the government and society as a whole would look at the economic issues in this country and the oppressive nature of racism and sexism instead of scape goating a few black men, than maybe change would occur. (Jan 17 93-j)

We express our deepest feelings to those whom we are In-Relation with, including our family members. Lena's journal excerpt about her "speak-out" in Circle will illustrate:

> I totally made a fool of myself in Wednesday's Cross Cultural class. I don't know if you'll remember by the time you read this but I cried yesterday when I started to talk about [my partner's] new job . . . . Sunday night he told me that he felt like people didn't like him because he was not white. I was blown away. I feel so terrible. I wouldn't have guessed that racism was the problem. For a week now I've been on his back to feel grateful that he had gotten the job. I am completely stupid. He must have felt so terrible when I was saying those things. I am so privileged because that would not happen to me. It is because of my

own racism that I didn't even think he was being discriminated against. The more I write about this, the more I want to go down to that office and scream at those employees. All I know now is that I want to be as supportive as possible for [him], but besides that I don't know what to do. (Jan 24 93-j)

Sharing Stories, Sharing Feelings

Creative storytelling is a good outlet for documenting and reflecting on emotions. I have adopted it as a method of assisting myself and students in releasing feelings and transforming personal pain into structural change.

Charnley advises writing as a form of personal activism—"taking action with the voice and hand":

On paper we can confront the enemy who is not embodied in one human being. We can question our thinking, we can address someone who is simply too powerful to confront in person. This is the power of writing, taking action with the voice and hand, moving thought into physical being, taking it further than one's mind will allow and giving it away to other people. (1990: 16)

In this Model-In-Use, participants have been encouraged to present their experiences and learnings both in class and in their lives in the form of a "story." They learn to make connections between their personal experiences and the cultural and structural realities that frame our individual, family and community lives. Students' stories of past racism reconfirm that we live our lives In-Relation, and that the experiences that have the most meaning are those we share with our relations. This is illustrated by the concluding remarks from the journals of two students who did interrogate past racial learning within their families of origin:

It's really hard for me to look back and realize how racist certain members of my family were (are??). It's not easy to come to terms with a less than perfect family. My family situation serves to show how racism can be learned at an early age, how racism effects those it's aimed at and the debilitating affects it can have on the person who acts upon it. (Gela Jan 18 93-j)

By doing this I feel that I will be getting to the root of where my own racism developed first, through socialization. I also feel that information is meant to be shared and if my family can become more aware, they can pass this knowledge on to others. (Tia 93-j)

The reality of the racist pain inflicted on ourselves as children and on children in our lives trigger strong reactions, particularly for those who are or who plan on becoming parents. An Aboriginal Community member, Redbird, contributes this story:

> My . . . [grandchild], the poor little thing went to school and they started racism on her, and I found that out by her coming home and saying, "Nannie, I'm ugly, I want to be different. I want to be different!" And I said, "Well how do you want to be different?" And she said, "I have to have blonde hair and blue eyes right away!" And I said, "Well who told you that?" And she said, "I'm ugly and I hate myself." And she'd go around and [her mother] would be so upset and I would be upset! And I tried to explain to her that you are beautiful, you know, you have two beautiful cultures in you and you are beautiful! It's so hard to tell a little five-year-old that and make her understand! She's just learning now the hard knocks of life, where I came from, the School of Hard Knocks! And she's learning that! And it's sad that in this day and age in the '90s, that it's still going on. (CC1:18)

Vada expresses her deep reaction to hearing this type of story:

> I just came home from the class about racism and oppression. I am not sure if I shall scream or cry. I feel so upset with my racism and the effect of racism and ignorance on other people. Tonight a mother told us about how her daughter is ashamed of who she is, her family, culture and her race. (Jan 24 93-j)

While this story was told early in the term, Vada concludes her journal, two months later, still reflecting on the impacts of the same class.

> The learning that has had the greatest impact on me, and that has stirred my emotions the most, is the growing awareness of the personal impact of racism. While I knew that racism had great effect on people's lives, it was the story about the little girl that was ashamed of her race, history and family, that really struck home with me. The learning after that day became so much deeper and emotional for me . . . . What made this learning as strong as it became, was that I thought about my own concerns about raising children that have a good sense of their identity and pride of who they are. I thought of how painful it would be to know that my children were ashamed of who they are and wanted to be different, as well as knowing that my children who have not done anything to anyone, are treated badly by others just because of their skin color, culture or language. The other stories about children growing up with racism, and the adult person's life with racism made my awareness, anger and my admiration for their strength even greater. (Apr 4 93-jsum)

I often draw on my own experience as a mother to share experiences of how racism affects my daughter's relationships with children in her school and in our neighbourhood. Illustrating through story that children are also capable of committing racial slurs towards other children provokes reflection on the responsibility of adults towards the socialization of children in their lives. Racially unaware students often react very emotionally to this form of teaching story. In one entry, Lena expresses her heartfelt reaction:

> I've also been thinking a lot about what you said in class the other night about your daughter's experience with racism. It sickens me to think that people raise their children to believe the things [your daughter's] friend believed. When are white people going to recognize that they are racist and that what they believe, say and do hurts other people. I am sick of we white people saying something racist and them saying "But I am not a racist"—Bull. This Saturday I am doing child care for my sister, she has two little girls and I am going to grill them as to what they think about people from culturally diverse groups. I don't have any kids of my own right now so they're the closest thing I have. I know that my family is racist so I am definitely going to check out what my sister and her partner have taught their kids. Hopefully, I will be able to take them to some Black History Month things so they'll learn through first voice. (Jan 24 92-j)

Self-interrogation and exploration of one's Self-In-Relation to one's family regarding responsibility for challenging racism can be seen as a positive step. Some students realize that, because children learn racism from adults, we must take responsibility to help them un-learn it as well:

> Children learn racism. They hear, see, and react to situations that are learned from other people, often these people are their parents, teachers or significant others in their lives.
> Children have to be educated in other cultures, and what better time to educate them than when they are young, influential, and eager to learn. (Nadine Jan 27 93-j)

Building Our Community Connections

Community is Multifaceted.
Community is as we define it to be:
Geographic . . . Social . . . Cultural . . . Racial
Spiritual . . . Intellectual . . . Political
How do you see your Self-In-Relation?
Who are your Communities? your Relations?
How do you understand . . . experience Community?
As a concept? An act of resistance?
As a feeling of togetherness . . . Interconnectedness?
As a strategy for Change?
Learn to recognize the complex interplay
Gender . . . Race . . . Class . . . Ethnicity . . . Age . . . Ability . . . Orientation.
Diversity is Enacted in

Necessary for Community.

What do you need to learn
About building your relationships with diverse Communities?
What lessons can be learned from past History
Present struggles . . . future Visions
Of those actively involved in community-building?

Recognize Community-building strategies enacted
In this Model-In-Use:
Sharing experiences and feelings Together in Circle
Storytelling . . . acknowledging First Voice
Heartfully Spoken . . . Respectfully Listened to
Enjoy together while we learn together.
Balance pleasure with work.
Consider the Four laws of living in Community:
Respect . . . Honesty . . . Caring . . . Sharing.
Learn what influences support? Run contrary?
Attempt to learn and teach Community-building
With and in the Communities.
Let us strive to be Heartfully Connected to Community.
Recognize our Self-In-Relation.

In Traditional times, it was understood that Community requires individuals to develop their sense of Self-In-Relation. We begin by expressing our feelings to our families. Through building our connection to our Community, we gain insight into the reality that we are all part of the larger Circle of life. Building and sustaining community was and is a deep concern to Aboriginal people. Our community structures, battered throughout the imposition of colonial measures, need to be continuously repaired. The Western definitions of community have been used socially and legally to weaken our tribal bonds. We have not been left to develop our tribal systems in a peaceful manner. We have been systematically stripped of our lands and separated from the beliefs that once grounded our Traditional identity formation. The enforced assimilation, detribalization and retribalization of Aboriginal peoples through the process of colonization is known by many Elders, educators, visionaries and activists as the root cause of our current well-documented social breakdown. Deloria expresses a common understanding of the governmental restrictions that interfere with exercising today our determination as a communal people:

> Tribes can no longer form and reform on sociological, religious, or cultural bases. They are restricted in membership by federal officials . . . . Indian tribal membership today is a fiction created by the federal

government, not a creation of the Indian people themselves. (1994: 243)

Collins (1991) points out that the type of community implicit in the market model is an arbitrary one based on competition and domination. For instance, she notes that Afrocentric models of community emphasize connection, caring and personal accountability. Rejecting existing models of power, she puts forth an alternate vision based on self-definition and self-determination. Fulani (1988) maintains that the system works to undermine our sense of community, history and solidarity, as community strength poses a threat to the current status quo. It is a commonsense reality to our Communities that the authorities are acting to erode community ties. Western society has constructed community as the dualistic opposite of individualism, as a threat to individual freedom (Fox-Genovese 1991). In today's society, dominant notions of "community" have arisen from lack of community, from the tyranny produced by the prioritization of the needs of some (specifically, elite European males globally) over the well-being of the whole. Individualism was produced and by now reproduces "communities" of people divided by norms of hierarchy and riddled with sexism, racism, classism, ableism and heterosexism. Individualism, fuelled by the capitalist market, threatens to swing the balance between personal freedom and social order wholly to the side of the individual.

Fox-Genovese identifies the dangers in the individualist Tradition: "the ease with which it has invited individuals to objectify everything that they perceive as other, to view other human beings as nothing more than obstacles in their path" (1991: 235). When one's place in the world is beneath that of others, community is severed. Society is becoming increasingly atomized, each individual increasingly relying upon a sense of morality that focuses primarily on social relationships as a function of our own personal choices. "Hence, obligations towards, and alliances with others, obtain a provisional character" (Jansen and Wildemeersch 1992: 9). The deconstruction of community has lead to an escalation of individual isolation, hopelessness and despair. One student reflects this perception: "Community seems to mean true connectedness and caring—what the world lacks today in our capitalistic alienating, cold, efficient society. It's obviously what we need more of!" (Lola Dec 92-jsum).

Because Self-In-Relation has existed as a foundation of a Traditional worldview, the value of community has been retained in the modern day. Maggie Hodgson, a Cree Elder, describes an Aboriginal women's group: "Their greatest strength is their community-mindedness built on self-help and peer support. In keeping with the Native way, what they receive is given back to the community as their spirits touch the community in a healing way" (1990: 38). This Traditional value is also reflected in statements articulated by Aboriginal participants in Circle Talk:

I guess that all comes out of looking at yourself as a Native person. Or as who you are! . . . . They feel that you have to bring, and you do have to bring it full circle, when you go out to university you have to come back. I feel you have to come back to your community and do something for your community. So that is a concept of the Circle that I believe in. That it goes, but it comes back, eh? (Jose VC2:13)

Coming together in a Circle, caring for each other, sharing with each other, helping each other gain a better understanding of our cultural locatedness, our Self-In-Relation is considered by Traditionalists to be necessary for the transformation of today's society. We must work continuously to re-establish the individual in connection to the community and In-Relation to Mother Earth.

Community is a sacred concept with high value in Aboriginal culture. The rebuilding of Self-In-Relation—the connection between the individual and the Community—is an act of resistance, given the level of individualism in society today. In this Model-In-Use, I take a highly community-oriented approach, which emphasizes Self-In-Relation to the Communities at many levels. Outreach to and networking with the Communities is necessary for the Model to be functional. The involvement of students in task-oriented work, which requires outreach to the Communities, helps to build the network necessary to deliver the Model. Students and I both arrange for diverse members of the Communities to come in and speak about their experiences in and against the System.

When participants compare what they have noticed in my class with the other Models for teaching and learning cross-cultural issues they have experienced, they noted that my class placed emphasis on learning from direct interface with community members.

I had cross-cultural issues with another teacher here in the School . . . and it was quite different. I think it's really special the way it's done now, and I hope it continues. Community input, the community being able to say, have some say to the School, some link open there, so that they can feel comfortable about what's going on at this School. What are we teaching here? How are we teaching professionals to deal with the communities? It's nice for communities to have the input there. I think it's really important. (Free TC3:4)

When I took cross-cultural a few years ago, the teacher was a white woman and although at the time I thought it was a pretty good class, because we were talking about other people, other issues other than ourselves, I realize now that the way it was taught was really ineffective and we were given a big pile of readings about other people, and we very rarely had guest speakers or people from the community. We just basically did our little reading package and sat around and talked about some of the issues and some of the ideas on the readings . . . . I can't believe the difference . . . . I just can't believe what I missed. What everybody else is getting the chance to experience and I'll regret it if they are talking, in any negative manners or not realizing the value of what they're having because I can't believe how much I would have liked to have had that experience. (Sis TC3:1)

Speak-outs from members of the Communities provide opportunities for critical analysis of the System. They help clarify educators' role, past and present, in oppression. This educational intention needs to be clearly communicated to participants. My contribution at one Circle expresses this insight:

> The Model . . . is really trying to teach from people's experience; to try to change the attitudes of educators so that they will do their work in a different light . . . . And I'm trying to invite the community to be involved in that because I can't do that on my own! I know that . . . our ancestors say—repetition, more voices can give the same message. Maybe your story will trigger somebody, whereas somebody else's story will trigger somebody else . . . . A lot of people think racism happened over 40 years ago, but not today. So those daily experiences from today is really what people can feel in their hearts, they can feel it's wrong. (Fyre CC1:2-22)

Talking Circles conducted with input from the members of the Communities provides crucial information about building good working relationships and lessons about community-building in the classroom. I have found that making the classroom a place where people can be connected with each other requires altering atmosphere and pedagogical forms in multiple ways. Through analysis of my own theme work, I reveal how culturally constructed our notions of community-building are.

> I've tried to make the class a place where people can be connected with each other, at a number of different levels, by doing teaching in a lot of different ways. To try to make people feel more comfortable about bringing their children in, bringing their Elders in to class. Talking from their hearts. Feasting after class, a social time so that people can socialize together and learn together from that. So that people can be together. Dancing, having dancers in, having [guests] teach dance. One day we had . . . thirty people from the [African Nova Scotian community group] dancing, singing, doing poetry in the class here . . . . It was wonderful! Those are the kinds of classes that I really remember as building community, as being times when people really got something more than just the theory out of it. They got a sense of relationship, they got a sense of community. They got a sense of understanding about what it means to be In-Relation. That's the heart of the West, being In-Relation. How do we notice that we're connected to other people? We notice because we have feelings . . . because we have conversation with them. We hug them. We dance with them. We sing with them. Those are the things that are the heart of the community. And we work together, we do things together to make a change. Those are the kinds of things I was trying to teach about community . . . . Our culture really defines what we see as community and what is important

in community . . . the way that I see community building is very Natively defined. The way Native people build community is by singing together, by dancing together, by eating together, by sharing stories together, experiences together. By sitting in Circle together . . . . How can we build that kind of community here? (Fyre TC3:9)

A White community participant relates my cultural identity to the enactment of community-building in the classroom:

When I think of how you brought community in to the classroom literally and figuratively, it makes sense that it happened because of who you are as the teacher in structuring the whole exercise, who you brought in and who the students were. When I think of the difference—Most of my classes at the School have been largely White students and always White teachers, and readings by White men and women usually. And how can you have community in that setting when our community is multi-racial and -lingual? It is filled with all kinds of people with different genders and sexual orientations and experiences. How can you have community reflected when everybody's from the same perspective and that's all we're talking about? (Sis TC3:16)

Community is illustrated and built into class through actively recruiting representation from more than one tokenistic voice from the group. For me, this was by far the most exciting aspect of developing community in the classroom.

As far as seeing community in action, I think one of the clearest times we had that, seeing all the diversity in community in action was when, [a student] brought in several members from the Chinese community and . . . other members from the Immigrant community. We could see all of the class/race and gender lines being drawn right there in the classroom as people disagreed on certain issues and represented their own voice, and it was a really beautiful illustration of how complex community is. Community isn't just what one person can say about it. Community is that all of these different people with all of their different agendas, all trying to live in community in some way . . . . That was one of the beautiful illustrations of . . . how in reality that all comes to be. (Fyre TC3:5)

Cal echoes my feelings in another Circle when he discusses a presentation in which several members of the African Nova Scotian community were involved:

That was so powerful for me. I can remember getting so choked up in the class feeling that degree of family and community in that class. And the fact that people who came, they all came, we were talking about culture but everybody came with a different perception of, not necessarily what culture was, but what the role might be in terms of dealing with issues in the community. I thought that was so . . . so interesting . . . people were really passionate about it. (CC2:15)

Traditional Community-Building Pedagogies

Storytelling . . . Testifying
Familiar to many . . . a Healing and Teaching tool
Builds rapport necessary to sustain Community.
Weave our personal traumas into the larger web.
Pain released as a Story to learn from.
"Old-style words are just like school" Says Elder Ned.
Culture and context influence the way we tell Stories.
Determines Who will hear them.
What meaning they will take from them.

Circle as Pedagogy.
Builds Community.
Listen Respectfully to learn what the needs are.
Gives everyone a sense of worthiness
Being valued . . . Listened to . . . Respected.
Circle as Pedagogy
Brings Healing.
Strengthening the Individual . . . In-Relation to the Community.
Strong role models Inspire others to Grow and Change.

Circle as Pedagogy.
A search for "dominance free forms of interaction."
Challenge the dichotomies between Knower and Knowledge
Reason and Emotion.
Build bridges between School and Community.
Personal healing and professional development.
Healing and teaching.
Heal and educate the Community . . . not only the Individual.

It is important to develop an atmosphere that allows a style of communication that is familiar to the Elders and guests, so that they understand the expectations and can contribute in a meaningful way to the process or topic. Storytelling is an excellent method of giving speakers an opportunity for uninterrupted voice in a manner culturally conditioned for many diverse groups and rich in learning for the listener. The ultimate value of storytelling is to recreate a situation for someone who has not lived through it, so the listener can benefit from the teller's experience. Stories told by Elders, shamans and other "authorities" have been documented as our main form of cultural transmission. Many Aboriginal people, particularly Elders, treat storytelling as absolutely central to conversation and base their evaluation of other people on their storytelling abilities. Students express in journals their appreciation for the opportunity to both learn from others' stories and to enhance their own storytelling skills.

> Tonight's class was wonderful, the dancing, feasting, storytelling was great! I loved to tell stories of my past because storytelling is not a great skill of mine and I would like to perfect it! It's so nice to listen to the Voices of women like yourself, and [the guests] because it allows me to listen carefully and to validate your experience, as well as my own! Wonderful! (Randi Mar 17 93-j)

Storytelling or "testifying" is also a familiar and comfortable ritual in African culture. Russell's (1985) pedagogy, "experience as text," encourages storytelling. She states that it is "[t]he oldest form of building historical consciousness in community . . . . Robbed of continuities, prohibited free expression, denied a written history for centuries by white America, black people have been driven to rely on oral tradition for our sense of the past" (1985: 156).

Buffalo reflects more specifically on the power of storytelling as a healing and teaching tool, used Ancestrally to share feelings and build the rapport necessary for sustaining community:

> Healing through stories is but one important aspect of synthesizing our relationship with ourselves and with the entire universe. As well as being entertaining and giving a sense of pleasure, stories arouse heightened mindfulness, a sense of wonder and mystery, and a reverence for life. As the story unfolds, a rapport develops between the storyteller and listeners. (1990: 120)

Cruikshank reinforces the role that relationship has in storytelling, as expressed by the Aboriginal Elders whom she interviewed:

> Storytelling does not occur in a vacuum. Story tellers need an audience, a response, in order to make the telling a worth while experience .... When they tell me a story, they do so to explain something else to me. The whole rationale for telling then disappears if I cannot understand what they are trying to teach. (1992: 16)

Starhawk also supports the healing, empowerment and community-building potential of "storytelling" our daily lived experiences. Stories can help us weave our personal traumas into the larger structural context:

> When an experience becomes a story, it is passed on, given away, made sacred. The story intensifies the value of the events that have passed. Pain and rage can be released, isolation broken, triumph and ecstasy celebrated. What was a singular experience becomes woven into a larger context. (Starhawk 1987: 123)

I express similar insights in my reflections on the power of storytelling in Circle. I emphasize how we are linked emotionally to others through recognizing ourselves in each others' stories:

> When you hear somebody's story that's similar to your own story, then you go home and you rework that story, it's like it becomes yours! And so a lot of the teaching Model and a lot of the emotions that people put out in class I take that home and I work it over myself. (Fyre TC3:8)

Storytelling is a form of reciprocity in which we each learn and share from each other. As Phil expresses, this can produce a healing effect: "I know that for myself, just coming in as a student and as a community participant; it's been very healing for me to talk and to tell my stories, and nice to hear what other people's stories are" (Phil TC3:14).

Story Circle

Several students reflect on the impact that a particular "Story Circle" on Aboriginal culture has on them. These excerpts illustrate the teaching and community-building potential available through stories:

> As story circle began, so did the beating of the drum . . . thump . . . thump, thump . . . . I learned that the drum with its drumbeat represents the center of life, just as the heart provides life with its heartbeat. I paid very close attention to the stories that were told . . . . The stories that are told in circle are all very important—and we all have something to learn from them . . . .
>
> It is the sharing of experience of others that helps us see things in ourselves that before we did not see . . . or in some cases, that we just *choose* not to see . . . .
>
> Through participating in story circle I was able to get a sense of the importance of oral tradition to First Nations people. I was able to see how stories that were told were very important in teaching a lesson to all who listened. I was told by a native friend that these lessons were not pointed out to you rather, it was often left up to you to identify the parts of the story that were valuable in helping you learn something. (Analee Oct 13 93-j)

This student, Analee, was able to gain insight into the importance of oral narration to the Aboriginal culture. She also acknowledges the aspect of personal responsibility for learning, which is embedded in Traditional pedagogies. Another White student, Bejay, journals more specifically about the content of the Circle and its emotional impacts on her. Her response illustrates the importance of the relationship built between the teller and the listener:

> Today's class was the Aboriginal presentation. It was a very meaningful experience. I really enjoyed the circle talk and the drumming. I felt connected to the rest of the group. The stories that were shared left me with a lot to think about. The story that one of the speakers shared about her partner's experience at the residential school was absolutely horrifying. I am so angry that white people thought they could just rip these children from their families and "educate them in the white way."
>
> I cannot even begin to know what it must have felt like for those families who lost their children, to those who had to attend those heinous institutions. I do know that it is very, very important that this never be allowed to happen again and that as a white person and a future [professional], it is my responsibility to fight in whatever way possible to prevent this form of atrocity from taking place once more.

I feel privileged to have the story of the Eagle Feather shared with me. The person who shared that story is very lucky to have been gifted with the feather, and to have viewed those eagles flying overhead. She taught me that there is more than one form of energy at work. It is not just the physical things we all see, and that some of us take for granted. It is also the spiritual.

Doing the dancing and singing the songs felt great! It was fun and relaxing, very uplifting, really set the pace for the day. The feast was very enjoyable. It gave everyone the chance to speak and socialize, to learn from each other. (Bejay Feb 15 93-j)

Rebuilding Respectful Community Relations

A Traditional approach to education reinforces that acknowledging immanence and giving respectful treatment to all participants is critical to the idea of community-building in the classroom. As Hart stresses, "The fostering of solidary relations among all the participants in a context of caring is therefore as vital a component of an overall libratory educational practice as the fostering of critical reflexivity" (1991: 135). Both critical and cultural philosophies support group interaction as a valuable learning process. Development of a strong peer culture through an emphasis on collaborative group process, including family and community members, reinforces Aboriginal values of community and helps to compensate for the "individualism" stressed in the learning site. Through First Voice, Talking Circle and storytelling, students are encouraged to seek diverse ideas in their learning and rely less on teacher as "authority." While guidelines are developed to help students engage in the learning process, it is actually the students themselves who must take responsibility for their own learning.

Building community in the classroom is linked to reinforcing connections between different cultures as well as cutting across the age and gender lines. Cultural ideals regarding the importance of family togetherness in building community strength challenges the Eurocentric "divide and conquer" mentality. Why are we forced to learn separately from our children, our Elders, our other family members? This is so ingrained it is rarely challenged in Western schooling. This Model-In-Use challenges this "commonsense" notion of schooling by encouraging family groups to come to class. Several family groups participated in the classroom and in Circle Talk. Many others have brought their children, sisters, partners, Elders and friends to share in class work. I express my heartfelt appreciation to the families present at Circle, as I always find it a very enriching experience.

One of the really strong things about my experience in university . . . the White Model of Education is to divide everybody into their right age group, into their right everything group, and have them learn separately from each other, and I think it's so rich to be able to learn . . . from our own family members and with our own families present. And I've always taken the opportunity to invite my family to come to Circle and I really appreciate you coming as a family group. I love that. That's really nice. (Fyre VC1:13)

An African Nova Scotian participant expresses very positive feelings towards being able to participate with his partner in class.

In the class of the several guests, one of whom was my partner, it was nice to see her in that form. As the feather was passed, I introduced her as my partner and mother of my two year old son. I welcomed her to the class and to a safe environment. I also attempted to point out to the class how grateful I was for her and for the courage that she has displayed over the years of our relationship. (Cal Jan 94-j)

Elders, children and families can play a vital role in transforming the classroom atmosphere, when a link is established between them and the classroom community. Elders can be used as a metaphorical bridge between the two cultural domains. Elders are repositories of cultural and philosophical knowledge and are the transmitters of such information. Using Elders in the classroom can help to combat the idea that degrees are the only avenue to knowledge. "Now, the elders speak . . . . Let us honor them by listening to them and learning from their wisdom" (Medicine 1987: 149). Many varied lessons are available from the words of Elders in the classroom. Analee journals the personal impact one Elder had on her:

This brings me to something that [name], an Elder, shared in story circle tonight. She spoke about how so many of us spend so much time wishing we had "this and that," or that we could lose weight, or gain weight, or be more serious, or funnier, or taller, or shorter, or smarter . . . wish, wish, wish . . . . I think most of us think by having these things we will be better people, or happier people, or maybe even better liked by others. [The Elder] said that even if these wishes were granted, who says that they would make us happier, or make us better people? She stressed the importance of being happy with who you are now and trying to be the best person you can possibly be . . . an important lesson for me. (Oct 13 93-j)

Tia journals the impact of the Elders' presence at the field trip we took to an Aboriginal community-based project.

[W]hat really made me aware was the fact that the diversion process values the voice of its elders and recognizes the importance of their presence in the community. Today we live in a world that does not respect its elders and listen to what they have to say. Instead we wait until our elders reach a certain age and put them in manors to basically die. However, from what I have learned this year the Micmac and other Aboriginal peoples respect their elders and they clearly hold a valuable place in the community. From what I have learned all people are valued and seen as unique parts of the community. In a way I feel envious of this bond and inner peace that does not exist in white culture. (93-j)

The need to show respect for Elders is a cross-cultural value and is expressed by an Elder of another cultural Community:

> We have always to learn to respect Elders, because we cannot overlook the fact that the Elders mostly they have learned from the experience of life. The book of life has taught them so many things which it never teaches a young person because we haven't gone through all those things. (Erma VC3:6)

Elders and other community guests must be treated respectfully. Beatrice Medicine, a Cree educator, challenges us to interrogate our "use" of Elders in the classroom. She asks: "Are they exploited as informants? Are they used without consultation? Are their duties explained previous to their entrance into an educational institution? Is their cultural mandate understood?" (Medicine 1987: 50). She cautions us that "asking an elder to bestow a name upon non-natives or to offer prayers delves into delicate cultural norms" (Medicine 1987: 150).

It is essential to learn local norms for asking Elders or other community guests to participate. I caution students, if they are unfamiliar with the norms, to find out first. Gaining entry into the "knowledge banks" of community members requires respect, patience, honouring and reciprocity. Certain steps can be taken to honour the Elders and other invited guests: invite other community members to help establish comfort in a dominantly White group; encourage guests to bring family members or friends from their personal network; adopt the Traditional practice of obligation towards feasting and gifting the Elders and guests for their contributions. One group of students invited several Elders from the African Nova Scotian community to the class. Nadine documents this process. It is a good example of respectful community-building through task work:

> [The students] then contacted one or two of the Elders and requested their time and assistance in participating in our presentation. A total of six were contacted, all female. Contact was made by telephone initially, then followed up by a personal visit . . . .
> Two of the four women indicated they were "shy" and were not certain if they could contribute anything to the discussion. We assured the women that their experiences were important and not to be intimidated as the students were small in number and interested in learning from their experiences. We informed the women that the

presentation would be informal, refreshments would be served and we would try to make them as comfortable as possible . . . . On the day of the presentation we provided transportation for them, babysitting services were not required. (Nadine Mar 29 93-t3)

Shifting the way we relate in the classroom is, at another level, an effort to model an egalitarian form of relationship, which can be translated and applied more generally to building relations with members of the Communities. Once we make the effort to build community in and In-Relation to the classroom, we then have access to "First Voice" stories. These stories help educate at a deep level about the need to challenge and change the hierarchical model currently In-Use when working with Community members. Given the disenfranchisement produced from years of Eurocentric practices, how can we as educators rebuild relations with the Communities? Free notes the importance of creating opportunities for community members to speak heartfully, to share with others:

Any relationship begins when we begin to speak about ourselves and about things that are close to our own heart. And that's how we learn, when we ask other people about the things that are close to their heart and how we begin to form a bond because we all know that people are very social beings and we need to interact with other people in order to survive . . . . We have to build these community relations with the people around us. And we do this by respecting them, and caring about them, and sharing, and being honest. (CC2:32)

She extends her analysis to reflect on the overall relationship between the School and the Communities:

If that is possible . . . if we could build that relationship between the communities around us and the School, the School will then get better rapport not only with the community, but a better understanding of what goes on here! . . . If we're going to be strong, this community, then we have to be able to reach out to the people in our community; to expand that community and to draw in other people. (Free CC2:32)

Free identifies the building of relations between the School and the Communities as a vitally important aspect of this Model-In-Use. The Communities themselves must have a say in the education process.

And that's why I think this whole Model and bringing things to the School is so important! If we can encourage the community to bring these issues to the School, or any issues that they feel that are pressing and are very important in the community . . . . And then the students will then in turn be able to then apply themselves to what they need to know about the communities they work with! (Free CC2:32)

I agree with Free, "We have to make it our business to know about the people that we work with" (Free CC2:32).

A Traditional understanding of the elements of a community-building relationship emphasizes the fundamental value of respect. Respect for the basic immanence of all of creation provides a solid foundation. Free's "speak-out" illustrates that respect is multidimensional:

> I think that respect is what is missing in society in general. People tend to be moving so fast in their minds, in their busy day to day lives, that they just tend to forget to pay that little bit of respect . . . . Not just to other people, but they never notice the flowers growing in their garden, they put them there but they never really notice they're growing there, and a lot of people don't even know what they smell like! It's basically they just don't have the respect for the world around them! (CC1:24)

She communicates another Traditional message regarding respect: you have to give it to get it:

> I am open to the teaching of respect, and we can only teach respect by giving it. If we want to get it then we have to give it. We have to respect other people. We have to respect all of creation and make that very visible in our daily lives! (Free CC1:24)

Many people do not listen respectfully to others. A participant from the non-Native community reiterates this insight:

> What we don't think about enough is listening and remembering or thinking of ways that we can be sure that we respect other people and think about it hard! Thinking about ways of being humble, because when you look at another culture, then you learn so much about your own. (Bea CC2:27)

Respect is shown when value is placed on sharing experiences, and caring about and learning from each other's experience. In a very caring manner, Sis remarks upon this to members in the Circle:

> I totally trust that this is a good atmosphere to learn in and a good way to hold a class. I've loved it! I can't believe how valuable it's been . . . . Just the strength that I feel to be in the circle, everybody's experiences are so valuable. And it just strikes me that . . . our society values the letters after people's names so much and when I hear someone with your strength (crying) it just makes me sick to think that someone can be twenty-five and have a couple of degrees and be really respected for no reason at all (still crying) and someone with your experience and your wisdom [Redbird], which I really, really appreciate, doesn't receive the respect that you deserve. It's really bad and I hope you know how

valuable you are! (crying openly now). (TC3:35)

Cognizant that respect is not the only value integral to individual and community healing, Free reflects on the four Traditional laws of living in community:

> The four laws of living in community can really work if people just internalized them and take it upon themselves as a responsibility . . . . I have taken upon myself to say to myself, I will treat people with Respect. I will Care about these people! I will be Honest with these people! And I will Share with these people who will be my [relations]. I will do these things. (CC1:23)

Circle as Community-Building Pedagogy

Respect, honesty, caring and sharing are the four fundamental "laws" of living in community according to Traditionalists. Student and community participants reflect on the "feeling of community" that Circle brings. As Char notes:

> It would seem to me that this would give everyone a sense of worthiness and being valued and listened to, and respected. It makes me wonder how different our society would be if we had adopted such traditions; perhaps we would have maintained the sense of community. (Jan 14 93-j)

Another White student expresses her learnings through Circle, reflecting a Traditional message very appropriate to the current classroom context: "The circle reminds me of a community where people join together in a sense of community where they are expected [to] and would be respectful of one another" (Eileen 93-j).

Participants' reviews of the Circle process were often a reflection of the Traditional values: respect, honesty, caring and sharing. Van recognizes honesty as a vital force:

> There's always someone who says something that speaks to you, and that's what's so important about this Circle, this method of teaching, and what I get from it. You have to be honest! The force is honesty. It's very easy to give what the person wants to hear, it's very easy to do that, but a circle for some reason, it really forces honesty! I think that's very important . . . to be reflective, honest, to appreciate what you can learn from people, what you can give back. It has to be real. (TC4:3)

Many highlight respect as integral to the Circle process:

> It gives everybody a chance to be heard rather than a discussion going on where some speak and some don't. And I think it's very powerful the

respect that comes with it. (6 second pause) I think it can be used in so many ways. I think it's a very respectful process. (Bea VC1:23)

A participant from the African community, new to Circle work through the project, has this to contribute:

I think Circle, doing Circle with others gives me the feeling of community as well. And how important community is to me. And that I don't live in isolation. Sometimes I think of Utopia too much too, but hopefully there's a point in our world that we can come to where we can live and breathe and love each other without necessarily putting limitations or conditions on that. (Liz VC1:20)

The Circle process itself helps build community connections. As a tool for personal healing and transformation, it provides reciprocity to community members who come in to share their stories and experiences with us. I reflect on the potential for community-building and healing through Circle:

Sometimes when you're in Circle . . . and you're having that Circle feeling of interconnectiveness, you do feel that other people's lives are as important as your own. You have that connection and even if you never met them before, and even if you never heard their story before, and even if you may never hear their story again, for that time you're there you feel connected to them . . . . I really have a lot of respect for people who can put out for other people. Who can take care of other people. I have a lot of respect for you [Redbird] and your story about your family. And I think that all of us women in the Circle today have had to be strong in our own families and in our own lives . . . . If you are not feeling as strong as you need to feel try to find some people to sit in Circle with you and have your own love circle, have your own sharing circle. I think that we all always need more love, we always need that connection. The circle, whether it's a big circle or a small circle, can bring that connection back for people. Heartfelt sharing can bring that connection to people. Wherever we do it! (Fyre TC3:42)

Some participants recognize Circle work as a form of intervention that can enhance a strength-oriented, community-based approach to healing and teaching. Phil reinforces the value of Circle work for strengthening the individual In-Relation to Community:

One of the biggest assets of the Circle work is that it builds personal strength for people to be able to bring up their lives and stories and to talk about it. And feel that they will be valued. And the strength of knowing that people care about what you value. And the strength in the community . . . . In people being able to be there for other people and build up bonds between everybody in the community. It provides all these strong role models for people, as they see women and men showing the strength that they had in dealing with difficult times and how they've come through, and how they can talk about it and learn from it. The strength that you gain from learning from somebody else being strong in the situation. (TC3:33)

The strong role models provided by some participants inspired others. Stories of pain, survival and success inspire ourselves and others and become lessons from which we can learn. Unless we have a listening ear, our painful experiences can become lodged in our bodies. Through Circle work, they can be released as a story from which we learn.

If you don't have a Circle or a way of talking about it or sharing, you become isolated and then you don't see the positive sides of what you're learning, so your difficult times are never used in a positive way. It's always just kept in yourself. You're just left to eat away at yourself . . . . Through the sharing you can find strength and you can see a purpose for what you've gone through, that it's making a difference in somebody's life if you do share it. (Phil TC3:33)

Phil reaffirms the view that Circle is a valuable tool and proposes applications of Circle work even without a formal Circle:

So I can see that it is such a valuable tool for people to be able to learn how to use Circle to help promote strength in people. Even if you don't have a formal Circle, the concepts, like the sharing of your experience and telling your story and listening to other people telling their story, can be woven in to almost any kind of [community] practice. (TC3:34)

Reciprocity is a critical aspect in developing community and in expanding our Circle of interconnectedness, and it is essential in working with the Communities. Phil reflects on how reciprocity is built into Circle work and this Model:

From my observation, having community people come in and be part of that Circle has provided a really valuable healing for people in the community as well, because it gives them an idea of being able to share things and feel validated to come in and be part of a Community Circle, which they might never have had been given the liberty, been given the chance, otherwise. It also helps . . . introduce people to other ideas about . . . trying to make changes and do things and their frustrations involved in changing systems that are so hard and stuck in their ways. I think that by bringing community in to the Circles and talking about these kinds of topics, the Circle becomes a living entity almost . . . . It produces change just from having gone through a Circle. It might give people new ideas and new stories and new ways of thinking about

> things and finding out about how other people have changed things and
> what you can do . . . . I can see changes in people being able to
> participate in Circles over a period of time and how it's valuable.
> (TC3:15)

Phil notes the impacts of divisions between teaching and healing and
between personal healing and professional growth and development:

> School work is so often separated into learning to heal other people and
> healing yourself. Healing yourself is seen as something you should do
> outside of your school work. It's not really part of it. A lot of classes that
> they bring up emotional support, talk about going elsewhere to get their
> support if it has emotional content in that class. I don't really see that
> you can separate the two. I think that it's part of being In-Relation.
> You're always learning from people that you live with and work with and
> that they learn from you. It's a reciprocal thing. (TC3:14)

It is a reciprocal relationship that this Model-In-Use seeks to inspire.
Whenever "power over" is enacted, it must be interrogated and transformed. I
wish to "nurture a new morality of non-oppressive, caring relationships among
all the participants in an educational situation" (Hart 1991: 126). Through the
pedagogical processes emphasized, the affective and relational dimensions of
transformative education are embraced along with the cognitive. Engaging in
Circle work in the classroom, which includes connections to diverse Community members across lines of age, gender and class, contributes to building
interconnectedness at the larger community level. The authority dimension is
minimized through Circle work.

> And that's why I really, really like this Model so much. I have really
> enjoyed participating in it because Circle takes away that authority! It
> takes away that perceived authority. In Circle Talk you don't have to be
> afraid of the person sitting next to you, or you don't have to be afraid of
> . . . a person who is facilitating the Circle. It's the distribution of power.
> (Free CC1:24)

These community-building efforts respond to the challenges posed by Hart and
Holton to develop pedagogies in which "[d]iversity and interdependence,
multiplicity and interconnectedness are inseparable, unifying all forms of life
beyond the many artificial separations created by our [Western] culture among
people of different races, sexes, ages, etc., and speaking to a profound spiritual
connection among all living things" (1993: 9).

I am joining Hart (1992) and others in the search for "dominance free forms
of interaction." I seek to reveal the current dichotomies between knower and
object of knowing; natural and social; critical judgement and empathic intuition;
reason and emotion; subjective and objective. Through First Voice, Circle Talk

and storytelling these Eurocentric worldviews are challenged. Traditional pedagogical forms harmonize rather than divide experience and knowledge, teacher and student, professional and community member. I concur with Mussell:

> [an educational experience] must prepare the learner, or educator as well, to be an agent of change who can help mobilize and help to build inner resources of other community members willing to join in creating the desired positive lifestyle. The ultimate of this healing/education is the community, not merely the individual worker. (1994: 8)

The relational work of building community inside and outside the classroom assists in forming the alliances necessary for change to occur in broader society. Following the path of the Wheel, we now move to the North and focus more specifically on change strategies enacted within and through the Model-In-Use.

The Northern Door: Enacting Change

The North corresponds to the Element Earth
Our bodies are our Connection . . . our link to our Earth Mother
Our plant and animal Relations . . . All our kin
All our Relations.
Picture Winter
Snow falling in deep silent mounds
A blanket covering sleeping Earth Mother.
A time to sleep . . . to meditate.
See the black sky . . . Midnight
A thousand stars blinking in the stillness
Grandmother Moon in her Roundness . . . Winking . . . Mysteriously
A time when the world is asleep.
From the North comes the Gift of silence

Restful . . . Meditative . . . Contemplative . . . Silence.
Take some time everyday to be silent . . . turn within.

Call to the creatures of Mother Earth
All the four legged ones
Buffalo . . . Persevering in the face of near extinction.
Wolf . . . Surviving to howl at Grandmother Moon.
Bear . . . Symbolizing Courage and Strength.
All animals hold and share their Medicine.
Recognize your animal Totems . . . your Guides.
See how they walk their path.
How do you walk yours?
Feel the pull of gravity . . . your attraction to Mother Earth
Breathe deep and Feel the power of Earth . . . of the Body
Be in touch with your own power
To See . . . Hear . . . Smell . . . Taste . . . Touch.
We live our daily lives in our Bodies
We learn . . . Know . . . Experience
Through our Bodies . . . through all of our Senses
Be aware of the Sights . . . Sounds . . . Smells
Of life . . . of learning.
Remember . . .
Times you have used your Body to learn
Learning through experience . . . Doing.
Methods more rooted in the Body
Art . . . Ceremony . . . Meditation . . . Smudge . . . Circle
Crystals . . . Feathers . . . Drumming . . . Singing . . . Dancing . . . Feasting
Traditional Spiritual teachings enhance our Connection
To our Bodies . . . to our Earth Mother.

According to Absolon, in following the path of the Medicine Wheel "the fourth direction involves creating a healing movement towards change—this is possible only when the other components have been acknowledged" (1994: 18). To move to the "doing" phase, the North, requires that we take the knowledge gained from all the Directions and enact it. Only in following this form of "praxis" is balance achievable. Evolving a Medicine Wheel analysis of healing and learning demands continuous and ongoing reflection of ourselves In-Relation to others. Attention must be paid to maintaining balance while embracing change. The teaching and healing process is evolutionary and cyclical in nature, as is the continuum of the Medicine Wheel. It begins with a desire to understand and identify with the balance, wholeness and interconnectedness expressed in the Medicine Wheel. We begin the process by identifying what a basic pattern of balance looks like. We might see it modeled in our Elders or reflected in the animal or plant worlds. Healing and teaching the Traditional way involve recognizing and respecting teachings that come from our experience, from our connection to Mother Earth (Absolon 1994). Through an experiential process, the seeker of knowledge begins to identify with the pattern of the Wheel. By modelling our lives and teachings on the Medicine Wheel, we will continue to gravitate towards a positive pattern of balance for ourselves and others. I work hard to engage in healing and teaching this way, as a role model to students and others.

This Model-In-Use emulates the wholeness of the Medicine Wheel in following the flow of the Directions. Enacting and teaching a change Model, in this instance, includes many aspects. Consciousness-raising and empowerment through First Voice does provide the insight upon which an activist position can arise. Being in and listening to First Voice can produce personal change for the listeners and the speakers. Enacting Aboriginal cultural practices, within the School context, can produce affective and relational change in the atmosphere and the participants. The healing and community-building influence of Circle produces a forum for change in individuals, In-Relation to their families and the Communities. Change in the philosophy and methods of education has been a consistent focus. Now attention will be paid to learning the process of "en-Acting Change." More specifically, activism will be theorized and analyzed as a teaching tool.

Learning from Experience

This teaching Model is rooted in experience. The reality of learning from experience is embedded in the Aboriginal worldview from which the Model evolves. In class we examine the daily lived experiences of racism and privilege; through listening to First Voice, the voice of experience, we can re-experience the pains of oppression and feel our own part in story; through use of ceremony, storytelling, song, dance and food, we experience the rich gifts of the cultures. We use Circle to experience our Self-In-Relation to members of the Communities and learn to develop this connection in a form that does not rely on hierarchical or purely rational models.

Weil and McGill define "experiential education" as "the process whereby people, individually and in association with others, engage in direct encounter and then *purposefully* reflect upon, validate, transform, give personal meaning to and seek to integrate their different ways of knowing" (1989: 248). This definition underscores the idea of direct encounter as a necessary base for experiential learning. This Model-In-Use allows for integration of different ways of knowing. It allows the learner to use more of his or her senses to learn, which reinforces the understanding that learning comes from many sources—including oneself—not only from the formal theory promoted by experts.

An experiential and embodied approach to teaching and learning can help students re-awaken the knowledge that their bodies are continuously giving them feedback. Griffin reaffirms:

> Our bodies reflect our emotions: anxiety becomes tense shoulder muscles or knots in the stomach; embarrassment turns into a blush on the cheeks. Sometimes, however, we feel the bodily reaction without having noticed the emotion. Sometimes we ignore the emotion, sometimes we deny it or repress it. The body knows it is there, however, and expresses it in some way. (1988: 115)

Having students pay attention to their bodies as a source of feedback about their level of comfort and helping them learn to breathe properly from the belly will help to reduce the stress that can be produced when dealing with controversial topics or listening to a painful retelling of personal narratives. Our bodies are constantly processing our experiences. In Traditional pedagogical forms, paying attention to our physical reality will help us learn and carry wisdom which our "minds" may not be "conscious." This is reflected in many Traditional healing and learning methods, which are meditative, ritual-based and earth-based.

Relaxation exercises, art, massage, ritual, herbology, crystals, drumming and chanting, all of which have roots in Traditional shamanic healing practices (Lorler 1989), can be introduced in the classroom context to help students be more in touch with their physical selves and enhance their "earth connection." Earth connection, a central form of Aboriginal pedagogy, focuses on feeling the energy of the Earth as a sensory experience, as a real, palpable connection that sustains us. We are told by our Elders: "Go out into nature in a quiet way. Listen. What do you feel from the earth, the trees, the sky, the sun, the rocks, all the natural elements around you?" Traditionalists teach that we are all interconnected by a form of environmental/ecological consciousness, which is becoming increasingly necessary to revitalize as our Earth Mother is dying from overuse and abuse. When we consider what the disconnection from nature, what the striving to "control" our Earth Mother, has done, we must rethink our relationship to her.

The Medicine Wheel, and the forms of meditational work that I have evolved through it, can be used to ground people, helping to re-establish their own connection to the Earth and to themselves. Several students note the "therapeutic" benefits of "earthy" meditative work:

> I felt so comfortable and relaxed—it was very inspirational. This exercise is very therapeutic—to step out of line and put myself into the world of Native, harmony, and tranquillity. I felt so relaxed during this experience. I hope to experience this again. If I felt stressed, this would be beneficial. (Dana Sept 15 92-j)

> Tonight's class was amazing. I find the whole concept of the medicine

wheel very earthly, I feel a real connection to what it stands for. The guided meditation was something I really needed at the end of this particular day. It helped me to clear my thoughts and release some of the tension that was built up through the day. (Bejay Jan 6 93-j)

I was then introduced to the Medicine Wheel meditation. This I found to be extremely powerful—powerful in a very relaxed and peaceful sense. By the end of the Meditation, the nervousness I had been feeling quickly faded away. For me, this sense of peacefulness was very therapeutic. (Analee Sept 15 93-j)

We can encounter ourselves and each other more fully if we can quiet the rational mind and learn to move into another state of consciousness. Comfort with silence is a gift of the North. Silence is necessary to build relationship to self, to others, to Earth Mother. To truly hear the messages intended for us we must be silent. Silence can be an act of resistance, a survival strategy. Restful, meditative silence is vital in everyday life. It can help us to focus, to be on target when we do move and act.

Throughout my life I have been taught reverence for quietly absorbing knowledge. This enables me to reflect on and value the lessons gained from experience, my own and others. I address this issue in one of the Visions Circles:

I really feel that most of the strongest and most powerful lessons that I've had in my life have been directly at the hands of other people. In a face to face encounter, or because I've taken on an action that I thought was small in the beginning, then all of a sudden it became huge, and then I learned from all the ripples and all of the things that came from that. I know that from my Elders, experience is the teacher. (Fyre VC3:23)

To the Traditionalist, our own experience with others and within various contexts is the source of many vital lessons. Observation and emulation of the example provided by the teacher/Elder is crucial. I express this insight and how this relates to the School context:

I strongly believe that we can't just say to our children, or to people, we want you to act that way. We have to be that way ourselves. We have to act that way ourselves. And by showing people what it is that we want them to do, or be like, they will learn that.... In [School] people are only used to learning from talking. They're not used to learning from watching and listening, and doing. I really had to adjust my mind-set and my work that way, because in our Aboriginal ancestry most of the learning is by doing. (Fyre VC3:23)

One participant reflects on the lessons learned by students from the "dominant" culture, and on how they have had to acculturate to the different teaching methods introduced throughout the course:

> One of the most important things that will be helpful in anybody's learning is introducing the dominant culture to a different way of learning. Giving them exposure to what it may feel like for us when we're constantly expected to learn things the way they do it. And I've really enjoyed that aspect of it as well. I think it opens a lot of people's minds—it's not easy just to adapt so quickly. (Unicorn VC2:23)

Mac, a White male, parallels his experience in class to his growing understanding of the feelings associated with oppression:

> Class has been opening up some new ideas to me. When the speakers come in they really talk from the heart. It is interesting how squeezed people feel by dominant ideology. I am starting to get a sense of being pressed into a smaller and smaller space, mentally and physically. It almost makes me feel marginal and invisible. I don't compare myself to an oppressed person; that would be presumptuous. However, I think that I am gaining a better sense of what it is like to be from a group that is stigmatized and excluded. (92-j)

This has reinforced for me the notion that experience is shaped by concrete social conditions and that knowledge gained from experience is linked to cultural locatedness.

Taking a Material Approach

Russell advises that to be effective in anti-racist education we must emphasize the concrete: "take a material approach" (1985: 165). A "material" approach has been enacted through various means. Having students continuously examine their daily lives is an ongoing exercise in applying new levels of consciousness about culture and race to their own concrete reality. Retelling experiences with racism as part of journalling and Circle Talk, engaging in Circle Talk and other structured exercises in the classroom and listening actively to oral narration of experiences by victims/resistors of racism all help focus on the privilege and oppression evident in these experiences.

Russell tells anti-racist educators to "use everything, especially the physical space of the classroom to illustrate the effects of environment on consciousness" (1985: 163). Groups or classes may be thought of as having an energy level and a flow of energy. "Some experiences stimulate high energy in us, and some seem to drain us of energy. Are you aware of what kind of learning experiences energize you? What deenergizes you?" (Griffin 1988: 114). Experienced facilitators learn to be sensitive to the energy flow and respond to it. Some tension and stress are necessary, but too much is a hindrance. "A relaxing learning environment can be created with color, softer lights, music and rearrangement of furniture" (Griffin 1988: 114). As noted by Medicine Eagle (1991) and other Traditionalists, eliminating rows of tables and chairs in favour of a circle of chairs changes the learning environment drastically. Moving the group out of doors to experience a physical reconnection to our Earth Mother can also provide stimulating learning.

> One of the things I really loved about teaching in the interior is that I had an outside teaching space. So we used to do Circle on the ground, outside, underneath this big tree. I would really like to be able to teach Circle that way again. There's something missing in Circle when we have to sit inside a box to do it! When we can't be sitting out on the ground with the beautiful sky over our heads and the grass on our bums, the birds singing, and feel the sense of interconnectedness to all of creation as we are there, because that's what brings the power to Circle. (Fyre TC3:42)

Altering the classroom environment, moving from linear rows to Circle, smudging with herbs and using music, drama, poetry, meditation, ritual and feasting are ways to materially challenge the dominant institutional atmosphere. Initial journal entries by students are illustrative of the difference in my classroom environment and what students are "expecting" to encounter in the context:

> . . . seeing how the class was conducted, so informally, and to further relax me was an intro to First Nations customs—burning sweet grass and participating in the greeting circle. What a pleasant experience and such a warm intro to aboriginal culture . . . . I feel excited to be part of this class—I can see my complacency regarding racism is going to [be] "jarred" in this peaceful learning environment. (Lola Sept 14 92-j)

Some students' initial journal entries illustrate the embodied paradox of introducing the Aboriginal "atmosphere" into a School setting:

> 1st class of Cross Cultural!!! Exciting, Challenging . . . . *Terrifying!* I have never felt so intrigued by a class yet so scared . . . . A very big contradiction in emotion—going through the calming meditative exercises and then being terrified by the expectations. I love the task choices that are offered. I love the meditative, first nations atmosphere of the class. I will learn, learn, learn, not only about cross cultural issues but also about myself. (Van Sept 15 93-j)

Excerpts from the journal of an African Canadian participant show how her reactions to the first Cross Cultural Issues class contrast with her experiences generally in the School context:

> By the time I made it to this class, I was seriously considering leaving the program. As this class proceeded, I felt my protective "shell" loosen. A glimmer of hope crept in and eventually took over. I sat in class wondering—how many people will understand or accept what they are about to learn? How many students know that this class is just the beginning of our learning? How many will care? Ah! I will. As I prepare for sleep I savour the relaxing cleansing effect the "Sweet Grass Smudge" has on me. May our People continue to stay strong. (Unicorn Sept 15 93-j)

Learning environments must be viewed through anti-racist lenses. How comfortable with our pedagogies and our programs are culturally located members of our Schools? Have we asked them? Many share their views of the school environment in journals and Circles. Unicorn journals frequently about her Self-In-Relation to her program and the School context:

> After my first class in the program, I felt that I had made the wrong decision. I felt angry and isolated from the others in my class. I stepped into this class feeling that I am here in body but not in spirit. In my first week of the program I have had two encounters that made me feel uncomfortable. (Unicorn Sept 15 93-j)

Adjectives such as angry, isolated, de-spirited and uncomfortable are commonly used by diverse members of the School community. How do we survive and learn to grow in these environments? The Model-In-Use is designed to provide a comfortable classroom climate for those who have this experience. Unicorn testifies to this need in a later entry:

> As I reflect on Wednesday's class, I may be able to survive the school set up despite it not meeting my expectations. I am more aware and sensitive of my history, race, and culture. I am open to learning to be aware and sensitive of others who do not benefit from "white privilege." I want—I expect to be included in all of the curriculum not just cross-cultural issues or anti-racist education courses. (Sept 23 93-j)

Taking a material approach also means putting community and world events squarely into the classroom. This becomes possible primarily by aligning ourselves to the anti-racist struggle outside the classroom, in the Schools and in the Communities. This relationship is facilitated by direct face-to-face encounters in the classroom and in the Communities, with members active in their community's struggles.

What to Do? "You Must Move and Act"

In the North we ask:
What to Do?
Brooke Medicine Eagle teaches:
"You can Talk about something or Think about it
All day, but to make it Real
You must Do it. You must move and Act."
Unless we take Action . . . Ground our plans
In the material world . . . the day-to-day lived experience
Nothing will change.
Our Elders propose: "Doing More Than Saying."

Take the knowledge gained from all the Directions:

Heightened consciousness of issues
Heartfelt commitment
Relationship to individual/community/world
Widely divergent types of Acts.

We each experience
Individually . . . Collectively
Opportunities for Action . . . Daily.
Learn . . . Recognize . . . Be open to them.
"Get in there and Help."
"Do something about it!"
Reaffirm your own Responsibility for Community well-being.

Do you know?
You Can Do It!
Small acts have Big personal meanings.
Each action is valid.

Silence Equals Compliance.
Challenge others on verbalized racism
sexism . . . classism . . . homophobia

Collectivity Counts.
Retell the successes . . . Build alliances.
Emphasize reciprocity.

Hope. Vigilance. Persistence.
Ripples move through the Water once the Stone is Tossed
My Elders say.

All the elements . . . all the energy of the Directions
Are interrelated in the production of Change
We must Move Cyclically:
Thinking . . . Willing . . . Feeling . . . Doing.

How can you use all or part
of this Model-In-Use
To create Change?
See applications to your "life work."
Links to struggles of your Community(s)
Anti-racist . . . Aboriginal
Acadian
Gay and Lesbian . . . Feminist?

What to Do? "You Must Move and Act"

Together we can actively Resist Acculturation
Through Aboriginal pedagogy.

Traditionalists believe that we learn, grow and change through actively using our thoughts, desires and feelings as vital components in the realization of our visions. Brooke Medicine Eagle teaches that "[y]ou can talk about something or think about it all day, but to make it real you must do it. You must move and act" (1991). This is the gift of the North: the need for activism. There is a call to action to challenge racist practices and structures in classrooms, Schools, systems and society. For change to occur we are all challenged to do more than unveil the existence of oppression or privilege. As well as acknowledging one's role in maintaining or resisting oppressive structures, activism requires applying the knowledge to a given target.

As feminists and critical educators before me have espoused, the raised consciousness that follows from transformative pedagogies may not lead to involvement in social change. According to Freire, the possibilities of "conscientizacao or conscientization" (1985: 185) refers to "the process in which men [and women], not as recipients, but as knowing subjects, achieve a deepening awareness of both the socio-cultural reality that shapes their lives and of their capacity to transform that reality" (1972: 51). Through the process of reflection, learning can result in individuals becoming agents of change, freed of the constraints of the social structures and enabled to act back upon those structures in order to change them. Education then becomes "the practice of freedom" (Freire 1973). Kenway and Modra are critical of feminist educators' "over-valorization of consciousness-raising" (1992: 156). As many of us have learned through experience, "one might very well develop a heightened aware-ness of pain and contradiction but may still feel powerless to resolve problems" (Kenway and Modra 1992: 156). They caution us not to stop short of action, the true goal of conscientization. According to Freirian praxis, it is experience, reflection and action, not memorization, that enables the individual to act as a change agent, to resist the hegemonic mindset.

This Model-In-Use radically challenges educators to see that the educa-tional process is not complete unless learners take concrete steps to physically apply towards change that which is learned. In this Model, I am proposing a form of community-building education, which engages persons in actively trans-forming the quality of their lives, families, Communities and societies. Rather than being an individualistic mental exercise, it is a dynamic process in which education, experience and social change are interwoven. Gela expresses con-cern about the lack of focus on change strategies in her educational experiences so far: "If we don't learn the basics of change at the school (an environment in which students do share similar goals), then how can we become effective initiators of change in the real world" (Feb 2 93-j).

To teach a change Model, it is necessary to understand the basics of community organizing. Awareness of the potential for activist opportunities within all locations is crucial. Piven and Cloward develop this theme: "It is the daily experience of people that shapes their grievances, establishes the measure of their demands and points out the targets for their anger" (1977: 21). They note that "institutional roles determine the strategic opportunities for defiance, for it is typically by rebelling against the rules and authorities associated with their every day activities that people protest" (Piven and Cloward 1977: 21). As people can defy openly those institutions to which they make contributions or have access, choice of targets is limited to those In-Relation to the activist. This leads us as activists within the School System to recognize our classrooms as potential sites of resistance. "Practising freedom" (Freire 1985) within the School—an institutional bureaucracy—poses particular constraints. I will return to this theme in "Learning from the Trickster."

Developing the classroom as a site of activism is a process of building new forms of relating. Students are asked to focus consciously on how to take action to challenge domination in our institutions and our society. Participants are encouraged to see all the opportunities for activism in their daily lives. Following the Traditional conceptions of Self-In-Relation, students can target themselves; their family and friends; their workplace; and their School. They may also engage with one of the Communities, or in coalition work.

"Personal" Activism

It is necessary to reframe "action" to embrace all forms and contexts of activism as vital to the transformative learning process. Engagement in action is a process of growth in itself. Targeting oneself and one's subjectivity for change is a possibility that students can explore in their examination of the range of possible actions available. Analee learned to reframe action to include her own self-talk:

> For me, I didn't really see that the changes I was making in my own personal life could be thought of as an action. I saw "action" as being more like taking part in an activity or putting on an activity or function.
>
> In giving this a lot of thought I came to the conclusion that action can come in a number of different forms—making changes and taking action in my own personal life being one of these. Since I have started taking this class, this has been an important priority for me. I have been examining my own thoughts, ideas and response to different conversations and situations. As I do this I try to identify for myself what I think may be racist behaviour—whether it be a thought, something I voiced, or an action. Once I identify this, I work on taking action to make changes in these things . . . . Whether or not you choose to communicate what you are thinking, does not make it any less racist! (Nov 24 93-j)

It is possible to target oneself. Students can reframe changes in their consciousness about race and culture as a form of "action." I strongly encourage students to find some way to externalize their insights at a level which they feel able to manage. I teach that change can be understood as a personal, transformational experience. But it must also be linked to structural change. I speak out about this in the Talking Circle on change:

> I really think that change is required in the structures. There's no way to get around that. And just making people see that change is required isn't enough for change to be there! People have to be doing something with that knowledge, and with that insight! Sometimes we can get bogged down in our own internal critique and our own rooting out of what it is that's holding our own selves in position. And if that's where our energy gets locked or stopped, I think that sometimes we do need to be patient with that and let ourselves go deeply into that and work on that as much as we need to. But at some point that has to become externalized again, and there's got to be that continuous external/ internal thing going on. (Fyre TC4:26)

Many of us learn to be active through acting out of necessity. We do not learn the lessons of oppression and privilege by reading or talking alone; much is embodied. While an understanding of theoretical constructs is necessary for gaining the consciousness of what to do and why, doing is vital to our survival and to change actually occurring in the conditions of our daily lives. As Unicorn tells it, transformation of daily life within this racist society is already consuming for some members:

> Please note as a Black woman living in a racist society, I find it necessary (personally, professionally and socially) to take actions every day. Some are short-term, some evolve into long-term. I have learned ways of actions from the history of my people and others facing a similar struggle. This knowledge was obtained through first voice story, storytelling, reading, television, community meetings, workshops and this course. Learning to adapt action(s) to reflect . . . the current situation or issue is the key to progress (no matter how small or large). It is important to do *with* others not *unto* them when doing cross-cultural work. (Dec 93-t4)

While critical theorists have been elaborate in their development of the terminology of oppression, less attention has been paid to the daily lived experience of resistance, our "activist" struggle to survive. Efforts to enact structural change can be addressed specifically as a personal journey. Benny, a member of the African Nova Scotian Community, reflects on the process of coming to anti-racist activism In-Relation to her own life experiences of racism. She expresses a commonsense reality for many activists. What seems a "small piece" to some may be perceived as highly challenging to another:

It initially starts off as a small piece. I'm going to go do this, but sometimes even just facilitating the workshop, talking about your experience, you're challenged in ways where people think you have two heads most of the time! You leave there sometimes thinking, maybe I am making too much of this, or when that consciousness comes on it's like you're critiquing everything—You see a commercial and you say, how come there's no Black kids in that commercial? How come there's no Black kids or Black people, period, on that poster? How come there's no Black people working in that store? Even within my day to day, whether it's I'm getting on the bus, or whether it's I'm watching TV, or whether it's I'm at work, it's a constant struggle, and I always have to find that I put myself in a position to try to create some change. (Benny TC4:9)

For Benny, the desire to communicate insights and experience, to create change, was one that grew with age and exposure to critical views:

When I was a few years younger I didn't make waves, but now it's probably to the other extreme. People know me as a person who's got to speak out. That's really important for me to feel that way! I believe that when I do it I don't do it in a confrontational way. I do it in a way that hopefully people will learn from my experiences . . . . That's the change that I hope to make, and the change that I'm making within myself, and hopefully it will work throughout the Black communities. (TC4:9)

Shifting the Blame: The Personal is Structural

Participants often speak about how the course helps them change their analysis. A shift from strategies of personal adjustment to identifying and attempting to alter structural forces is noted. This represents a form of empowerment that is personal, yet politically inspired and collectively achieved. Phil notes that becoming conscious of the extent of racism contributes to being able to externalize rather than internalize it:

It's really made me aware of how to go about making changes, and to have the confidence in what I've been doing, and that it's worth fighting for, and that there are other people who feel the same way. It's also made me realize that all the racist kinds of things that have happened to me; they've not just happened to me, they've happened to everyone, but I've realized that on a deeper level than I did before . . . . I realize that the extent of it is built right into the whole social system. I find myself looking at everything, and noticing things that I wouldn't even have recognized as being racism. And being surprised when other people didn't realize that what's happened was racist, and even people that it's happening against, often think that it's just something that's happening to them. So I've been starting to be able to when I see things like that, even letting the person understand that what's happening is racist. It makes a big difference to have the person perceive what is happening instead of internalizing it. If you understand that it's coming from someone else and it's not you personally, it makes a big difference for being able to deal with it. (TC4:23)

Sharing "personal" stories of oppression and change helps to promote the consciousness necessary for activism to occur. Collectivizing our understanding of oppressive experiences helps depersonalize racist trauma and refocus our energy on an external target. Being an activist does take a certain amount of personal clarity—the feeling of being able to "en-act" requires a conviction that systemic and/or personal change is possible. Redbird reflects on the everyday "overcrowdedness" that makes us bitter but helpless to do anything about it:

I have so much on my mind, I think it's overcrowded! I can't seem to think of anything else except maybe injustice and that type of thing. It makes me so bitter. I feel really helpless to do anything about it. Because I can't do anything about my own life, but I'd be more than willing to help change the system if I knew how. But I don't know how, and until that day comes, and if I'm still alive, I will be more than willing to help change. (TC3:12)

Having the "know how" is essential to breaking down internalized and externalized barriers to change. Shifting the focus from personal adjustment solutions to social change is seen as a challenge by some. Members of the Communities are continuously forced to assimilate, to adjust to the "commonsense" norms of White middle-class life. Activism, in this case, is "personal"—challenging the internalization of "self as problem." Cindy gives a clear depiction of empowerment—the gaining back of personal strengths which are available when the sources of alienation are located in systemic rather than individual deficits:

The whole society can come together, and they function real well; how come I feel I'm isolated and marginalized, and cannot fit in the society? And I still damage myself. And people around me say, because I'm not tolerant, or I still have to do something good to fit in the society. But when I come here, then I realize, it's the system! ... When I share with the classmates, and listen to the feedback, I start to get my power, I start to realize it's the system . . . . So, suddenly, when I'm in this system, I find that I gain back my strengths. And I feel good about that. I hope, if personally, I can face all these critiques, all this attack, maybe I myself can be a person to demonstrate to other females how we can come together and change the environment. (TC4:5–6)

Resisting Assimilation Through Embracing Cultural Identity
One form of "personal" empowerment, according to McLaren, is "gained from knowledge and social relations that dignify one's own history, language and

cultural traditions" (1989: 186). This Model-In-Use uncovers systemic oppression while validating the importance of cultural gifts, including teaching reverence for the rich heritage of resistance. This combination encourages participants to actively resist assimilation. Dealing daily with a racist environment means engaging in a continuous ongoing struggle to maintain/embrace a cultural identity in the face of institutional assimilatory forces. I "role model" resistance to assimilation in the classroom through the use of Aboriginal process. I know and teach that it is an essential survival strategy to embrace your cultural identity. Participants from the Communities often reflect on the importance of preserving cultural roots. One African participant expresses embracing cultural identity as a daily lived expression of resistance to White cultural domination:

> Because our society is ruled by the dominant culture, white—privilege and power, they judge us based on a mirror image of themselves. The message that this sends is—the white way is the right way and the only way. Based on my readings (for class and others), guest participation in class, and my experience—the white way, right way and only way does not ring true to oppressed peoples. (Unicorn Dec 2 93-j)

Acadian participants often stress the necessity of their community's resistance to assimilatory forces. One Acadian Elder has this to contribute:

> I could go on forever to tell you how the Acadians have changed or how they've evolved and how precious we are now, but, because the time is short, I'm just going to say that we have gone a long, long way and I would say the last 15 or 20 years, even about . . . from 25 to 50 years: there were job applications, people would put up jobs and say "Acadians need not apply!" And we walked down the streets here in Halifax and people would, if we spoke French, people would gawk at us and call us names. Well that gradually, that has disappeared. And just the fact that I've been asked to sit here as an Acadian, I think shows one of the ways where we have finally, somebody is recognizing that the Acadians exist and we have our French schools. (Celi CC2:35)

Cindy links the Model to my cultural identity. She discusses what she has previously learned through her efforts to assimilate to White norms:

> This is the only course that I'm not taught by a white teacher . . . [and] that validates all different ethnic groups and different cultures. I find it's very important because no matter how we learn from the white community, unless I say I will completely cut off my culture, my community, and completely tune in the White community, those things that I learned from the White community may help me survive in a White community, but then if I do that, I face the problem of when did the White community accept me to integrate to the society?—Because in the past

> I tried to learn the white's strategy, but I feel that all the time I cannot fit in to the White's society. I know no matter how much I try to be completely assimilated to the White's culture, there's drawbacks. (Cindy TC4:27)

She concludes by discussing the construction of a bicultural identity as an alternative to accepting assimilation. According to Cindy, there are "two levels of understanding." One is for the cultural group—"you can never cut off the relation with the Community and the Culture;" the second is for the dominant group: "given the choice, the white people will pass some comment. Maybe they are intangible, but they try to push you to assimilate to the white culture" (Cindy TC4:27). Her solution is to do her best to validate her culture and to learn creative approaches to avoiding the assimilation tactics of Whites.

The validation of cultural identity, necessary for our survival, also simultaneously provides a challenge to the System.

> Once we get over the fear of being ourselves, our own identity, what makes it a contested terrain here is when we decide I'm going to stay who I am, I'll learn when I have to of your stuff, but I want to be who I am when I get out of here still! So I think that was part of my struggle; yes, I'll learn your stuff, but yes I want to stay who I am too. (Free TC2:5)

Hattie clearly draws the links between her experience, her cultural identity, her resistance to assimilatory forces and the impact of the teaching Model-In-Use:

> I look at this School and I look at the [teachers]; I had these [teachers] telling me that I should start thinking different thoughts and writing differently. I should not spend my time talking about racism, its pain, I should begin to think about different things. My response is that I'm not white, so I can't think white. I don't have a different cultural background and I can't think that. I am because of my culture and because of my experiences. I might be able to change my life in certain ways, but I'll never be able to change my culture. And your experiences are what they are. I found I just wanted to be here because it would have been the only time in my [school] life, except as a [teacher], where I would have any control. I would be able to feel like I was a person. I felt I didn't even have to explain myself to anybody, for one time in my life. That it was ok to be me. And I think that experience in itself is the thing that really kept me joyful. (TC2:21)

She voices her experience of embracing a positive/resistant cultural identity as an ongoing challenge in multiple but converging assimilatory contexts:

> The thing that I find with society, what they want you to do is assimilate. Assimilate, assimilate, assimilate. And if you don't assimilate, it's nothing. It's pain, it's pain, it's pain! I've always been this type of person.

I have to be who I am regardless of what the cost is. I will always be that in Circle. I was allowed that in this class. And I guess that's why I really appreciate this class. And that's why I really didn't care for once in my life. I felt like, oh, this is how white people are because they don't have to apologize for who they are, they can just be themselves. I was allowed that in this class. And I appreciated it! (Hattie TC2:22)

The pain produced from contact with the constant assimilatory forces present in the context is poetically spoken by this participant. Simultaneously, Hattie testifies to the validation she feels when participating as a student and Community member in the Model-In-Use. Her speak-out reinforces the practical/applied link between validation, cultural identity and political change. Guiding/learning on the journey, in our struggle against assimilatory forces, I deeply appreciate these testimonies of cultural resistance inspired and nurtured by my teachings.

Activism as In-Relation

For some, our daily lived experiences motivate us to work to create change in our own lives and the lives of our family and community. Brandt links Black activism to first- or second-hand experiences of continuing acts of overt and covert racism in their daily lives and the lives of their children: "street violence, racist laws and educational oppression" (1986: 123). While the "fight against racism has been led by those who suffer most its effects" (Thomas 1984: 23), this Model seeks to "engage the energies of both those who experience racism and those who are members of the dominant culture in the challenge to racism" (Thomas 1984: 23).

Aboriginal, anti-racist and feminist organizers and educators would agree with Howse and Stalwick: "[O]ne cannot learn second hand in an authentic way about change and social movement. Merely associating with those who struggle is not enough. One must 'get in there and help' to realize and learn participatory alignment" (1990: 106). In this Model-In-Use all students are expected to engage in, process and share their learnings from actions taken during the period of the course. Guiding students to undertake "en-act-ed" forms of expressing their learnings has been a constant effort in the production of this Model. Students are challenged to show their learning through doing, while engaging in theory-building. This is an often sought after balance for educators. The activity-focused task work lends itself to this process, as does the explicit demand for activism:

Task IV: Do something about it! Take an action. For example, anti-racist community work (join a local organization and work with them on a project); an analysis of racism in an organization or a piece of policy; a class project on racism or cultural diversity could be organized . . . . (Appendix: 310)

Following the Model, students are encouraged, as am I, to be continuously engaged in learning how to "get in there and help." Activism can include a challenge to any of the various forms of oppression and hegemony that create and sustain the current status quo. European domination of our geographic and cultural spaces is visible at nearly every site we experience daily. The educative processes, course content and research strategies In-Use are intended to help participants recognize oppression and injustice and act on it. Action is seen as an integral and dynamic aspect of the process, as both educational and transformational. As Khosla poetically expresses:

> From the navel to the fist—from individual reflection to political action—depending on what route you chose, can be a long, personal, abstract, meandering journey that safely explores every corner of our victimization, but never quite makes itself into a cohesive social resistance. Or it can in fact be a risky, collective snap into consciousness that is rather startling, and quite liberating. (1991: 98)

Students become engaged in hands-on action In-Relation to self, family, workplace, School and the Communities. This provides them with opportunities for risk-taking activity. While multiple possibilities and sites are encouraged as targets for intervention, the readiness of the student strongly influences the level of activism in which he or she is engaged. Consciousness and access to community or collectivity impacts on choice of target. Some students require specific guidance, but more race-conscious and activist students will readily select forms of action that are challenging for them and those around them. I have come to frame action, in this Model, as interactive and requiring: a) a heightened consciousness of the issues (East); b) a heartfelt commitment (South); c) a form of relation/access to the individual/community/systems (West); and d) widely divergent types of *acts* (North).

I teach that it is possible to enact change in any possible context. We each experience daily individual and collective opportunities for action. We must learn to recognize and be open to them. Collective action requires reciprocity and must be community directed. Through taking action you learn, and you give back to your "teachers" the gift of your time and energy. In this Model, students are asked to take an active approach to a cross-cultural situation within their immediate environment or within a negotiated Community context. They are to plan the "intervention," enact it, reflect on it and share in Circle with their peers. Vada expresses her learned definition of "activism": "The class has made me feel that I need to be more active in promoting cultural diversity and awareness, and to fight racism in any way it is expressed" (Apr 4 93-jsum).

Student action has taken many forms to achieve this expectation. These include: challenging racial slurs with friends, family, co-workers and teachers; writing letters of protest to papers, magazines, companies, agencies and the

School; organizing and/or facilitating race relations training (including sessions on White privilege) for peers, agencies and children; lobbying for change in policy, service provision and staffing of agencies; revising core curriculum in Schools; joining existing community groups working for change; working for change at Schools through committee work, workshops, video production and Open Circles. Students express learnings through activist efforts in journalling and in Circles.

Talking Circle on Action

Targets vary, as does the magnitude of the actions. All students have opportunity to raise possible actions for which they want peer support or to consult with me regarding their plans for action or lack of the same. While some students report on the progress of their activism in journals or in Circle throughout the term, all are encouraged to report on actions taken at the Talking Circle on Action which is held each term. Students often express appreciation for this Circle. They comment on what they learn and unlearn about their own and others' roles in anti-racist activism. The following excerpts capture some of this: "I liked tonight's cross-cultural class. It was mostly a talking circle on Actions people have taken. There seems to be a lot of diversity and some of the group actions have been very complex" (Char Mar 31 93-j). One Aboriginal participant journals a common reaction of members of cultural Communities to this particular form of Circle:

> The talking circle on taking action was great, it allowed me to verbalize my experience . . . . It was my first political move, it was quite a big step for me to be vocal and be heard . . . . It was great to hear of some of the actions that others have taken, it's nice to see that white society does take some sense of responsibility for some of the oppression that exists! (Randi Mar 31 93-j)

Talking Circle on Action gives students an opportunity to share their experiences, to speak publicly as an activist, to hear peers address their efforts at social change and to reaffirm their own responsibility.

> Talk in class was good today. I feel that it is important to hear from each other how we handle racism, how we fight it, and from first voice, how it is lived with. I have gained so much knowledge through first voice experience. It always used to be that I would ignore my racism, seeing it as someone else's problem. I see and hear from those it affects, I have learned that I am responsible in challenging myself and the larger institutional forms of power and oppression. (Bejay Mar 22 93-j)

This entry illustrates a shift in level of commitment to activism and reflects an internalization of Aboriginal sentiments regarding Self-In-Relation. Bejay expresses having learned the sense of personal responsibility to act on one's knowledge. Participating in Talking Circle on Action can be experienced as validating, empowering, informative and hopeful. For others it is overwhelming. Paradoxically, and true to Circle form, some students receive an inside-out lesson about what they have not done. One student's entry tells this tale:

> Listening to [a student's] description of their involvement with a native organization in taking an action—I was blown away—totally impressed with what they have done but horrified at what I *hadn't* done. At this point I'm quite overwhelmed by my deadlines and can't or haven't even given any thought to this task. I think I thought by some miracle an idea was going to fall from the sky, since a few weeks ago I put it on hold. This may say something for my own hesitance to get "involved," and also for my procrastination . . . . (Lola Nov 30 92-j)

"I Can Do It!"

Some students are most inspired by the fact that they do find an avenue by which to undertake an action over the term of the course. Often this is something they have never previously done or even thought they could or would do. I recognize that the levels of entry into activism are different for different students. Some students need indepth consultation even to become conscious of what access is available to them. I reflect on this in Circles on CCI.

> For some people it's really hard to get to that first action! They never, ever, took one in their life. They never confronted a joke. They never said anything back to people. I see that struggle in my course all the time, for people who did never do anything before at all, and now it's their struggle to try to figure out anything at all to do! (Fyre TC4:2)

The empowerment experienced through taking action is expressed in a heartfelt manner in some journals. As Randi comments in one entry: "And of course I took an action, even though it may seem minute to some, it was gigantic for me, and I really felt so empowered doing it!" (Apr-jsum). The small action with big meaning is a common theme.

> For me, I see now how important this is if we want to work towards any kind of positive change. These changes that I have been making may seem small to some, but for me it is a big step—it is personal action that I will be able to continue to build on. (Analee Nov 24 93-j)

Each action taken needs to be validated as an important source of learning and personal empowerment, although some targets are larger.

> I feel very good that I was able to get to a place where I could initiate an action that would have such a far-reaching impact on so many people, and more especially that I had to overcome great feelings of personal risk to do it. It was empowering to me, and I hope will be the beginning of further political action. (Char Mar 29 93-t4)

Silence Equals Compliance

Often students practice/enact their activist role through language, which is a comfortable medium for most middle-class Whites. They learn to challenge others around them on their verbalized racism. I encourage them to "storytell" about these actions and what they learn from them. Bejay reports, in her first entry, a clarified understanding of the activist role regarding slurs—silence equals compliance, not disapproval:

> I have been learning over the past two years how harmful racism is to those whom it oppresses. I always thought that if someone was making racist remarks or telling racist jokes, and I remained silent, I was letting

it be known that I did not approve. I know now that silence equals compliance, and that it is important to speak out and educate people as to how harmful these things are. (Jan 13 93-j)

Speaking out about racism can be taken as one sign of the development of a heightened awareness about racism.

I realized in this incident how much more aware of racism I have become. A few years ago I would have ignored it and not said anything, even if I disagreed. I now cannot keep quiet and I am glad. I have developed a heightened awareness about racism!!! Thank goodness!!!! (Dana Sept 21 92-j)

In practicing their speaking out to challenge racism, many students express their Self-In-Relation by engaging in an educational process with their own family members. This reinforces the aspect of the action theory In-Use that specifies that access or relation often defines/confines our activism. Tia tells the story of challenging her mother to examine her racial consciousness:

After this first class and critically analyzing my flashback, I phoned my mom to share my feelings and thoughts. When I explained what I had remembered she apologized to me and agreed that she was still unaware of her own racism. I explained that permitting herself to be unaware is not acceptable and that apologizing may make her feel better, but it doesn't change attitudes, values and beliefs. Actually, this discussion was a bit more heated than how I have described it on paper. (93-j)

This student was not alone in her desire to share insights from the course with other family members. Others tell tales of family interventions:

My husband paints statues for various churches, he paints them skin tone, which is white. I mentioned to him that Jesus was Jewish and therefore should at least be represented with olive skin. We debated over this and the next night I came home to find my husband painting a darker skinned Jesus. (Van Oct 93-j)

Another level of handling racial situations is gained when peers and co-workers are targeted for race awareness. Analee expresses her transition to activism in this way:

For me, an important part of the learning is actually putting what you learn to practice. This week I had an opportunity to do this. I was involved in a situation where I was able to identify and address what I saw as a racist comment. I was meeting with someone and we were discussing his financial situation when he made [a slur]. I decided to address this comment right away. I discussed how negative, offensive, hurtful and *racist* this comment is and tried to point out some other ways that he could express what he was trying to say.

I was feeling a little apprehensive at first because I did not want to offend this person, but, in the end it worked out quite well. He looked at it as being "just an expression" but I helped him to see that it was *much* more than that. For me, this ended up being a very positive learning experience in that I was able to confront this individual in a non-threatening way and help him to see that we must really think about what we are saying because what we may think are "just expressions" may be very racist . . . and very hurtful towards others.

This may be a very small gesture to some but to me it was a very big step . . . . [I]t gave me the opportunity to put into practice what I have been learning. I think it is very important to address these small comments because it will help us to get a little further ahead in our struggles against racism. (Oct 15 93-j)

Reframing action to include verbally challenging racism in our day-to-day lives allows many a "glimpse" of activism. As previously noted, the "small gesture" of resistance can be a very big step in heightening consciousness and commitment to act. A later entry by Analee expresses continuing growth in this area:

. . . I don't feel as scared about addressing certain issues with people. In fact, a big step for me was addressing an issue with a co-worker. I was absolutely terrified because this person was almost twice my age! I thought they would think I was just trying to be smart . . . or that I would offend them in some way. It turned out to be a positive experience in the end . . . . I actually think this person may have learned something from me . . . not that he would ever admit it, of course! (Nov 24 93-j)

One student from the Aboriginal community provides an excellent example of applying her learnings about activism in every area of her life, including at the School. Her journal illustrates the many forms "speaking up" can take. One day she directly challenged a teacher by responding truthfully to the question, "Do we make you comfortable here?":

I felt very proud of myself for having been able to speak up about this. At one time I would have felt silenced by it. I think that I am starting to feel confident about confronting people when I am hurt by their racist remarks. (Phil Mar 16 93-j)

Further motivated to continue her activist learning, Phil took an assignment in another course and turned it into a lesson about racism in the classroom. She enacted, with a White male colleague (Mac) playing the role of Native student, the multiple forms racism in the classroom can take and has taken. The video includes the psychological impacts on the student and a culturally appropriate style of intervention in dealing with the trauma.

> I felt very good about having done this video. It was a good way to make [the teacher] think about racism, without making her lose face. It was also good for the people in my group to watch because it brought out a lot of issues that they had been unaware of. I felt empowered by taking an action against something that I had felt so strongly about. (Phil Mar 23 93-j)

In her journal summary, Phil reflects on the progress she made. She notes her shift from being conscious enough to make "self-protective remarks" and address racism with children to now being empowered to raise issues with people who have "power over" her. Her journey includes several interventions within each context of her life, including the School context:

> I think that the most important thing that I have learned this year and largely as a result of this class, is to be able to speak out against racism. I feel empowered in a way that I have never felt before. I feel that I have a voice, and that people will listen to what I have to say, and take me seriously. I can see the progress that I have made in this way through my journal. In the beginning I made only self-protective remarks, like I did with the counsellor. I had always spoken out about racism in children before, but never to anybody who had any power over me . . . . Since then I have been empowered enough to confront students and [teachers] on their racism. I would have been terrified to do this last year. I know that I will continue to develop and gain strength in this area. (Phil Apr 93-jsum)

I teach that speaking out against racist slurs whenever we encounter them is a step on the path of becoming an anti-racist activist. Acknowledgment of the transition from an "anti-racist wanna be" is expressed by Lena:

> At the beginning of my journal I wrote about an incident where another white woman said something racist and I did not respond. Later, towards the end of my journal I wrote about two incidents where I called people on their racist behaviour. I feel I have grown from practising non-racism to anti-racism . . . . I feel I went from being an "anti-racist wanna be" to actually taking action against racism . . . . (92-jsum)

Collectivity Counts

It is both a comfort and a source of distress to me, often the sole Aboriginal teacher on staff, that it is not by my actions alone that systemic transformation will occur. I take courage from the writings of Razack, who says:

It is within my control to name the dilemmas of speaking and working across differences at this historical period, even to the point of whining, and to work at the same time to ensure that the ratios that I live with ultimately change. It is not possible for me to speak with integrity till then. (1991: 46)

Speaking with "integrity" as a culturally located teacher is difficult. We need to critically interrogate employment equity for its potential as a "mask of reform." Our positions within the institution can be theorized as the "indigenization of social control." Historically and recently, Indigenous peoples have been recruited to "enforce the laws of colonial power" (Howse and Stalwick 1990: 105). Mama acknowledges the same theme in Black organizing: "[I]t is clear that putting a few Black faces at service delivery points does not address the inegalitarian character of service provision . . . . Rather, it is a question of collective power as well as politics" (1989: 38).

Challenging the hegemonic code, Leonard observes, "effectively requires collectivity and not simply individual refusal, however heroic that may seem" (1990: 23). As Thomas states, "Racism is not an individual problem—it is lodged squarely in the policies, structures, practices and beliefs of everyday life" (1984: 24). Collective action is crucial to the development of an environment in which racism can be discussed and resisted. An important part of anti-racism is about "making explicit, the implicit" (Brandt 1986: 127). Once the issues are defined in explicit terms, targets can be set and resistance enacted. Working with others in the System who have common aims, building networks and gaining allies and advocates is essential. As the magnitude of the issues are revealed, including the commonalities and differences across the Communities, coalition-building must be reflected upon as a necessary strategy. Journal excerpts from members of the Aboriginal and African Canadian Communities illustrate this. One Native student journals: "I learned a lot about the struggles of other oppressed groups and can join in their struggles to help themselves, for it is the power in Numbers, collectivism that helps!" (Randi Apr 93-jsum). Nadine shares a similar realization: "I can't help but wonder what would happen to our society if all of the racially visible peoples and those discriminated against, banned together to promote changes that would benefit them, rather than having to fight the larger powers solely?" (Mar 3 93-j).

Change, when envisioned as a structural issue, requires community participation. Stories that illustrate effective change strategies enacted by our Communities must be encouraged, told and retold. We need to remember and retell our successes as well as our pains. Positive role models are essential. Field trips to sites where change efforts are being enacted are rich in learning potential. Phil told how the women of one Aboriginal community banded together to stop men from abusing women in their community by collectively, with their children, moving into the home until the abuser moved out. She concludes:

> How important it is to have everybody working towards the same thing—a group of people working . . . . It made a big change in that reserve. It just put that message out that women weren't going to take that any more and that they weren't about to let men continue it, and there were consequences. It really shows how you can make changes if everyone sticks together. It wouldn't have made any difference at all with just one person left to themselves, but having the whole community react and finding a creative way of solving something that seemed like an impossible task before. (Phil TC4:41)

I consistently work to expand my connection to the Communities by providing an opportunity to listen actively to First Voices from the Aboriginal, African Canadian, Acadian, Asian and Lesbian and Gay Communities represented in the School. I engage in reciprocal relations with many Community members, using my own resources to support and advocate for others. As I continue to encourage and require an activist position in all participants in the educational process, several avenues to create sustainable change are open.

Enacting Change within Communities

Some students take their activism outside their immediate lives and the School. On occasion students seriously take up learning by doing, by volunteering in the Communities for a special project or for an established period of time. In making efforts to join with existing community organizations to contribute to change efforts, I encourage students to focus on an entry point as defined by the group. Some students from the Communities target Systems relevant to their group. One African Canadian student, Nadine, emphasizes the objectives and learnings she obtained through intervention with her own Community members. She stresses reciprocity for the Community members, which will bring about learnings and benefits for all participants involved:

> I feel that the presentation accomplished a couple of things. One in particular was the opportunity for Black parents to network and share experiences. Since being a part of the White structure can be intimidating many Black parents choose not to participate. Currently, there is no homogenous group or support for Black parents to come together and talk about their experiences.
>
> The presentation was also a great learning experience for [the students]. Present and future [professionals] need to hear that cultural difference is an important part of a child's life . . . .
>
> I feel strongly that the presentation was a valuable learning experience for all who attended. The letter composed and sent to the officials will hopefully promote change within the program as it affects Black children and parents who work within the system. (Nadine Mar 31 93-t4)

Her assessment of the learning experience and the impacts on participants is supported by Randi's journal entry: "During second round I wanted to speak to the Black women in the room and to let them know that their experience and wisdom has impacted on me greatly this term" (Apr 7 93-j).

When White students wish to offer assistance to Aboriginal, African, Acadian or other cultural Communities of which they are not members, reciprocity is stressed as crucial. If a Community is offering a learning opportunity to an individual or small group, then the students must consciously work to contribute what they can to the site. What the student learns about working across cultures is to be documented along with the action accomplished. Respectful and reciprocal relations are expected and validated in any communication I have with the students who are embarking on these journeys into "helpfulness." An excellent example of such an intervention involved three students who engaged in a voluntary relation with a local Aboriginal organization to aid in doing background research for a proposal that the agency wished to submit. At the outset of the term they communicated to me their intention and we discussed the appropriate way to approach the agency and the kinds of service they could offer. They collectively negotiated their own terms with the agency and wrote up their learnings jointly in a task report. While the nature of the work they undertook is contained in their full report, the section quoted here illustrates the depth of their learning through doing. They emphasize the necessity of learning and unlearning when working to build cross-cultural alignments.

> Throughout our contact with the people of the [agency], it must be said that [the co-ordinator] and others have been most accepting of our group coming in as virtual strangers. In our learnings about First Nations people, we have needed to learn and unlearn some of the ways in which we have been socialized to interact in White society which are in conflict and sometimes seen as offensive to the people. We have needed to suppress our urgency for information and to learn to sit back, relax, and develop a trusting relationship. We have learned to be quiet and to be still as we were like intruders. We also learned to go outside ourselves and our learnings. It is also significant to state that we needed to learn to be patient and to appreciate any contact that was shared with us . . . .
>
> Overall, this project has been a great learning experience for each of us. We have learned that Aboriginal and mainstream cultures need to learn to appreciate one another. It is the consensual opinion of this group that White society could stand to learn much from the Aboriginal values and beliefs towards child care, community interconnectedness, and respect for our relationship with Mother Earth. (Group Report Nov 23 92-t3)

Mac, one group member, shares his cultural learnings, expected and unexpected, more specifically in this journal entry. He illustrates an interactive pattern between what he learns theoretically, from the "books," about cultural difference and his actual lived experience in the Community:

> Well I finished with the [agency]. I am not sure that my experience there was quite what I expected . . . . Most of my learning came from sitting and listening. From talking and asking questions. It was through those moments of sitting around the office discussing issues of racism and the history that I really came to know more about Aboriginal people, culture, and oppression. I feel that the other work was secondary. It is interesting how quickly my expectations changed. At first, I thought that when I started to work that at least some acknowledgment was due to me. Also, when I greeted people I was a little disturbed by the apparent lack of response. Then I read that in Native culture that there is no onus on the other person to return the greeting and that this does not necessarily mean an insult. Also in Native culture, a level of participation that in White culture would be considered above what people would deem acceptable and, therefore noteworthy of praise is expected as a regular contribution. So, there is not as much concern given to "extraordinary" acts as the individual is expected to contribute what they can toward the survival of the community. (92-j)

These "realizations" allowed the student to stop worrying about "being accepted" and to *do* what he could to contribute to the Community. Mac learned that acceptance is culturally expressed: in Aboriginal culture acceptance rests more on what you do than what you say.

> I don't think that I was totally accepted but I also don't think that, that was important. I was there to learn that there are good reasons why I might not be accepted . . . . By doing this I feel that I have become a little more accepting of other cultures and ways of seeing things . . . . Perhaps it also lets me see that there truly are different ways for doing things and that this does not mean that the world will come tumbling down. It simply means that other ways are different; not better or worse. (Mac 92-j)

Perceived acceptance or lack of acceptance outside of the White environment is a common theme for students from the dominant culture. This is vitally linked to hegemony: their own acculturation to implicitly adopt White values and to not accept others' cultural ways as equally valid. Also, Whites are accustomed to being accepted in dominant culture, so are often "uncomfortable" when they are not openly welcomed in the ways to which they are accustomed. This reaction is graphically displayed in Dana's reflections on having attended, with two White peers, a majority African Nova Scotian community event:

> I have been reflecting more on my experience at the [event]. I did feel

> oppressed there, as one of the only white persons. To be in a setting like this, for the first time, it was very educational. For the first time, I was not a member of the dominant group. I felt very uncomfortable. I was hoping that someone would come over and say hello, or introduce themselves to me, as I did not know anyone there, except for [the two students], who I went with. I could feel the discomfort. I felt like a fish out of water. I was hoping that someone would introduce us, include us into their circles of communication. I felt like we were being watched; people were probably trying to figure out who we were and our reasons for being there. It was a great learning experience for me. Never before did I feel so alienated and uncomfortable in a crowd. I have learned first handedly how difficult it must be for Blacks and other minority cultures, who must face this everyday in our white, dominant culture. I could feel myself that day looking for other white faces in the crowd to help me to feel more comfortable. (Nov 20 92-j)

Students need to learn that some uncomfortable feelings are necessarily a part of entering into an unfamiliar racial or cultural context. As Dana notes, it can be reframed positively as a first-hand experience of what others from the Communities face every day. Van's entry reflects how her embodied experience of "minority" status was made visible to her in task work:

> Being the only white person involved in this presentation [racism] was quite an eye opener for me. I did not just hear the rhetoric of whites can't speak for blacks, first nations or any other non-white groups, I experienced the reality of the words . . . . The most illuminating aspect of this presentation was my being on the outside looking in. This was my presentation and I was expected to do the work for it, yet I was on the peripheral.
> The boundary of color and the uniqueness of the black experience put me in the position of uncertainty. This helped me to understand, on a small scale how a person of color feels when they walk into a white room in the education system. They are expected to learn, do their work and succeed, in spite of the barriers they face daily, hourly, minute by minute, second by second. (Oct 93-j)

Van reports her action of joining a White anti-racist coalition. She emphasizes the role played by her experience with the Model-In-Use, both in motivating her to join and in her analysis of her experience with the group:

> My action is that I have joined the [anti-racist group]. What brought me there—my belief in the respect for all peoples, my desire for peace among people and the need inside of me to do something. I have always known that my lamenting and verbal support for fighting racism, were not cutting it—This class was the door of awareness that I could not close.
> The words "do more than say," were/are the representations of

truth to me—"my door jammers." I knew I could not be inactive any
longer . . . .
Being a member of the "white group" at first seemed strange to me,
I thought that a unified group of blacks and white would be more
effective. I now see the necessity of having a white group—it is our
responsibility to educate other whites, but I also now know the power
of first voice and the dramatic effect this has had on my learning,
hopefully it will have the same impact on others. (Dec 93-t4)

This type of act, another small beginning, can result in activism that
continues beyond the conclusion of the course. These acts are a spark of hope
for sustainability of White anti-racist activist initiatives begun through participants' involvement in the Model. A learning Model that emphasizes an action-
oriented approach, lodged in day-to-day life, can help students more clearly
identify the symptoms and causes of oppression. It helps concretely support
efforts to learn ways of challenging structures of domination once visible.
Hands-on activism helps to equip all of us to recognize the need for personal and
collective strategies for change.

Hope and vigilance are required when attempting to promote change in the
overall structure. An understanding of the relationship of persistence to successful activism is also required but difficult to teach in a one-half credit course. In
the first year, an action group began the process of initiating an anti-racist policy
at the School level. In each year at least one group followed this up, providing
a lesson in the sustainability that is critical to successful social change processes.
While some limited progress has been achieved in this area, many proposed
changes have been successfully resisted. We began an annual Open Circle to
honour International Day to Eliminate Racial Discrimination. This event,
organized by a group from the class, is an educational event open to the School
and other Community members. The first was the hottest topic that year: Racial
Harassment. Due to the backlash produced from several Community members
speaking out about their experiences at the School, I advised a less radical topic
for the second year. The group wanted to focus on "Whites'" role in anti-racism.
We settled on "Working Together for Anti-Racist Change: What Can I Do?"
Both Open Circles were very well attended with many members from the
Communities and the School. One Open Circle can be produced per term, as
they have resulted in incredible learning for students and School alike and
promote systemic change. Ripples move through the water once the stone is
tossed, my Elders teach.

The combination of pedagogical strategies enacted through this Model-In-
Use has produced impacts and reactions, which can be labeled as dialectical,
paradoxical, contradictory and sometimes endangering. I will now highlight
several of the most frequently recurring themes, including those issues that
arose directly from the activist aspect.

Learning from the Trickster:
Classroom as Contested Terrain

Aboriginal egalitarian practices
Re-located . . . Adapted
Within a Eurocentric Hierarchical setting.
Using Ancestral forms
The Medicine Wheel . . .
Smudge . . . Talking Circle
In this context . . . in this location
The Rational Patriarchal School
Is fraught with Contradictions . . . Risks.

School culture
Where rows . . . linear arrangements

Force us to crane our necks to see who is speaking.
Except, for the Teacher . . . the focal point, the Expert.
Hierarchy . . . Grades.
I teach, You learn.
Chalk in hand . . . theories in Head.
Rational arguments . . . thoughts Objective
Severed from the Heart . . . from our Will
Our subjectivity . . . Our lives.

This context does not revere Female
Aboriginal . . . or the Personal.
Being "Open" can be demoralizing.
Multiple interpretations of the "same" reality
Are always produced from my "speak-outs."

I courageously question . . . examine Western values.
I Challenge Oppression
Racism . . . Privilege . . . Culture . . . Resistance . . .
Inherent in the classroom Context.
Dare to imagine a classroom
Where Eurocentric Domination is Not possible?
Where all Voices . . . All cultures are valued?

Aboriginal philosophy Adapted
Enacted through Circle form in the School Context.
Refreshing . . . Stimulating
Intensifying . . . Contradictory
Non-authoritarian Authority
Non-equal Egalitarianism.
How well does the Spirit of this pedagogical form
Re-locate into the School context?
Work together to Willfully Resist Cultural Hegemony.

Our Ancestors embraced humour as a sacred and necessary part of our struggle and survival: "human beings are weak . . . and our weaknesses lead us to do foolish things" (Beck and Walters 1977: 30). An Iglulik proverb says, "Those who know how to play can easily leap over the adversaries of life. And one who knows how to sing and laugh never brews mischief" (Rasmussen, in Beck and Walters 1977: 32). Ben Black Bear, a Plains Elder, acknowledges the centrality of humour to Aboriginal existence:

When you are alive, you give homage to the Great Spirit, and you will do favours for others, and then you will enjoy yourself. If one does not do those things, he will explode within himself. These three things are the highest in law. Realize this. These are truths, so be it. (in Beck and Walters 1977: 40)

The knowledge of relationships and how they are arranged and interact with each other is instilled in youngsters by Traditional teachings. Many stories and experiences tell us how this harmony can be upset and what tragedies can result. "Too much of one thing can lead to imbalance," "Don't take life so seriously," "Don't take yourself so seriously," "Don't make yourself bigger than you really are," my Elders taught. Too much power and too much seriousness are feared, for they can "unbalance" life in the Community and the environment. We are taught by the Trickster and others not to take ourselves too seriously, not to make ourselves too important. No one individual is indispensable. In the modern age of individualism, in which "stronger" individuals or nations dominate, this philosophy can be misread to mean internalization of external cues of inferiority. But Trickster's intention was and is to assert the Self-In-Relation. Humour is used to destabilize the individual who wishes to see her- or himself as "better," more powerful than others. The human who wishes to forget his or her dependence on other life forms as he or she exerts "power over" or superiority is challenged through humour. Humility is revered in a Traditional worldview. The ability to see oneself as dependent on and interconnected with other forms of life is an aspect of intertribal wisdom reinforced through humour and stories of reversal.

The Trickster is evident in some form in every Aboriginal culture and is responsible for the changes that took and are taking place in the world. The Trickster, often a male figure, can change his shape at will and can change into the shape of an animal.

He does not plan, he is impulsive, he is jealous and he imitates others without thinking of the consequences. The consequences are usually disastrous for him, but he must suffer alone; no one comes to his rescue. He is neither good nor bad, but is responsible for both because the reader can learn from the trickster's actions what is good and bad. (Grant 1992: 25)

The Trickster, the transformer, represents the power of learning through reversal, through "inside out lessons" (Medicine Eagle 1991). He/she shows up in many of our stories.

In such a story the protagonist meets a super human being (usually an animal disguised as a person) and is taken on a journey from the secular, material, temporal world of everyday life to a supernatural, timeless domain. The two domains—ordinary reality and the unfamiliar realm—are marked off in some physical way: the protagonist may pass under a log, into a cave, beyond the horizon, or may be given a "slap" causing temporary amnesia. The physical characteristics of this new domain are the reverse of those found in the more familiar world. It may be a "winter world" where everything is white, including people and animals, usually the customs, food, and behaviour of human beings are offensive to the inhabitants. Often the central organizing principle is a refraction of the human world from the perspective of animals. This view of human social order is not a mirror image, but one that (like myth itself) simultaneously unbalances and reorients the protagonist, revealing the ordinary in new ways. (Cruikshank 1992: 340–41)

Lenore Keeshig-Tobias, an Ojibwa author, laments that the Trickster has not been regarded as relevant to both Aboriginal and non-Aboriginal societies since the arrival of Europeans on this continent: "you, what ever happened to you, Trickster?" (1992: 102). Trickster, who helped us see our own mistakes, who helped us laugh at ourselves and each other, a necessary strategy to keep us strong and sane, was seen to have deserted us through the colonial period:

Now if there'd been a story, just one new story, even a little one—if only to make people laugh, things might have been different, might have been okay, might have been bearable. But there wasn't. There were no new stories. No wonder no one was looking for him, watching for him, waiting for him. He had just kissed-off and who cared. He hadn't even warned the people about treaties! (Keeshig-Tobias 1992: 103)

However, Trickster, as a teacher and caretaker of indigenous values, is once again being revived in Aboriginal Traditions. Keeshig-Tobias points out the similarities between the Trickster and the White Man. According to Iktomi prophecy, Trickster warned: "He is like me, a Trickster, a liar . . . a new kind of man is coming, a White Man" (Keeshig-Tobias 1992: 101).

Retracing the path of the Medicine Wheel using Trickster Tales will allow me to reveal the several layers of contradictory dynamics, which resurfaced in various manifestations of the Model-In-Use. Absolon advises us to ask: "Where do I sit in relationship to the Wheel and where must my own healing begin? What are the dark forces that contribute to my imbalance and dysfunctional behaviours?" (1994: 7). We learn through reversal, from inside-out lessons, the difficulties that are produced from imbalanced living. As Ellsworth reminds us, as "[u]ninvited, uncomfortable, threatening, and confusing as they may be, these moments become the curriculum when they erupt in classrooms" (1992: 9). Dr. Battiste reminds us that "contradiction and incoherence are inevitable in and indispensable to successful transformation" (Battiste and Barman 1995: xiv). She cautions that we must not allow the fear and doubt that arise to lead us back to assimilationist models of Eurocentric education.

This chapter is an effort to make visible both the "internal" factors—that is, issues that arose from the curriculum and pedagogies In-Use themselves—and the "external" or contextual factors that have intensified these dynamics. I will begin with myself—with an exploration of the difficulties of a "personal" embodied approach to teaching. Circling to the East, I will discuss issues of language as a medium of "knowing" and understanding identity and difference. In particular, the contradictory elements of First Voice as pedagogy will be discussed. Moving to the South, the difficulties of "adapting" Aboriginal Tradition to a Eurocentric School site will be noted. In the West, emphasis will be placed on the "negative" feelings produced for some participants, and how these "repressed" feelings feed into covert patterns of resistance which, in turn, blocks rather than builds community across diversity. Finally, in the North, the endangering potentials of taking an activist position are revealed. Backlash is theorized as continuously intertwined with activism.

Contradictions in all Directions: Trickster Teaches

216

Learning from the Trickster

Trickster Teaches
Embodied Teacher Revisited: Can I Be
"Personal" as Teacher?

Working in the Traditional way requires an "embodied" approach for both teacher and student. This is articulated in the Aboriginal "lifeworld" as "walking the talk." Walking the talk in this case means actively putting into practice the learning from the Model-In-Use. While many direct and positive lessons are learned from this, there are also Trickster tales. As an Aboriginal teacher in a Western School context, I face many struggles and contradictions. Walking the talk is, as Absolon tells us, "easier said than done" (1994: 30). The experience of being a "minority" teacher who is teaching race relations based on Aboriginal philosophy in a White Western context is an "embodied" experience. Following Bannerji (1991), one becomes an "embodied teacher" when one's body, and experience within that body, is part of the lesson. She tells of how she becomes aware that she is "a body in a space": "I am speaking particularly about my own non-white Indian woman's body, in a classroom where the other occupants are mostly white, and in a classroom in Canada" (Bannerji 1991: 6). As I identify myself and am concurrently constructed by others as "not White," I become the "embodied" other. Embodiment is a contradictory position in a Western educational context, where to be "not-mind" is to be excluded (Gatens 1991). This experience, and therefore this narrative, is highly contradictory, very personal and ultimately political. "It is nevertheless in these contradictions that I exist, and therefore think, speak, and write" (Ng 1991: 10).

Confusion is inherent in the undertaking of teaching critical, alternative content and enacting Aboriginal teaching methods while engaged in surviving a Eurocentric context. Eurocentric educational methods practice separation of teacher from learners, healer from "patients," worker from "clients." Traditionalists are expected to be engaging with others in the teaching-healing cycle and working on ourselves first and foremost. In the Traditional worldview, as teacher/healer, it is our responsibility to courageously share our own "personal" journeys. As Aboriginal educators, we need to know—acknowledge and communicate—our own past pains, our present struggles and our visions for the future in order to assist others on their own paths.

One recurring source of connection and disconnection for me was that of being a First Voice contributor *and* the teacher. First Voice requires speaking about your own experiences and insights gained. In the Traditional way, we each tell our own part in the greater story. As we become Elder teachers, we learn to understand/know more parts with greater depth so that we can speak of them. It is understood in Traditional teaching that we learn and teach through our own experience/voice. This Model requires divulging of "personal" stories in a "heartfelt" manner. This is *not* an "expected" practice of "teachers" in Eurocentric School settings. In Circle Talk on CCI, I spoke about the experience of recurring "cultural clash." Trickster has taught me that when some students hear the "personal" stories of my life, because I am their "teacher," they are shocked.

> White students aren't used to knowing personal things about their teachers. They're used to having that big separation between their teacher and them. And usually by the time the course is over, students know quite a lot about my life because I tell stories every class in Circle about different things that happen; right then as they're happening, or things that might have happened in the past that I think are important in terms of my own experience. I'm trying to encourage people to share their experiences and encourage guests that come in to share their life experiences, and students to share their practice experiences. (Fyre CC1:27)

As an "embodied" teacher, I am a model for other storytellers. The split between personal and "professional" is rampant in society and in the School context overall. Once personal but political stories are told, the authority that is invested in the "aura" of teacher is demystified. This is especially true when "inside-out" stories are told, when the learning arises from what the Western mind would categorize as "mistakes." It is Traditional to teach through reversal, through Trickster tales, and I do practice this story-form. The contradictory results are contextually-based.

> I even tell things about mistakes I've done and things I've learned from them .... That's one of the ways that power is equalized, in that we're all then equal members in the community together; just because I'm the teacher doesn't mean that I know everything. Or that I've never made a mistake in my life. Or that I'm really not making a mistake right now! ... What I'm saying is really my own experience, and what I know from that. I think that's quite shocking, for people ... to have a teacher that's talking about their own life, and talking about making mistakes, and sometimes actually even making them right there. (Fyre CC1:27)

One Elder who participated in Circle Talk on CCI expresses a Traditional approach to mistakes:

> You must always be ready to acknowledge your own weaknesses also. Because acknowledging never makes you small. It makes you much bigger! ... If you think too much of yourself, then nobody else thinks of you. Try to set an example for what you want. If you want something then for you, think for others. Do for others. And then, you see, the others will do for you .... (Erma VC3:8)

Being open with your own evolving subjectivity, particularly in a context that does not revere female, Aboriginal, the personal or "mistakes," can be demoralizing. Rather than inspiring respect and community, this kind of sharing can have the opposite effect.

> Sometimes I get negative feedback from students—they often don't say it to me, but I'll feel not respected from students. Not the same way that they respect teachers that are bosses to them. Sometimes that hurts my feelings because I'm trying to be equal with them, and sharing, and trying to be a participant with them. When they don't respect that I am the teacher and that they still need to do the work and they still need to come to class, and they still need to meet the obligations as a student, and that I'm still meeting the obligations as a teacher, even though I'm not really acting the same way as they expect teachers to act. (Fyre CC1:28)

Trickster has taught me that the institutional authority as evaluator is embedded in the need to produce the relevant grade, so true equality is unattainable. I continue to learn that to be "in charge" of a Traditional process in an educational setting requires a great deal of sensitivity, awareness, self-reflection and patience. Too much direction can stifle and inhibit the flow, creating blocks to people's mindful participation. People will concentrate more on what "the teacher" expects and less on their own process. Too little direction intensifies misunderstandings and widens the cultural gap.

The Eastern Door

Mono-cultural reality presented as the Norm
Racism and Privilege Spoken but seldom Challenged.
Naming a list of slurs and stereotypes can Increase racist vocabulary
When slurs are repeated they perpetuate the existing social order.
Language is political.
Usage is not accidental but part of an ongoing power struggle.

When White is spoken in stories of Pain and Resistance
White Privilege becomes understood through Reversal
By pain *Not* received.
Uncomfortable Feelings can arise:
Guilt . . . Embarrassment . . . Anger . . . Fear . . . Responsibility.
Reframe these feelings as a starting point
For cultural equality.
Pedagogy of Disorientation disrupts Silent Dominance
Of Eurocentric hegemony.

We the too few in number

The "minorities"
Charged with the mission to create anti-racist change
In Eurocentric Schools.
Is First Voice pedagogy re-enacting the service role?
We are held Continuously Responsible
For the curriculum development on Difference . . . Diversity.
The School Context is Not a "safe place"
To disclose stories of Racism . . . Oppression
Efforts to educate result in Denial
Minimizing . . . Incomprehension . . . Overt Racism.
First Voice . . . Empowering or Oppressive?
Freedom to Voice is always mediated
By power relations.
Empowerment through Voice requires actually being Heard
Validation . . . Support . . . Recognition . . . Community.

Language, as a cultural qualifier and a political process, and the various meanings of words have been strongly emphasized in this educational process. First Voice, with members of the Communities visibly represented in the classroom, alters who speaks. Circle Talk is a process of designating how, when and about whom people speak. What is said or not said by whom becomes political and a very hot topic in this classroom. I am reminded of the words of Minh-ha: "Words are think-tanks with second and third-order memories that die hard despite their ever changing meanings" (1989: 21).

Trickster Teaches
Are Slurs and Stereotypes in the Classroom
Actually Teaching Racist Language?
Helping people unveil their own racism is a difficult and emotional task. Strategies are often linked to the uncovering of racial stereotypes and slurs. Racial slurs make many "uncomfortable" because they make people's biases visible. Vada notes her reaction to a race relations exercise done by African Canadian participants, which required writing the ends to sentences that reflected traits of Blacks and Whites respectively:

> I also feel very upset with my thoughts when I wrote the ends to the sentences. How can I have learned racism when I do not remember any negative stereotypes spoken in my family. Is socialized racism that subtle that we do not even know we are racist before we are looking honestly at ourselves? I am very upset about the realizations that I may have been oppressive and expressed racism unintentionally and unknowingly. (Jan 24 93-j)

Uncovering and speaking racial biases is upsetting. Discomfort is present for those who recognize that the use of slurs and stereotypes produces pain for those categorized. Lena expresses her concern for herself and her peers:

> In class this week I was uncomfortable because of the things I have learned about myself and how I was racist in ways I never knew . . . . I was also uncomfortable in class because of the things the other students were saying . . . . I felt worried that the things being said would hurt the culturally diverse students. (Jan 24-31 93-j)

While some advocate direct confrontation of racist language, the use of slurs and stereotypes as teaching tools can have unintended effects. This classic debate is poetically addressed by Vada, who was not previously exposed to certain racial qualifiers. She articulates her experience that using racial slurs can reproduce them rather than stimulate unlearning: "What has concerned me the most in my first week in this class is how new negative statements and stereotypes of black people affect me. I had never heard about [slurs] before our last class" (Vada Jan 10 93-j). She has concerns that the more she learns about slurs and stereotypes, the more negative labels will be newly lodged in her thinking:

> Even though I have learned a great deal about my level of racism and about the black community, I am afraid to learn more about other stereotypes or negative statements that I have not heard before. This experience has made me concerned about how I will react to examples of the racism that native people are experiencing. Will I start to think these negative statements or stereotypes also? (Vada Jan 10 93-j)

By term end, she was able to reconcile "unlearning" stereotypes as a positive aspect of challenging racism: "I also unlearned many stereotypes about different cultures. This felt good" (Vada Apr 4 93-jsum). Naming a list of slurs or stereotypes is not enough to pose an anti-racist challenge. Critically examining the power relationships that are made visible through negative qualifiers is required to stimulate unlearning.

Because of power relations structured into the educational environment, confusion can easily arise from the articulation of racial slurs by presenters and teachers. Spoken by some, slurs perpetuate the existing social order, yet First Voice storytellers have used them to challenge the power of dominating discourse. This was illustrated vividly in class one night when Ela, an African Canadian participant, told a childhood story in which she was called a common racial slur. She tells her own version in Circle Talk on CCI.

> I remember one night in class I was relating a story about my experiences . . . and I used the word [slur]; and I used it because I had to use the word in order to get across the message that I was conveying. So

> somebody else, when we went around the circle, used the word too. Somebody white used the word . . . . Maybe they should of given a little introduction, or softened the blow when they used the word because it came out not quite the same way! (Ela TC2:3)

When that same word was re-used by a White student, it became a weapon of oppression. The experience served as a Trickster tale to several present. We witnessed how large a role cultural locatedness plays in understanding the meanings of language. That night, when the slur was spoken by the White student, many of us visibly flinched. When my turn to speak came, I addressed the issue of racial language, speaking of the need to avoid slurs and why it was improper to use them as qualifiers for group members. If and when some members of the targeted Community feel it necessary to say it as they tell their stories of resistance to racism, it is their right to do so. It is not the right of an "outsider," certainly not a member of the dominant majority.

The power of lessons learned through reversal is illustrated by the lasting impression made on the Black participant and on the White student. As Ela re-told the story in Circle Talk on CCI, she mentions that the student had approached her after class and at the last class again. She recreates the dialogue:

> They said that they had felt they were chastised for using the word in that context . . . . They said, when you used the word I thought it was safe to use it. I said, ya, but I used it from a personal experience because what other word could I use? That's what I was called so I had to tell you that that's what I was called. (Ela TC3:3)

Further, she clarifies the conditions under which she felt that it was all right for a majority member to use a slur. In her opinion, a verbal "cushion" or warning is necessary:

> So if you, from a white perspective, are using that word, then you say, I'm going to use this word and it's going to be an offensive word but I have to say it in order to get my message across. So you explain why you're saying the word, not just blurt it out! Cushion the blow a little bit! (Ela TC3:3)

Although I had spoken about it in Circle, and she had offered her wisdom to the student at the time, she concludes the story by indicating that she felt the person still "needed an explanation." She perceives that the incident left the student confused, creating a block to learning rather than promote unlearning: "So that person carried that all through the course . . . . Feeling slighted about that and wondering why they were slighted. Why I could use the word and they couldn't, and never said it until the last class" (Ela TC2:3). The Elders would counsel: deep lessons take time. When the time is right, he'll learn what he needs to know from the experience. Ela wisely concludes with a now recurring theme: "[E]verybody gets something different out of Circle, and everybody interprets things differently" (TC2:3). Potential contradictions arise because the multiple interpretations within the English language itself interact with diverse cultural locations present in the classroom. Ela returns to this theme at a later Circle:

> English is such a stupid language at times. I can say something and everybody in this room will interpret it differently. It's a matter of what's relevant, and again it's because of your belief system. You interpret what I say on the basis of what you believe. So that's where it all comes from and where it all goes. (TC4:37)

Ela's experience is part of what I have come to describe as "multiple interpretations of the *same* reality." Cal offers his version of the same theme: "But I'm still questioning what the other students, the White students in the class, really got out of it. And I'm not sure whether or not what I had wanted them to see was what they actually saw" (CC2:15).

When exploring the contradictory dynamics of racial language in the classroom, it is essential to keep in mind that everybody interprets the learning/teaching from their own individual/cultural location. Usher notes that "the difference in reality interpretations are not accidental but are political by nature, because power relations and power-struggles interfere with and influence personal experiences" (1989: 25). As a teacher, I now strive to avoid speaking and writing racial slurs and stereotypes. I have learned that once they are spoken by the teacher, they become part of what is considered acceptable classroom discourse. Zero tolerance for slurs provides many teachable moments.

Trickster Teaches
Can "White" Be Used as a Cultural Qualifier?

Slurs are not the only kind of language that becomes part of this contested terrain. Names for various Communities are often changing—Coloured, Black and African Nova Scotian or Indian, Native, First Nations, Aboriginal and Indigenous are two such progressions in the naming of cultural Communities. Most contradictory in this Model, and least discussed in hegemonic literature, is the use of "White" as a cultural qualifier. As earlier theorized, a label like "White" is politically constructed in a particular historical time period. "White" has become a racial qualifier, so it is also a political category. A general dissociative pattern is shown by those of European descent towards being named (Katz 1985). This has combined with the blurring of cultural diversity, created by the history of colonial migration patterns (Blaut 1993). According to Jay, "What holds white people together is not a common language, religion, cuisine, literature or philosophy, but rather a political arrangement that distributes power and resources by skin color" (1995: 124). These factors reinforce the historically established and continuously recurring deconstructionism of "Whiteness." Vada expresses the difficulties she experiences in being labeled by a construct named "White." She has concerns that all Whites, regardless of ethnicity, class or country of origin, will be categorized by this qualifier.

> I'm white, but I still feel that I've gone through a lot of experiences. I don't see my culture everyday. I don't speak my language. I don't celebrate my holidays. And every time it is something special that our [group] celebrates, I would have to explain to people and so, where do I fit in? I'm white, I'm western, I'm . . . struggling with the word "white" . . . when we're talking . . . . There was a lot of talk about White and Black, and White and Native, and I had never thought about the term "white." Who did it mean? It was always giving white privileges. I was so confused, because I was thinking of the immigrant community, about many whites that had experienced different type[s] of discriminations and I couldn't just see "whites" as one line, and White fit there and the Black fit there, and . . . the Native fit there. For me, I always think how different cultures and the different experiences in all these different groups of culture. (Vada TC2:19)

Vada has highlighted a critical debate in the postmodern. If we accept the label—the category as constructed—White, Black, Native or Other—are we merely reiterating our place in the "colored hierarchy"? (Vada TC2:19). According to Nicholson, "[T]he extent to which we insist on difference and how we describe the 'difference that makes a difference' is itself a political act" (1990: 10). Said's work acts to deconstruct notions of clearly definable cultural groups. He asks: "How does one *represent* other cultures? Is the notion of a distinct culture (or race, or religion, or civilization) a useful one?" (Said 1978: 325). The questioning of fixed categories of gender, class, race and culture comes at a time when groups need to consolidate the fragments of their identities in order to challenge the hegemony of Western metanarratives. It also comes at a time when "Whiteness" is being unveiled as hegemonic by post-colonists and others.

When members of cultural groups share the painful and common stories of their racial and cultural oppression, the unification of "White culture" takes on a particular meaning. Bejay describes her Self-In-Relation to her culture:

> I am white, anglo-saxon, protestant. My culture feels it has an inherent right to dominate, that it is superior over all other cultures. What white culture feels is important in other cultures, it appropriates for its own benefit. I have voice because I am white. I have privileges and power bestowed upon me by the mere colour of my skin. What is my culture? My culture is technology, competition, looking at the future, disregard for nature, oppressive, respectful of individual success, a heavy thing to live with. (Bejay Jan 93-j)

Bejay expresses her culture as understood through an oppositional perspective. She has recognized the structurally oppressive nature of the White privilege from which she personally benefits. When students are first internalizing this insight, it can be hard for them to celebrate the gifts of the dominant culture. Gela discloses why it is difficult for her to see "White culture" in a positive way:

> It is difficult for me to consider white people as having a culture. I have always associated culture with tradition and have perceived it as something positive among groups who celebrate their origins and act on traditional values and beliefs. Because of my personal definition of culture, I feel at a loss to describe white culture in the same positive light. (Jan 25 93-t1)

Gela describes what she now has uncovered as the basis of her people's culture; "a set of sanctioned rules and by-laws":

> White people certainly celebrate who they are and their values and beliefs have come to be the prescribed guidelines by which all people should follow. However, as I gain an increasing awareness as to what defines white culture, I am beginning to recognize that white people don't identify with a cultural heritage as much as they identify with a set of sanctioned rules and by-laws. (Jan 25 93-t1)

She identifies the values of "White culture" as reflected in "patriarchy, capitalism, competition, advantage, and an unyielding instinct to control" (Gela Jan 25 93-t1). She has named the philosophies that underpin Eurocentric domination as the basis of White culture. Through becoming conscious of a critical analysis of race relations, she has come to express an essentially negative assessment of the guiding values of her own group. Gela then documents specifically how these values were passed down to her through her family's definitions of an "acceptable lifestyle":

> I have been encouraged to receive a secondary education, obtain a financially rewarding job, and to someday marry and raise children. The ways in which my parents socialized me are very much within the expectations of white middle-class status. Although no one has ever taught me to be cruel or harsh to others in order to insure I will succeed in life, my membership in the white culture is enough to ensure I will be somewhat successful in life providing I adhere to white mainstream ethics. (Jan 25 93-t1)

Finally, she unveils White supremacy as a commonsense reality for those with White privilege:

> What white people consider to be important for them is the basis for white culture. I believe that membership in this white culture leads us

to assume we will succeed in everything that we do because our "superior culture" (otherwise known as society) is set up to meet and fulfill our own white needs. (Gela Jan 25 93-t1)

When students are put in the position to interrogate their own Whiteness and to realize simultaneously the impacts of their privilege on others in society, uncomfortable feelings may arise. These feelings are akin to the anomie produced when members of racially-defined groups try to acculturate to White norms. Guilt and embarrassment, which are often characterized as "negative" feelings, can be a result of a critical reflection of cultural locatedness for Whites. Hearing the "facts" of history from an Aboriginal or Afrocentric perspective is an emotional eye-opener for many students who have been acculturated to understand the colonial version of the story as "truth." Embarrassment, anger, fear and responsibility are all expressed in Tia's entry:

When I truly think of how history actually happened, I find myself extremely embarrassed and having minimal things to be proud of. I also find myself being angry. Throughout my life I was taught to believe the white man's version of history. Which obviously was not very accurate. I feel like I was brainwashed into believing that what I read was factual .... I feel that we have to acknowledge what happened in the past, and that acknowledgment must include rewriting history as we now know it. As white people we must take responsibility for our ancestors because the garbage they wrote as the truth (true history) is wrong, and it is still being taught in our education system. As white people we need to finally stand back and listen and stop enforcing our power and privilege on to others. . . .

To be honest, I'm scared because I don't want my children growing up believing the lies I was taught as a child. (93-j)

Tia later expresses the feelings of confusion and embarrassment she experiences in her work to reveal her Self In-Relation to her culture:

Not surprisingly I ask myself what my culture is and how am I a part of that culture? To be honest, when I look at myself as being a white person belonging to a white culture it is confusing and embarrassing. Feeling embarrassed because of the actions of people belonging to my culture fragments me as a person. When people ask me what my culture is I state that I am German, Acadian, French Canadian, Dutch and British . . . . I have never recognized myself as having a white culture. When I consciously look at the wire cage Marilyn Frye describes, I see little to be proud of. I don't want to be a part of the oppressive values and roles our society states as being the norm . . . . (93-j)

These "negative" feelings need to be reframed. While discomfort can be produced when we face the "negative" aspects of our own selves or society, this is a crucial step in critically examining our lives in relation to social structures. Gela describes her embarrassment as a "starting point for cultural equality":

> Throughout this entire journal I have attempted to describe, explain, and identify white culture. What seems ironic is my obvious resistance to describe "my" culture. I guess I'm a bit embarrassed to call it my culture. I just wish more white people would agree to understand and share this embarrassment. I believe this would definitely be a starting point for cultural equality. (Jan 25 93-t1)

Conscious awareness of White culture is an essential dimension when transforming cultural imperialism. As Katz tells it, "[T]he bonds of culture are invisible and the walls are glass. We may think that we are free. However, we cannot leave the trap until we know that we are in it" (1985: 623). By making visible the bonds of White culture, we may then examine how they serve to entrap. Due to hegemony—the domination of all institutional forms—Whites become blinded to the values that are used to dominate themselves and others. Through this lens, acts of resistance to Eurocentrism are framed as personal hostility rather than necessary acts of survival.

Theorizing White as a cultural qualifier can create confusion for White students as they try to define their cultural identity. As Jay notes, "To be a white person is to have certain advantages, socially and politically and economically, but being white does not provide you with a culture" (1995: 124). He is not surprised, then, when students end up writing that "they do not have a cultural identity" (Jay 1995: 122). But, as Stuart Hall argues, "[Y]ou have to position yourself somewhere in order to say anything at all" (1991: 18). These experiences, then, can be considered as one way in which Jay's proposed "pedagogy of disorientation" can be enacted:

> The exploration of otherness and cultural identity should achieve a sense of my own strangeness, my own otherness, and of the history of how my assumed mode of being came into being historically. I could have been someone other than I think I am. And maybe I am. (1995: 125)

Trickster laughs: this "pedagogy of disorientation" has been imposed on us as Aboriginal people through colonization. As Todd argues, the term "Native" is "inscribed with meaning from without" (1992: 77); it has become a knowledge that blocks our own "certain subjectivities and ways of experiencing the world" (Todd 1992: 77).

While this Model seeks to critically challenge dominant constructions of "culture," Dana poses a poignant example of someone who is lodged in, yet critical of, the Western view of culture. She expresses her definition of "culture" as linked to "oppressed" group membership. Because of this, she is unable to capture her own identity within the construct "White culture."

> When I think of what my culture is, and how my culture defines me, I do not think in terms of a "White" culture but instead, as my culture as a female. Is there such a thing as "White Culture"? Is this the same as "Western Culture"? I probably do not identify so much as a White person because I am not oppressed as a White person. I am however, oppressed as a female living in this patriarchal society, governed by male culture, values, and beliefs. (Dana Oct 19 92-j)

Her efforts to understand the construct of White as a culture are further impacted upon by a positive connection made with a Traditional person from within the Aboriginal Community. Through a process of reversal, a negative assessment of Whiteness is produced alongside a positive acceptance of the gifts of another Community.

> When I left this man, I felt lost and empty. He shared his native culture with me, the hand crafts, the medicine wheel, the dream catcher, and aboriginal culture, community, and values with me. It seems to be a culture that any feminist would like to live in, a world of democracy and equality; a culture based on community and sharing. I feel empty because I do not have such an exciting culture. Our culture is so mainstream and ordinary. I do not feel that I have a true culture. Can we really call the white culture a "culture"? This was a *valuable* learning experience! (Dana Nov 15 92-j)

Dana has become conscious of the value of a Traditional worldview. She has begun to challenge at a deeper level her culture's lack of connection to their own material representations. Days later another entry reveals more specifically how she begins to unveil her own Self-In-Relation to Whiteness. An artifact she had purchased from the Aboriginal person stood in stark contrast with the rest of her living decor. Trickster reveals a reflection of her own Whiteness through this. It is an image which she vows to change.

> Today, I hung the dream catcher up in my bedroom. I just realized how much my bedroom, and home reflected the white culture. I have two pictures in my bedroom of children—all white children. I do not have any decorations except this new dream catcher, that reflects the aboriginal culture, or any other cultures. I feel the need to change this. I want to create a feeling of Cross Cultural awareness in my home. I will find pictures of other children, other than white, to hang in my room. It took me this long to notice this. (Dana Nov 18 92-j)

In this case, the student finishes the course with her ideas of culture as "material" firmly entrenched. She concludes her journal with this entry, expressing discontent with belonging to a culture that is not "distinct":

> I feel empty. I wish that I belonged to a *distinct* culture, such as Aboriginal or Black. I do not like to feel like an oppressor. And, I do not consider the White, oppressive culture to be a culture. What is so distinct about it? (Dana Dec 10 92-jsum)

A combination of uncovering White hegemony and an uncritical acceptance of the material and spiritual gifts of Aboriginal culture produce a shift in her alliances, at least temporarily.

> I especially enjoy the Aboriginal culture's link and spirituality to nature. It makes so much more sense to be—more spiritual and inspirational. I hope to learn more about it. It is a belief system that I could aspire to live by—a culture of sharing and democracy. (Dana Dec 10 92-jsum)

In the postmodern we are warned not to essentialize African, Aboriginal or White as "distinct" cultures. Diversity exists among all cultural groups and cultural expression takes on individual and communal traits. While I personally do not experience the teaching of "White culture" as contradictory, others have pointed out that it is highly controversial and not accepted within dominant discourse. White, when recognized and named as a culture, becomes a political category. The naming of it clarifies—and disrupts—its silent dominance. Denying its status as "cultural" and "political" reifies White norms and White privilege.

Trickster teaches that members of the Communities continue to suffer under the criticism that unveiling hegemonic Whiteness is somehow "White bashing." Negative criticism of our work is accepted as "fact" under this rhetoric. Certainly the reality that I am teaching this construct in a Eurocentric, White-dominated context adds to the difficulty. Context plays a big role in implementing any and all alternate forms of pedagogy, including First Voice.

Trickster Teaches
Is First Voice Pedagogy
Re-enacting the "Service Role"?

Face-to-face encounters, where First Voice is spoken, is a highly effective tool in challenging privileged students to gain an empathic understanding of the pains of racism and oppression. This strategy, however, is not without its perils. Given the historical roots of anti-racist pedagogy, concern must be expressed about reinvoking the longstanding "service role" of our peoples. It is contradictory having myself and other culturally located educators and students placed in the position of educating White privileged students. As Carty aptly reminds White feminists:

To turn to us and ask that we offer the knowledge of our experiences—in short, to explain our absence and educate the oppressors how they oppress us—is hardly evidence of anti-racist feminist pedagogy or feminist inclusionary praxis, but a denial of responsibility, and an act of exploitation. It is not the responsibility of women of Color the victims of racism, to teach white feminists how they practice racism or how it is manifested on a daily basis. (1991b: 17)

The Aboriginal, African, Asian, Acadian and Gay and Lesbian members of our classroom Communities should not have to be continuously held responsible for the curriculum development on oppression or their cultural Community. This is one recurring form that discrimination takes in the classroom context. Trickster's voice is articulated very poetically by one African Canadian participant:

I grow tired of having to call people on things that are obvious to me. If they are attempting to be aware or sensitive they should stop hiding behind politically correct affirmative action programs that are all appearance, no sensitivity. Stop looking to the oppressed to educate people and make the changes. Stop hiding behind ignorance and white privilege. (Unicorn Oct 1 93-j)

Participants from our Communities face a contradictory position when they are or become the content. While efforts have been made to de-tokenize members, a fundamental contradiction remains. How can we call on Community members to share their experiences in First Voice, in a context that is dominated by White patriarchal norms, without contributing to their further oppression? African Canadian Community members who were ongoing participants shared their feelings in their journals and during Circle Talk on CCI. The first entry from Cal expresses this sentiment clearly. When he first learned that personal experiences of members of the Communities would be used to teach, he felt "uncomfortable."

This initially made me somewhat uncomfortable again as I am so tired of giving testimonial to White people as an explanation of just how they should act. To have them become more aware of how they have brutalized me and my race. Though I feel it is their work to do and understand their Racism.

I also have a role, but sometimes I am not sure I want to take on this responsibility. (Cal Jan 5 94-j)

His concern is in part related to the current conditions within the School context, which inevitably means the "few" educating the "many."

> I was somewhat disappointed to see that there were not more people of color from the majority cultures . . . in the class. The immediate bonding that usually would take place will need time as my present class mates have little understanding of the things that have ravaged my life. (Cal Jan 5 94-j)

A culturally-loaded and commonsense reality is expressed in Cal's question: "Why do we always have to be the only one or two 'people of color?'" (Jan 5 94-j). If we make up the "majority" of Mother Earth's people when embracing this construct, why are we consistently understood and labeled as a "minority"? Being in minority, while being First Voice in Circle, means sharing heartfully "personal" racial and cultural experiences with people who have "little understanding." As Cal tells it, "Few of the students in the class really understood what it took to make this statement and to talk about my feelings so passionately" (Mar 23 94-j).

The experience of First Voice on a weekly basis can produce many feelings; sometimes there is reluctance to share with peers. Cal reflects on this contextual reality in his final entry:

> In the beginning of each class, there were so many feelings and emotions that I had, sometimes I felt as if I would explode. There was so much I wanted to share and so much I knew that this particular group would not understand. I would just once like to be in a situation where one does not have to explain who they are. Where you don't have to make justification or defend who they are but have it accepted as a given. I had hoped that there would be Blacks in the class and that there would initially be a safe environment where we would not have to explain. (Apr 7 94-j)

First Voice participants often clearly perceive and articulate that the majority of their White peers do not understand or relate to the amount of pain that engaging in First Voice pedagogy can produce. When we are present in First Voice as teachers, students or Community guests, we are very aware that we are in a White-dominated institutional context. We incur pain to present our stories and ourselves in an effort to encourage other participants to support our brothers and sisters in addressing the issues of race and cultural difference. The painful reality is that retelling our experience means reliving it. Listening to other's experience sometimes means remembering our own similar ones. Unicorn graphically describes this:

> I did have a difficult time talking in our first few classes. My reasoning is because I breathe, smell, taste, touch, sleep and live with/through racist experiences/situations of my own and others seven days a week and twenty-four hours a day. To constantly relive this is emotionally and physically draining enough amongst my family and friends. By the time

I reach your class I've had my fill and did not wish to bare my soul and most intimate feelings to white strangers whom I believed not to have grasped enough of the course content at that point. Near the end I became more comfortable with classmates. (Oct 93-j)

"Comfort" is again a critical issue, this time for participants enacting First Voice pedagogy. Some students do express an increased level of understanding and respect. Vada's entry reflects a recognition of the Trickster medicine in this situation:

Today I also felt that it is so ironic that I need to be educated about my racism by the people that I oppress. Have they not gone through enough, and is it not our responsibility to educate ourselves about our weaknesses? (Jan 24 93-j)

More often students learn if told directly about the costs of Voice. The next two excerpts from students' journals illustrate this new awareness, gained through a "speak-out" by Unicorn:

[Unicorn] mentioned in-class another aspect that I had not thought of: That every time someone speaks in class it's her speaking also because she relives all of her pain. The presentations were painful for her—This learning helped me to see that I cannot allow myself to believe I know anything because I don't!! (Van Oct 93-j)

Analee states this learning in her closing entry. While she did not specifically mention the "speak-out," clearly the message is received.

I realized the importance of First Voice to our learning. For some, the sharing of these experiences was very painful because as they share with us, they are "reliving" things. As a result of this I have even greater respect for these people and I appreciate my learning even more. I have certainly learned a great deal from First Voice . . . it really brings things to life—the happiness, the heartache, the reality of the lives of those of different cultures. An excellent learning opportunity for me. (Analee Dec 93-jsum)

While First Voice provides an excellent learning opportunity, the institutional reality is that the School context is White-dominated. It is not a safe environment in which to disclose "personal" experiences of structural oppression or to be validated for sharing emotion. Contextually, because of these institutionalized relations of White domination, First Voice can work to position participants in highly contradictory relations of visibility and appropriation. Trickster asks: How do I/we take the risk to speak when I/we know not how or by whom my/our words will be tak n?

The impacts of this pedagogical method—the face-to-face encounter—on students' consciousness is continuously mediated by the limits of our understanding of others. According to Schutz, "[O]ur knowledge of the consciousness of other people is always in principle open to doubt" (1967: 107). Given that the "whole stream of lived experience" of another is not open to me, "I can catch sight of only disconnected segments of it . . . when I become aware of a segment of your lived experience, I arrange what I see within my own meaning-context . . . thus I am always interpreting your lived experiences from my own standpoint" (Schutz 1967: 106). The "habit" of interpreting another's experience from your own standpoint is a central feature of cultural imperialism.

According to Weir, "[N]on-white students addressing race place themselves in a vulnerable position, for they realize their statements may result in denial, minimizing, incomprehension and down right racism from white students: they have every reason to feel that their knowledge and contribution to discussion will be undermined" (1991: 23). Aboriginal and African participants address this reality:

> Tonight as I ponder over last class I feel as though some things will never change, I see the looks on people's faces around the room and wonder, do these white middle-class students have any idea what this whole course is about? I shouldn't be so harsh it's hard not to be!
> I see anger, dismay, defensiveness, and it makes me angry to think that these people have the nerve to be defensive, we've been defending ourselves all of our lives and we are tired of it! (Randi Jan 27 93-j)

> Because of the topic, I felt it necessary to arrange the evenings class with variety to hold the class's interest. I see the non-verbal grinning and rolling of eyes when classmates hear about Racism . . . . As my Grandmother says, "In one ear and out the other." I even heard one classmate say I hope we are not doing that brown eye blue eye thing again. I kept all of this in mind when . . . planning the evening. (Unicorn Oct 7 93-j)

Anger, dismay, defensiveness, grinning and eye-rolling are all visible in posturing and body language when sitting in Circle. In a context where "rational" explanation is expected for all that one gives voice to, verbalizing one's painful experiences can be exhausting. Storytelling to a disbelieving or disengaged audience is tiresome, discomforting and dangerous. Developing a level of comfort to speak in the Western School context about racism and oppression is a journey. Achieving comfort in the face of peers' well-developed denial is difficult. Anticipation of and recovery from occasions of outright racial harassment is ongoing. According to Weir, "[W]hen the classroom becomes a site of anti-racist political struggle, the racism present massively among white people will be spoken" (1991: 24).

First Voice can be experienced as "personal turmoil" for the speaker. As a teaching tool it has the potential to reinforce "service" relations with a personal cost to the speakers. It can also, simultaneously, be an enjoyable and empowering experience. Unicorn and many other First Voice participants conclude with a positive review of the experience and Model overall:

> Despite my personal turmoil, I enjoyed the class. I enjoyed and learned from our talking circle. I expressed viewing this class [as] the one that keeps me at the school. It gives me the opportunity to re-experience and learn from new experiences even if it hurts. This course keeps me in touch with current issues based on first voice as opposed to theory from a textbook written by someone who has nothing in common with me. (Unicorn Nov 19 93-j)

I endeavour to have First Voice representation be an empowering experience, one that is central to the classrooms rather than tokenistic. I have paid particular attention to the feelings, thoughts and stories of students and Community members who have represented their experience and have recorded what was positive and empowering and what remains oppressive. I have strived to be very aware of my own feelings of being oppressed in this role, and have found communicating openly with students to be enlightening for us all.

Trickster helps me to recognize that learning occurs "among multiple, shifting, intersecting, and sometimes contradictory groups carrying unequal weights of legitimacy within the culture and the classroom" (Ellsworth 1989: 317). These "problems" of difference are left unaddressed by most critical educators, who fail to acknowledge both the conflicts among differentially located students and the impact of their identity on their subjectivities and those of others. I agree with Jansen and Klerq (1992) that the experiences of participants in learning processes cannot be isolated from our integration into larger political, economic and cultural connections. These relations not only leave marks on our concrete experiences but, to a large extent, they determine "which experiences and interpretations of the world are acknowledged and which are marginalized" (Jansen and Klerq 1992: 99). We must remember that "the degree to which students [and teachers] will feel free to voice experiences will be mediated by power relationships in the classroom" (Brah and Hoy 1989: 73). The difficulties inherent in teaching from First Voice, a tool designed to invoke an altered state of consciousness about what we need to know and how we know, are primarily context related. So are the following contradictions about introducing forms of Aboriginal philosophy and pedagogy to non-Natives in a non-Aboriginal context.

Learning from the Trickster

The Southern Door

Non-Natives aspire to adopt the process.
Appropriation?
They lack proper attention to Form.
Acknowledgment of the Source.
Profit gained from our Ancestors' Pain.
Who speaks?
Who listens?
To whom?
Words spoken most quickly
Most often . . . most loudly . . . most complicatedly.
One interrupting another at Will.
Rudeness Not Respect is expected
Domination of air time by a few Consistent.
Who listens?
To whom?
Stop competing
Analyzing . . . Arguing
Trying to Change . . . to "Fix" the speaker's "Problem."
Really listen . . . Experience Silence.
Profound for White middle-class students.
And the Teacher.

Talking Circle in a non-Native context
Can become a Negative Hurtful experience.
Clear and compelling narratives Voiced.
Can be heard by Ears open to "accusations."
Some wish our silence.
Project their Fear as our Negativity.
"Facilitating" Circle is complex.
Simplicity is an Illusion.
Caution is wise.

In Western institutions, Eurocentric culture is most often the dominant form of expression. While members of the Aboriginal, African Canadian and Asian Communities may be occasionally present as students and teachers, their numbers are not great enough to balance or challenge hegemonic authority. The Circle process can be used to begin to address this. Many who are accustomed to being silenced and treated marginally are welcomed and given opportunity to tell their stories in Circle. In a Circle primarily of those steeped in "colonial consciousness," care must be taken to hear rather than to silence, to honour rather than to appropriate First Voice or the Circle method itself.

Trickster teaches that we must always be aware of the colonizers' propensity to appropriate. Many definitions and examples of appropriation are possible. Central to the act of appropriation is the misrepresentation or partial representation of an idea or artifact without recognition of the Traditional sources of knowledge or inspiration, often in combination with gaining prosperity, success or benefit from others' ideas. In the modernist period, it was the lands and resources which the colonizers sought; in the postmodern era, the experiences, the sensation, the artistic and the spiritual have been objectified as commodities. Todd is poetic in her analysis: "We have become the source of spiritual merit badges for the politically correct, and conduits to the cosmos for the instant shamans of the New Age" (1992: 72).

Since the late 1970s and continuing through present time, the literature on Native peoples has included "not only books on Indian religion written by non-Indians but also anthologies and treatises on ecology allegedly using Indian principles" (Deloria 1994: 42). This is usually done without acknowledging the appropriative act involved. Appropriation contributes to sustaining the status quo, reifying the White expert voice as truth while suppressing Aboriginal people's voices. Lenore Keeshig-Tobias says publishers have returned manuscripts submitted by Native writers with "too Indian" or "not Indian enough" scrawled across them (in Godard 1992).

Trickster Teaches
Circle as Pedagogy:
A Gift or a Stolen Treasure?
In this Model-In-Use, Traditional Aboriginal philosophies and pedagogies have been introduced to non-Natives and have been "imported" into the Eurocentric School context. I address the inherent contradictions in my opening remarks at the Circle on context:

The South is about the heart and the spirit, and to me, my heart in this project and in this work has been trying to make enough space in this white western [School] to teach as an Aboriginal person and not feel that I have to be using white methods or that I have to be white to be here . . . . I have been consistently trying to bring Aboriginal spiritual forms into the classroom through using the Smudge, through using the Circle, through using Circle talk, and trying to get people to get into the spirit of being respectful to each other and trying to get into the spirit of heartfully speaking about the subjects, instead of what is generally the context; which is staying in your head, only talking about your thoughts, not getting in to your heart at all. In a system where people are competitive, not cooperative. In a system where the teacher is expected to tell everybody what they're supposed to know and not engage in a learning process with them. (Fyre TC2:3)

The Traditional way of teaching is in contrast to the "commonsense" expectations of students and educators. I address some of the struggles in using a Traditional Model in a Eurocentric setting in Circle Talk on CCI:

> The Aboriginal way of teaching is that something happens!, and we're all part of it, or a story is told and we all hear it. And then we all make sense, each for our own selves, and sometimes we talk about it, about what learning we may get out of that. And so trying to operate from that Model of learning and teaching has been . . . a real struggle for me here. Trying to avoid the pitfall of being the expert, while still understanding that people have a lot to know . . . a lot to learn! And try to provide some learning opportunity. (Fyre TC2:3)

I have been taught that Circle is a gift of Aboriginal culture. I am attempting to introduce the "gifts" of our Tradition in ways that would bring beauty and honour to the Ancestors. This has been, and necessarily must remain, a very large challenge. I reflect on this in my comments at one Visions Circle:

> I think the richest and most difficult part of the learning has been trying to apply the Model in a Non-Native environment. It has been a real struggle at times to try to do it in a respectful way, that would bring beauty and honor to the Tradition, as opposed to feeling like it was being treated badly, or inappropriately, or misused. And to really try to be firm in myself about what it means to use this Model respectfully in a White setting. (Fyre VC1:15)

Trickster reminds us that the undertaking is inherently paradoxical due to longstanding relations of appropriation. It is an ongoing struggle to balance the desire to share our gifts to inspire respect with the fear of having the offerings appropriated and stripped of spiritual intention by "well-meaning" Whites. I raise this concern in one Circle:

> I really struggle sometimes with feedback from members of the Native community who feel maybe sharing Native ways with Non-Native people is losing something. And I hear from other Native people that say, maybe sharing things of beauty from our culture will help people respect and share in our culture and learn from our culture. (Fyre TC3:23)

Free envisions Circle as bringing peace, acknowledging Ancestral use as a tool in conflict resolution:

> As a person with Native ancestry, I learned a lot the last few years, just how much our people have been silenced over the years. My ancestors and my relatives. I am envisioning Circle work, and the Circle process, as a way for our voices to be heard, for us to be able to find the courage,

and the safe place that we need to say the things that we have to say. I think it's important that we label our own oppressions; that we label our own needs. I see Circle work as being really important in that way. The time is not right to confront and say, HEY!, look what you did to my people. What is that going to solve? It doesn't solve anything, but puts more conflict out there. What I like to envision us doing as Native people, is using the Circle work and putting that forth as a gift. As a gift from our culture to help towards healing the Earth. We have tried it the white way for many years, according to my people. That's not working for us and we are saying, we have a gift here to try to put forward to initiate into mainstream a way of listening. A way of hearing and a way of really being able to act on the real needs, what people are saying. It's very difficult to claim ownership. But I think if we try as Native people, or people with Native ancestry, to put forward that this is a gift, and put it forward as a gift, that maybe we'll just get enough attention that the Circle will spread. And if the Circle spreads, so will the peace that it brings. (VC3:28)

Ownership is a contradictory claim in this era of postmodern diffusion. According to Said, "[T]he history of all cultures is the history of cultural borrowings.... [A]ppropriations, common experiences, and interdependencies of all kinds among different cultures . . . is a universal norm" (1993: 217). In contemporary times, writing about culture and cultural "exchange" involves thinking critically about structures of domination and multiple historical precedents of forcible appropriation. Throughout the history of cultural contact in every colonized location, "someone loses, someone gains" (Said 1993: 195). Trickster reminds us that the appropriation of Aboriginal gifts is an ongoing process. Arising from and embedded in teaching an Aboriginal process in a Western context is the history and current reality of appropriation of our cultural processes. How do we teach respect for Tradition to those who are still embedded in colonial consciousness and who have an ingrained practice of destroying what they fear? One White activist, Charlotte, expresses this relation eloquently. She links internalized domination with current educational models:

In order to teach people the power over system, from either side, to teach people to either be crushed by it or to dominate in it, you have to hurt them when they're young. The injury is part of the teaching. I think it's the heart of the teaching because you have to teach people to protect themselves. When they walk into a situation look around, if they can take control, take control. And if they can't, obey, grovel. That's the reaction that being hurt teaches. So this whole system that we live in, that is based on, like a ladder. You dominate those below you and you grovel to those above you. It requires that kind of education! You can see it around this place. You can see how much it's based on criticizing people, tearing them apart, making them feel small. Dividing them into bits and isolating bits of the person or isolating people from other

> people. It's based on that and it's not just some intellectual exercise. This is really deep! It's an addiction. It's a built in thing that education is supposed to hurt. (Charlotte VC2:26)

Recognizing domination as a "pain-full" educational foundation, she expresses the need for all people, including Whites, to heal from the continuous projection of power onto others. She theorizes that all of us need to become self-governing. This struggle will require models of education that focus on healing and self-knowledge.

> So when you're trying to experiment with Models like this which are intended to heal . . . when you start seriously trying to heal through education you are going to run into people for whom that's deeply disturbing. And who's first reaction will be to lash back. (3 second pause) We must recover education as a healing function in order for all of us to be self-governing. White people aren't self-governing either. We've learned so well to project everything. Like to project the important decisions on our lives to the experts and to project our leadership on to the leaders. And then to project everything we dislike about ourselves on to scapegoats, and then punish them for it. Project, project, project! Self-knowledge is just unheard of because we haven't been educated that way. So to recover education that's based on self-knowledge and healing is going to be a long, long struggle. But if we're going to become self-governing enough, all of us, in order to save the planet, we've got to do it! (5 second pause). (Charlotte VC2:26)

Trickster Teaches
Can Tradition Be "Adapted"
for Non-Native Use?

Recovering education based on healing and self-knowledge is an ongoing but necessary struggle. Aboriginal consensual Models offer many important avenues to challenge Eurocentric educational practices grounded in "power over." Teaching of this sort requires both learning and unlearning for all participants. Because I am using an Aboriginal method with non-Native participants, I have to become more and more adept at articulating "Circle rules." This learning is based on what has happened when I have failed to state specific rules at specific times. Other innovative educators express this as clarifying the "terms of engagement" (hooks 1988). hooks' description of her own experience resonates with mine: "For a time, I assumed that students would just get the hang of it, would see that I was trying to teach in a different way and accept without explanation. Often, that meant I explained after being criticized" (1988: 53). I have found, as have other "minority" scholars (i.e., Ng 1991), that students are much quicker to "criticize" than to inquire or clarify. The need of

Circle Works

students for clarification or justification of processes unfamiliar to them can be seen as Eurocentric intrusion into the sacredness of Circle. Circle Traditionally is taught primarily by example, sometimes combined with oral narration by Elders on "proper conduct." Most students are unaccustomed to learning by example and often do not recognize non-verbal cues. Only once they are told directly do they recognize the need to adjust their behaviour. Even then, they may be unwilling or unable to do so. I express this concern in Circles on CCI:

> I taught for quite a few years using [Circle] with Native students and never thought to be that clear about the instructions because people seemed to understand what was expected and once we sat in Circle people were on the same wavelength . . . . How to acculturate non-native people in Circle talk. It's been probably the largest struggle. (Fyre VC2:21)

> At first when I was doing Circle with Non-Native people . . . I was constantly shocked at how come Circle didn't seem right? How come people couldn't get it? How come people didn't know what to say? I've learned that it is a learned thing . . . it is something that people do need to be taught. I've become a lot more conscious of teaching Circle, not only to the White students, but to Native students that haven't had an opportunity to learn. To Black students who don't have this as part of their cultural understanding . . . . It is not something that people know, it's something they have to learn. And so to me that's been part of my learning . . . . Now I see how using it consistently over time, what it can do and what some of the limitations are, given who we all are in a Circle. (Fyre TC3:27)

In order for Circle to function as a teaching tool in a School setting, serious consideration must be given to the make-up of the Circle. Circle conducted in a cross-cultural context is very different from the healing gift it is in Aboriginal Community. In a School context, Circle involves much more information sharing—the expected norm of dominant Eurocentric pedagogies. We get to hear and share each other's opinions, occasionally feelings surface. In an Aboriginal context we would have much more heart. We use Circle for deepening, deepening to the bone the processes of healing.

> Like the onion skin, as you deepen in an Aboriginal Circle, and you've been around say, 5 or 6 times, what you get is a peeling away, peeling away, and peeling away, so that we're all finally in Circle together, towards the end, we all have cleared out everything and we're just there in our spiritual sense, or in our most closest to our heart sense. (Fyre VC3:31)

It is a critical realization to note that the Circle process In-Use in this Model is an *adaptation* of the spiritual/healing process used by shamans and Elders in

Aboriginal Communities. While efforts are made to articulate the Ancestral wisdom that guides this process, the differences as noticed by myself and as pointed out by Aboriginal participants need to be highlighted. One example will illustrate the simple yet complex transitional process that occurs when using Circle as a data collection technique. I began one Circle by saying:

> So I'm going to try to take a few notes while we talk. I always forget to. And so I'll take a few and then I'll forget. The last Circle I got home and I remembered that I had forgotten to take notes the whole time. (laughs) So let's see how it goes. My data collection has got its own set of problems using this method. (Fyre VC2:1)

Sarah, a Mi'kmaq Elder present, immediately spoke up to remind me and others present: "Jean, I was going to say, this is not the practice, taking notes . . . in a setting like this" (JA VC2:1). Another Aboriginal speaker later in the Circle reiterates her position:

> The only comment I wanted to make was that . . . it wasn't really emphasized that this is an adaptation of the Circle . . . . Like [Sarah] said, you usually don't write in the Circle, so that's one adaptation of the Circle that's been done in this Circle, because of the fact that it is part of research. (Jose VC2:24)

Is the adaptation of Traditional methods for use in the School context a problem in itself? In introducing Aboriginal ideas and processes in this context, I use material representations of energy to aid in enhancing the spiritual and experiential aspects of the process. The use of material energy forms is a Traditional practice, and using any Traditional forms in a context with non-Natives must be interrogated for potential appropriation. As Deloria points out: "The first wave of appropriation, therefore, was simply the symbolic costumes that non-Indians believed would place them closer to nature" (1994: 40). Local norms must be explored, or offense can be given. For example, using eagle feathers can be controversial. Mi'kmaq Elders teach that no one who has indulged in alcohol or who is on her "moon time" can touch the sacred feathers. Mi'kmaq participants present at Circle Talk on CCI raise these concerns:

> The rules aren't exactly the way the Native people's rules are for Circle . . . . Recognizing and acknowledging that we have more stringent rules of the Circle . . . . I haven't been to one Nation that hasn't mentioned that about women and asking them to stay on the outside of the Circle to support the Circle [when] they're on their cycle. (Jose VC2:24)

> I wasn't sure how you handle people, whether they've been drinking or using drugs, and then you're using sacred objects, because I know some people prefer that they stay off of alcohol and drugs for at least 4 days. (Ray VC2:25)

The specifics of Circle Traditions do vary according to teachings, and this does create a potential for confusion, especially for those new to the practices.

> In some ways they're universal teachings, but in other ways . . . there are variations that branch off. It is important to keep that in mind and be respectful of it . . . . I guess that's the only thing I wonder about is how it's addressed—all these things regarding alcohol and drugs or the moon time, and any other, I want to call it rules, but laws are better. (Ray VC2:25)

In adapting Circle to the School context, I emphasize aspects related to the teaching process and I use it primarily as a learning tool, rather than highlighting the spiritual or shamanic healing properties. I have also been taught that abstinence and other "laws" exist in Traditional forms of practice. These vary by tribe and geographic location and often are linked to women's and men's participation in different types of ceremonies, times and places. I rationalize that I am primarily using forms of Circle as a teaching tool, rather than implementing it as a healing practice. While there are healing effects, we are not primarily engaged in a shamanic healing ceremony. Requiring classroom participants to disclose their substance consumption over the last four days or for women to be required to sit outside the Circle on their "moon time" would be viewed in a School setting as unusual, if not "abusive" of students' rights to privacy. Having discussed these matters with several Elders, I have learned to see adaptation as a necessity to be engaged in very cautiously.

I believe that our Traditions need to be taught to others to assist in healing the Earth. Phil emphasizes the value of teaching Circle as a practice tool:

> I learned a great deal just from participating in Circle and seeing what I can and can't do when sharing with other people, and how that works or it doesn't work. How deep to take it and what kinds of things to say to promote the understanding of what's being done. Since that's happened I've been able to use it more on my own, to be able to use it and teach it as well, because I do think it's something that's been taught. (TC3:34)

While my intention is to use Talking Circle to teach and not specifically to teach Circle, it happens. I feel Trickster's energy begin to arise for me when non-Natives express a desire to use Circle to work within their own Communities. Blanche explores the theme of White acceptance of the gift of Circle:

> That's a great concept the Circle as a gift. If the white culture can accept the gift because, the white culture has dominated for so long . . . I'd feel personally prepared to accept it as a gift. It's a wonderful gift. But I know people that I work with and come in contact with would find that real difficult to accept. Circle is a process that people have to open up to.

> That's the real trick. To get people first to come, and then to get people to open up. It's been positive, very positive for me. Professionally and personally, so I can see it as a worthwhile process to pass on. (VC2:8)

Several White participants consider specific applications to their fields of interest. Blanche sees it as useful for work with the Deaf Community:

> I'm finding that Circles . . . give a safe arena for venting . . . . People speak from their heart. There's no disguise or no political agendas, it's all just real emotional information. So I'm hoping that this will be useful in my work with the Deaf community.
> We have to come to terms or accept the venting because there's been a lot of oppression in the Deaf community! The hearing people have to be responsible for that oppression. So the information that I'm learning in Circles and in the class is very helpful in terms of my work . . . . Circle is a way of working together, instead of trying to work things apart or separately. Building community and change and conscious-ness, and it all really fits with what has to happen with the Deaf community. (VC3:13)

Other examples will serve to illustrate the potential diversity of applications, one in business and one in counselling battered women:

> I hope to try to have some sort of a modified Circle of some sort in the team that I'm trying to build now. Hopefully the people will accept it the way that I have because I certainly think it's an opportunity to voice your frustrations and your feelings without being worried about someone else, like me, interrupting you and saying, well, this is the way it is. So, I think my biggest challenge will be to remain silent while we do it. But I think it's very valuable. Absolutely! (Cat VC3:28)

> Another thing I have been thinking a lot about this week is how, if it is appropriate, could I incorporate more of what I've learned about circle and healing into the Liberty group I am co-facilitating. I do not want to appropriate things from the Aboriginal culture and I am not sure if it is respectful to incorporate these healing techniques into my framework of practice. I am going to try to get the opportunity to talk to you about this. What I would like to do is have the Liberty group structured more like the circle time we have in class. We do check-in the Liberty group now, but it is time limited (i.e. say in a few words how you are feeling) and I feel this does not give the women an opportunity to address the issues they feel are relevant and necessary. (Lena Feb 21 93-j)

Some African Canadian participants also express an interest in adapting Circle to work in their Community:

> My reason for being here is to try to decide what I need to do to include more Black people, to allow them to incur the benefits that I have from this, to create a larger support network for myself, and to be able to draw on it, to feed the energy that I need in my own situation in my family and the community. (Cal CC2:31)

Unicorn wisely realizes that "sharing" Aboriginal gifts has not always been respectful:

> I would like to be one of the people that when the Native people share their Circle with the Black community, one of the people that would be on the sideline to ensure that it's being used with respect, and when it's introduced, that it's adapted in a way that, in my terms I always say people tend to rape what we share from our culture, and I would like to be one of the vocal people that would work with others to try to not have that happen. So we would form more bonds and a better relationship. (VC2:8)

I find myself issuing a warning to zealous new recruits who want to run out and apply to other contexts what little they have learned. I strongly encourage further consultation with me or another Traditionalist who has used Circle in different contexts:

> It's really important when you're thinking forward to Circle work, that you talk with somebody who's done quite a bit of Circle work. Just in terms of talking about the kinds of issues you might be approaching with it, the kinds of things that might come up, because it's really important to set the right stage for Circle work, and it's really important that people are informed in an appropriate way about how to use it . . . especially if you're moving into a highly conflictual topic area, it's best to have the ground laid prior to engaging in Circle work. If you do a Circle process, even if it's modified, and I did talk in advance with you about the ways to modify it, given various circumstances, it would be really good to have a follow up conversation to discuss how it went and here's what was learned from it, before moving on to other locations. (Fyre VC3:29)

As this text intends to document, Circle work does have its complexities, in spite of the appearance of simplicity. Trickster is always ready to teach the unwary that there are always multiple and competing realities. While the physical form of Circle work may be easily comprehended, the spiritual and other dimensions are not. I attempt to articulate this in one Circle:

> Everything I ever learned about Native culture, whether I learned it as a child or as an adult, was always really deceptively simple on the surface. When I first learned it, it was: Oh!, this is so easy. How come

everybody doesn't know how to do this? But then as I've explored it more and took the gift on and then tried to use it and learn from it, then I found I learned many, many lessons from it. And not all of them painless. (laugh) To use it—be cautious and be clear in your own heart about what you want to put out. Especially moving into corporate arenas where people have learned competitiveness, they'd need quite a bit of instruction in Circle talk before they could begin. (Fyre VC3:29)

My warning ties into one Community member's expressed concern about the ingrained potential for appropriation of the Model by members of White culture:

When you introduce people from White culture into it you're dealing with such a deep old habit of control, tear apart, criticize, judge and I think it's fine at the first level, like when it's you or someone else who deeply understands the Model, guiding it, but what happens when they/ we take it and try to apply it. Like in the old habit that White people have of assuming it's an intellectual thing and it's just like a model, like a leggo model. This is neat so you just put it here without really deeply understanding it. (4 second pause) The question is: Are you or are all of us concerned about that happening? What do we do about that? I just don't feel it would be ok for me to take your Model and use it. It would be appropriation. And I understand that some White people with all goodwill appropriate because they don't understand that we do have some models of our own too.

It's very tempting just to borrow wholesale from North American Earth Based Tradition because it's much more recent. It's much more intact. It still exists in living memory, which ours does too to some extent, but not nearly to the same extent. So it's tempting just to borrow. But it's not right. And I don't even have a reason for saying that, it's just that it doesn't feel right. So that's just some questions about using Circle with White people. And with people of all races . . . who are not yet far enough along in healing from the North American/European Damage Education Model. Any Model we use will become a negative, a hurtful thing (Charlotte VC2:28).

Trickster has taught me and others that using the Circle in the School context has the potential to become a negative, hurtful thing. Sarah, an Aboriginal Elder, responds to Charlotte's words. She speaks out based on her experience of the Circle process when it had been used for a political forum within the School context.

It's so very real because we've had an experience here. Right here in the School. Where we did have Circle. We did have people not using in respect. Because when I see the Model being used by the dominant society . . . who will be the participants? I think, do these people really understand? I question it. Are they really truly sincere in trying to understand? . . . After the Circle was held . . . one of the teachers or administrators made the comment that she felt that the students were coerced into saying what they did say. And I was so hurt! I was really, really, hurt over that. And I felt maybe we shouldn't be doing this here. They don't understand. They don't understand. They shouldn't even be in the Circle . . . . This is something that belongs to our culture and I look at it with respect and so do all you people here. And I'd like the dominant society to learn from this. But I don't want them to exploit it or do damage to it, or make fun of it. That's my biggest fear. (4 second pause.) (Sarah VC2:28)

What specifically concerned the Elder was the backlash received by Aboriginal participants who did heartfully speak out in that Circle. Their acculturation to Circle norms and their lived experiences of racial harassment produced clear and compelling narratives. These stories, heard by ears open to the "accusations" but closed to the "lessons," continue to impact on all our lives. Circle is supposed to bring community healing through shared voice and experience. For this to happen, the talk has to be framed in a healing way. A balance must be struck between the pains of our oppressive experiences and the rich gifts of our heritage of resistance and activism. Creating movement with the collective energy of our shared insights is possible. When not all members of the Circle are acculturated to Circle norms about the type of speaking, or if some members hold power over others and are acculturated and known to enact it, risks are magnified. Care must be taken to avoid placing speakers in vulnerable positions by sharing too "personal" information. Some desire our silence. Some are shocked and afraid of the stories of pain and resistance. Some project their fear as our negativity. Beware of listeners who are acculturated to using "personal" information as data to maintain the institutional status quo. Trickster teaches us that the power of voice in Circle Talk can be used against the "heart-full," "truth-full" speaker. This experience challenges me to be cautious in using Talking Circle as a forum for taking up community issues in non-Native settings.

Several forms of appropriation of Aboriginal gifts are possible given the context. The most challenging concern is the adaptation of Circle process by non-Native users with little or no cultural sensitivity. This remains a real possibility and, knowing the power of Circle, it will undoubtedly produce many Trickster tales for those who attempt its use. Circle has other contradictory elements built into the process itself, a topic to which I now turn.

Trickster Teaches
Can "Silencing" Be a Tool
for Teaching Empowerment?
Given that Circle is a tool that empowers speakers to voice their stories, it is paradoxical that the process itself provides much more opportunity for listening than speaking. Is teaching silence, named

by some as "silencing," contrary to a pedagogy that emphasizes experience, voice and egalitarian relations? To value silence and listening challenges the "commonsense" overvaluation of speaking in School settings. Cultural conditioning for domination rewards speaking and devalues listening. Posing specific questions, which then have concrete answers that can be supplied by the teacher, is the expected norm in Western educational endeavors. This impacts on people's openness to the Circle process.

I acknowledge, overtly and positively, the necessary relationship of silence to voice. I embrace the gift of silence—respectfully listening—as a form of teaching balance, as a relationship-building tool itself. I recognize silence is often arrived at contradictorily. As some participants express in their opening phrases, silence can be spontaneously experienced in Circle: "Suddenly I've blanked out everything I was going to say, I've been listening to everybody and every time there's something more that I wanted to talk about" (Vada TC2:16). Bea expresses it this way: "The interesting thing I find about Circle, is that when you really do listen, when it comes to be your turn to talk, I have nothing in my head. It's like I haven't prepared anything" (VC1:22). "Nothing in my head" is not necessarily a problem when the focus is on speaking from the heart. Some participants do learn reverence for listening. One White participant reflects on this process:

> The first time I attended the session which was specifically about the Circle concept, I found it very difficult to shut up, to finally listen to what other people had to say. Even at the beginning of this Circle I thought, it would be a lot more productive if we were allowed to ask questions . . . . But in listening as we went around, I realized that not only does it offer you an opportunity to talk about what you have on your mind when the feather does come, but also as people are talking, you're constantly thinking about different things. Specifically about yourself and how you feel about different issues. And I think it raises your conscious level as to what you're actually all about. (Cat VC3:22)

Through silence, many participants realize heightened consciousness, "a clearer picture," but the issue of "silencing" retains its negativity. I reflect on the contradiction inherent when processes designed to allow voice also serve to silence some:

> A controversial part of the model is embedded in the first voice expectation, particularly as it is reinforced in Circle Talk . . . you have to have the experience or live the experience to talk about it, you're not supposed to talk about other people's experiences, you're supposed to talk about your own. But when people, particularly White students, begin to speak, they realize that they have very little number of things they can actually speak about with any insight! Sometimes that makes them silent completely! So instead of sharing what little they do know,

> or sharing their lack of insight, or sharing their fear, or sharing their hurt about not knowing, or sharing their feeling of stupidity, or whatever it is that's happening, instead of sharing whatever is on their heart, they feel overwhelmed by it and don't want to. (Fyre TC3:25)

Vada expresses her feelings of being silenced through lack of validation of her particular cultural background:

> I did not speak about my feelings as much as I quietly thought about them. This was partly caused by [the fact] that I wanted to spend my time learning more from others, and by my feeling that my experience of immigrating and my cultural background were not understood and validated. (Apr 4 93-jsum)

Vada revisits the topic in Circles on CCI. She gives a more detailed account of how her internalized comparisons with other speakers interferes with articulation of her own voice:

> I don't like to talk myself. I like to listen. Talking Circle was important because I could listen to people. I usually don't say too much because I felt that those things that I have experienced weren't that important compared to much of the other things that came out. And I was trying to figure out and compare them, the more, the very traumatic experiences, they came out through the Circle, compared to mine, that mine didn't seem that bad any more .... That was one of the other things that maybe hold other people back too. (Vada TC2:37)

Vada recognizes the value of her Trickster lesson. Her internal "silencer" simultaneously allows her to listen and gain empathy with others who have experienced a lifetime of silencing:

> It was very valuable for both me, and other people that are White, to have to listen. Even though I felt sometimes that I couldn't speak, even though I wish maybe I had spoken, it also gave me a lesson at the same time. I felt many times that I was put through the same situation that Black and Natives have been experiencing. That, this is how it must feel. Even though I knew that I could never totally understand. But it gave me the place and the feelings that went through my body, listening to many of the things, I think, it was good that I had to, that I was forced to sit down and listen. It gave me a clearer picture of how it actually is. (Vada TC2:37)

Learning from the Trickster

Trickster Teaches
Silencing the Teacher

Although as an Aboriginal Community member I have been acculturated to listen respectfully to other's stories in Circle, I found at times a contradictory relationship to silence in the role of teacher.

Sometimes when you're trying to use Circle in class and not everybody is really committed to the concept, or the philosophy behind it, sometimes things start being said that are really difficult. Because, with Circle the rules are always in effect, even as the teacher you can't interrupt. (Fyre VC2:21)

When sitting in Circle, I also do not have the right, as I would in other educational processes, to respond after each student to question, process or reframe their response to meet the learning task. This in itself has contradictory aspects. It is a teacher's privilege, and often students' expectation, that I use the "after remark" to acculturate students to the classroom norms. By validating some, by cutting off or negating others, we "teach" what is considered valid classroom discourse. Trickster asks: Could the limited opportunity for teacher response be hampering efforts to acculturate unfamiliar students to appropriate Circle Talk? Perhaps, if I took up the practice of responding to each speaker with this intent, students would adjust to Circle Talk more rapidly. More likely the whole process would break down or lose its integrity. I discuss this dilemma in Circle Talk on CCI:

> Sometimes when I'm sitting in Circle in my class and people are saying things . . . a judgment or some racism that needs to be confronted . . . I don't know if I should intervene and cut this off or let it be said . . . . I've found with using Circle consistently, the speaker who says it . . . . if not right in that moment, recognizes by seeing the reaction of everybody else in Circle, by the tension created by making the remark in a group of 20 people, at least a few of them that recognize that it wasn't quite on. And how that shifts the speaker in itself, without any active facilitation. The Circle tends to facilitate itself. (Fyre VC2:21)

Unicorn's entry illustrates how her peers' level of sensitivity to "remarks" is made visible to her in Circle:

> She really put her foot in her mouth. I'm positive she embarrassed whomever invited her. A true case of saying something just to say something. She thought she had something to offer yet she showed her ignorance—I'm not even sure she knew. I did take comfort in the fact that the non-verbal of most students displayed their new awareness. We were in circle and could not say anything until our turn. (Nov 10 93-j)

Circle Works

Silence in the Circle does function in its own way. Use of this process reinforces to me that it takes time, patience and perseverance to teach in Traditional ways. I strive to acknowledge and interrogate my own internalized acculturation whenever I contemplate direct intervention, and resist the impulse. I choose instead to remain true to Traditional forms, using stories, example and reframing to guide the Circle process.

> If you stick to the rule, speaking from your own heart about your own self, you have to break the rules of Circle to get to the place of condemnation . . . . People do become more acculturated to Circle and to talking in that way after a routine period. At first there may be real glitches in how people speak and sometimes people are offended, but it is very hard for people to be condemning people in the same way, when they have to sit in Circle with them and have to put their own hearts out and speak about what their own issues are. (Fyre TC4:43)

If someone has been acculturated to use voice as a tool of "power over," Circle has its own Medicine.

> The rules of Circle do also work . . . where you have a dominant member who is maybe not operating at the same level who needs to learn to listen to others and who needs to learn to speak from his/her own heart, as opposed to projection. (Fyre TC4:43)

Trickster teaches that we all get the lessons we each need from Traditional teachings. Silence or Voice: both are necessary to meaningful communication. Both are ultimately unrepresented in everyday conversations.

The Western Door

Time . . . Industrial clock Time
Governs mentality
Time's up . . . Sorry, have to cut you off
Not enough Time . . . turn it in on Time.
"People need Time" to adjust
To accept Change.
Don't rush the Council the Elders tell.
Time . . . Now a commodity
To be spent or wasted.
Circle as Pedagogy is a Flow
Patiently move through and with.

Be Aware
Learning environments are Contested Terrain

Learning from the Trickster

A field of competing energy forms
One site of the larger struggle for cultural space.
Some do not feel Comfortable and Suppress in class.
Express later in the lounge.
Passive Resistance . . . Projection.
Some target others who "instigate" stressful Feelings.
Fear of the new . . .
Fear of their own inner turmoil.
Fear of being Labelled . . . Judged
Blamed . . . Uncomfortable.

How can their Resistance be Reframed?
Some are not embedded in the daily "problems."
Surrounded by their Privilege.
Can Whites be expected to be seriously invested
In challenging White Domination?
Unsupported by peers, family or community
Many can afford to remain Uncommitted.

Encouraging consciousness-raising through encounters with others from different cultural locations is complicated by the reality that our ability to understand others is mediated by comfort.

> We humans are most uncomfortable when confronted with differing values and practices from those [with which] we were shaped. As a result, we tend to resist any force which interrupts or challenges our own well-established behaviours or patterns of thinking. (Forbes 1979: 146)

Trickster Teaches
Can Community Be Built across Diversity?
Trickster has shown that it is essential to acknowledge that not all students are appreciative of all aspects of the process. Some do not feel embraced by the Circle process or other community-building efforts in the classroom. I recognize that the competing and contrary energy contained in a diverse classroom context has definite impacts on trying to build community in the classroom. In essentializing the difficulties, I dichotomize the participants into two different groups of consumers:

> There are two different camps in my classroom work: those people who have the experience and have been silenced, who are from the various groups and haven't learned to value their culture and have learned to

be marginalized and have learned to be oppressed, and they have the weight of oppression. They've learned a whole bunch of lessons in that. Then there are a whole, large group of people who have learned the exact opposite. They've learned to ignore oppression. They've learned to take people's voice. They've learned to have the privilege of speaking whenever they wanted, or to feel safe when many people have never been safe. In my work, it's always trying to engage both of those groups. To encourage the Black, Acadian, Native, Asian, Gay voices to come forward and to articulate themselves while simultaneously encouraging those people who have been voice-full to listen respectfully, to get a different place of learning than just their own expert model. (Fyre VC3:29)

Within these groups, differences in experience and perception are expressed by participants. Not all members from the diverse Communities embrace the Model; not all from the privileged population resist it. Gender and class also play a large role in determining whose voice gets spoken and heard. While we may be present together in a current learning context, that relationship is informed by our past. As Said reveals:

Past and present inform each other each implies the other and . . . each co-exists with the other . . . . Neither past nor present . . . has a complete meaning alone . . . . [H]ow we formulate or represent the past shapes our understanding and views of the present. (1993: 4)

One participant from the African Canadian Community, Ela, expresses her lack of comfort with the process. She links it to cultural identity and context:

I had a lot of things to work out myself because of the experiences I had going through the entire education system. I don't think I would have been comfortable in any [educational] context . . . unless it was an absolutely total "Black" experience for me . . . . I did feel really anxious about doing Circle work. And I felt sometimes . . . called upon to speak sometimes maybe when I really didn't want to speak, but knew that it was important that I did speak. And so I had different mixed feelings about that. I sort of felt like being put on the spot at times. (Ela TC2:6)

Being "put on the spot" as First Voice is one difficulty encountered by this Black Community member. She continues on this theme later in her "speak-out":

I still find Circle difficult. It's not my favorite thing in the world to do. Some people will come into Circle Talk and be very relaxed within, it hasn't been my experience because it hasn't been part of my culture . . . . I suppose to some degree we might do this type of situation, but it would be in a different format within the Black community. The level of comfort when you're all coming from the same mind-set, as far as your cultural roots are concerned, then a particular format is a lot more comfortable for you because it's something that you can all relate to together. (Ela TC2:12)

Ela reflects a Traditional view when she proposes that "people need time":

I think it's a good process and people need time to get used to it and to relate to it. Changing a particular format is not always easy for those who are going through the process and those who are trying to put that process in place. (Ela TC2:12)

Failing to address Gays and Lesbians as an integral part of the curriculum promotes feelings of exclusion from the process for Gay and Lesbian students. Homophobia remains unchallenged. Kate speaks out:

When I would speak up in cross-cultural last year, and share experiences that I have had with homophobia and heterosexism, I felt like, sometimes, people were [thinking] . . . we're here to deal with racism, just be quiet. I was trying to make links. I was trying to share my experience, trying to have a voice. I think that if [the course] were a year, that kind of silencing wouldn't happen. Sometimes that was my own internal homophobia silencing happening, but sometimes people made comments or I felt the mood in the room of some people was very tense, and impatient . . . . [C]an't you just be quiet about this? I really felt like a lot of the students in the class were just rolling their eyes whenever I talked about heterosexism, and to a certain extent about sexism. I was doing that in the context of making links. Trying to figure out my own privilege and oppression and means of resistance . . . . (TC1:3)

Through this student's direct challenge of the curriculum, I am able to see the impact that the exclusion of Gay and Lesbian issues has on members' First Voice from that cultural Community. I address her and the issue directly in Circles on CCI:

I realized in working with you, working through that with you, and watching you locked into that, and seeing that happen in class, was a really good lesson for me about having it overtly on the agenda, and really making a place for it in the curriculum, because it needs to be there! . . . It really motivated me to do something different then . . . . (Fyre TC1:4)

Kate's voice and experience provides a Trickster tale about being excluded from an inclusive Model. Gay and Lesbian content has now been included in the curriculum—the readings, the course outline and the course progression. Members of the Gay and Lesbian Community are encouraged to emphasize the gifts of their Community as well as to express the pains of homophobia. Classes that have looked at Gay and Lesbian issues across the cultures have been an excellent illustration of diversity and unity within a given Community. I acknowledge the impact of Kate's First Voice in the changing curriculum.

Trickster Teaches
Does Sharing Feelings
Build Community in the Classroom?
The challenge of embracing many different cultural groups is one level of contradictory energy. The content itself poses many barriers to building positive community relations in the classroom. Interrogating ourselves and our families about racism produces many complex emotions, including anger and guilt. These, when expressed outwardly, are considered "negative" emotions. When repressed, they can become internalized and directed at self and one's own cultural group. They can also become externalized and projected onto others.

I am learning that challenging people's worldviews can be an "uncomfortable" experience for all involved. This often needs to be contextualized so that people do not feel alone in their own process. Along with feelings that arise based on our personal histories and struggles, anxiety, insecurity and disorientation can also result from "sociocultural dissonance." This term is defined by Brown (1990) and Chau (1989) as the stress, strain and incongruence caused by having to adjust to competing cultural demands. Dissonance is certainly an integral aspect of teaching Aboriginal and anti-racist methods in Eurocentric institutional settings.

One example of the dissonance produced is illustrated in Mac's self-reflection. It is clear in this entry how deeply challenging the emotional aspect of the learning can be. These processes can shake the foundations of a Western worldview and can result in internalization at a very personal level for some.

> I can't believe that I got so emotional in class the other day. But at that point it just came out. I don't know if it was more anger or frustration. I felt like I have been in the dark for twenty eight years. I knew about the things that happened to the First Nations but this was the first time I really felt it. That is the problem. It is too easy to turn away. To forget. I feel like I am starting over again. From the beginning. Questioning every assumption. Questioning what it means to have your history erased, your culture destroyed, your life blunted. I want to learn more, come face to face, but it is like I don't feel that I have the right . . . . I'm going through a real existential angst. Not the meaning of life again. I mean that I am desperately seeking my own place in all of these issues. My values used to be like bedrock. Now they are like sand dunes. I feel vulnerable but I feel open. I sometimes feel defensive.
>
> I have to sieve through what I feel and think. Suspend judgements.

Learning from the Trickster

To be totally open.
To be with the moment.
Things are. (Mac 92-j)

Lather (1991) offers tools to use with students to view the process of transformation with them and their reaction to it. I am learning that helping students name the process, the alteration of consciousness, including an articulation of the possible feelings generated, can be useful in many ways. To share information is to share power. Participants need to know that a wide range of feelings is "normal." This includes embracing and reframing "resistance" as a "healthy" and expected reaction. Providing an opportunity to reflect on the experience as it unfolds and to understand it from a critical perspective can reduce anxiety and resistance to the process.

Trickster Teaches
How Can "Negative" Feelings Be Positive?

The power of anger and the use of anger in the classroom are discussed by Culley as the "energy mediating the transformation from damage to wholeness" (1985: 211). She theorizes that as the person passes from denial to anger, the journey to affirmation and change becomes possible. "Only when our anger has been felt and acknowledged, not denied, when it has been demonstrated to be grounded in a personal and collective sense of worth and not their opposite, can we hope that our students will join us in the remaining work to be done . . ." (Culley 1985: 216).

Anger is an often expressed emotion. Anger is frequently part of the stories told by First Voice participants as re-living oppression and exclusion re-produces the feelings. Many speakers are very direct about how the everyday nature of systematic racism produces "multigenerational" anger, which needs to be released somewhere. Releasing anger is a form of healing, as many times loss and anger have been turned inward. As Charnley (1990) tells us, because of the pervasiveness of the dominant belief system, it is hard to make out who is "the enemy." Often there is no target at which to aim our very reasonable and natural anger. The dilemma is found in Maracle's poem "Hate": "Blinded by niceties and polite liberality we can't see our enemy, so we'll just have to kill each other" (1988: 12). We have learned that when an external target is made visible to the victim, the release of anger and "bitterness" will produce a healing effect. Self-blame can be reframed and redirected as resistance to oppressive forces.

Because most people are unused to embracing anger as a healthy emotion that needs expression, anger is repressed, misdirected and displaced. In this Model-In-Use, emotional discharge is expected and planned for in the process.

Circle Talk is a process that gives opportunity for voicing strong feelings while restricting opportunities for direct confrontation or targeting of others to occur. This process is complex in working with oppressed individuals, and even more so when working with members of the dominant culture. Many students are uncomfortable with direct expressions of what they have been acculturated to understand are "negative" feelings. Students respond at times by blocking or resisting hearing these stories/emotions expressed and wish to continue the safety of denial. Some have their own emotions stirred by the stories and by the process, and anger is co-produced along with guilt.

Guilt is a commonly expressed feeling of students at various points in the learning process. It can contribute to the desire to change, but it can also create and sustain defensiveness and promote resistance to the overall process. One White male clearly represents this as his reaction early in the course:

> In circle tonight those of us who are white tended to express feelings of guilt for having white privilege. I was glad to hear these white female students express feelings of guilt, because as a result I did not feel as alone with my feelings of guilt. However my feelings of guilt, which seem to be increasing on a weekly basis, are based not only on my white privileges, but also on my privileges associated with my gender, sexual orientation, age, and class. I just hope I will be able to do something constructive with my feelings of guilt, instead of just feeling guilty. (Ken Jan 26 93-j)

Privileged students are faced with challenging something that they have internalized as part of themselves and from which they have benefited. This can result in complex forms of projection and denial and the "fixing" of one's "negative" emotions on others. As Culley notes, "[A]nger felt by students in the classroom often fixes itself upon inappropriate objects, particularly upon other students" (1985: 213). One way of coping with the anger, guilt and "self-hate" engendered by uncovering the parameters of our own racist culture is to direct these feelings towards others. Rather than exhibiting an increase in racial tolerance, some students react by further targeting as the "problem" those who have voiced their experience. Trickster has taught me that sometimes student's anger is projected upon me as the instigator of the stressful learning experience. Culley expresses a similar insight regarding feminist pedagogy: "If she initiates a process challenging the world-view and the view of self of her students, she will surely—if she is doing her job—become the object of some students' unexamined anger" (1985: 213). This reality is conflated by issues of race and gender. Ng (1991, 1994), James (1994) and many others share stories of how this has happened to them as "minority" teachers, particularly when challenging the belief systems of privileged students.

Trickster Teaches
How Can Students' Resistance Be Reframed?

In my classrooms, resistance is a continuous dynamic unfolding in multiple variations. It is a theme that I occasionally address directly in the classroom. Not surprisingly, it is mostly absent in the journals, which are originally submitted for grade, but it was reflected on at the Circles on CCI. Most often the forms of "passive" resistance enacted by students towards the Model are similar to common patterns of resistance to dominant practices. Resistance is talked about a lot in Aboriginal and African Communities. Mostly it is

> behind the scenes, behind closed doors, and usually in a humorous manner . . . people don't usually sit down and talk about it in an analytical way, but it's understood, because without having to say it, as to why it occurs and to why it's necessary and why it will continue to be necessary. (Ela TC:10)

Resistance has earlier been theorized as universal and as existing in an ongoing and complex relationship with authority. Resistance can be described as a continuous process visible to and impacting on many, but mostly unacknowledged in any direct way. Regardless of efforts to engage in egalitarian processes, a teacher cannot be relieved of the authority embedded in the context. Both the context itself and the Model as enacted within the context catalyzed resistance from students. Trickster reveals a paradox. Sharing Aboriginal Tradition across cultural groups, particularly in the hierarchical School context, while an act of resistance to dominant forms of education, produces resistance from those who do not feel "empowered" by processes unfamiliar to them. This resistance impacts on the efforts enacted by me in this Model to challenge and resist the dominant and dominating structures. I articulate my understanding of resistance as a foundation of this teaching project:

> [This Model is] really an act of resistance. Resistance to the dominant forms of teaching and learning. There's got to be a lot different experience[s] of Circle and a lot different understanding[s] of Circle for people who are just coming to it, than for me. I'm looking at Circle when it's happening here and when I'm doing it in class; I've got a whole long history of Circle behind what I'm seeing and what I'm hearing when I'm using Circle . . . I'm hoping that people can share with me what their experiences have been with that . . . . It's competing and contrary energy going on there. Trying to use Aboriginal methods, which are very much about being open and receptive and comfortable in our learning, and being ready to accept this on our journey, [in] a classroom, which is very set in terms of the ways of learning and the expectations. (Fyre TC2:3)

Resistance by students to the process or the content can be reframed as a healthy reaction. Kea, a respondent in Lather's research on feminist pedagogy, defines it as "a word for the fear, dislike, hesitance most people have about turning their entire lives upside down and watching everything they have ever learned disintegrate into lies" (1990: 142). As she tells it, "'[E]mpowerment' may be liberating, but it is also a lot of hard work and new responsibility to sort through one's life and rebuild according to one's own values and choices" (in Lather 1990: 142). Trickster has taught me that not everyone is prepared to undertake this "life work," and many innately resist that which will move them in this direction.

Participants reinforce the link between resistance and feelings of discomfort with the process. While First Voice, Talking Circle and storytelling can empower "minority" voices, it can be a different experience for some privileged students. The level of affect in the classroom is addressed as a central contribution to resistance. Expression of feelings in a heartfelt manner is "expected" in the Circle process and mandated by First Voice pedagogy, but it is not common in Eurocentric learning models. The processes In-Use emphasize depth of feeling and this produces a contradictory response from students unacculturated to such an experience. I have realized that while emotional expression is structured as part of the Model, some people are "uncomfortable" with heartfelt expression. Tradition dictates that "in Circle if you don't want to share your feelings, don't start doing it if you don't have the heart for it. But people have to at least be able to absorb others' feelings" (Fyre TC3:25). One form resistance takes is the deflection of feelings being expressed in Circle.

> One of the things that happens is that people sit in Circle and deflect the feelings . . . . [B]ecause they've spent all that time barriering and deflecting they only get to their own feelings after the fact. And so they find themselves at home or they find themselves in the student lounge or they find themselves outside of the Circle and outside of the class, then sharing their feelings. Part of that is because they're blocking and deflecting because they don't want to have feelings in class. They don't want to relate to it. They don't want to have to know that. (Fyre TC3:25)

Phil, a student from the Native Community, expresses her understanding of how students' general lack of acculturation to the feeling content generated by the process led them to express their feelings about the class outside of the classroom context:

> With every Circle that we had, afterwards, in other parts of the school, you would hear all these things that never got brought up in Circle. You would hear different perceptions and . . . people's ideas about what Circle was like and what was happening. And . . . you would hear all these things that no one would ever bring up . . . but be talking, like, two or three students in the lounge . . . and you would overhear conversa-

tion . . . . Bringing the feeling content to the class and how doing anything in Circle forms brings out emotions and makes people feel safety in talking and relating things from an experience of your own . . . . A story about your own experience brings up so many things for other people. But there are no other classes in the School that really deal with things on a feeling basis. And if feelings do come up in class it's always from an analytical point of view about why people feel this way and how can you make people feel differently . . . . It's never actually just having the feelings and how you feel about feeling this way and coping with, that kind of thing. (TC3:14)

Ela expresses her surprise at finding out the level of controversy that was going on behind the scenes. She feels that fear is playing a big role.

I was a little surprised at some of the feelings and things that were going on behind the scenes but weren't coming out in Circle. And a lot of it was anxiety. And a lot of it was fear. One of the biggest things was that students felt that they had nothing to contribute, because they weren't speaking from First Voice. The emphasis on First Voice really terrified them. And they felt that they couldn't speak about experiences with racism or anything . . . . It would have been nice to have heard some of those things a little bit earlier on when we were actually involved in the process, instead of at the very end of it . . . . Authority and resistance, it really entered context . . . . It was unfortunate that people couldn't talk about that type of resistance that they were embarking in behind the scenes among themselves and spreading throughout the School. That they couldn't have talked about those particular feelings that they had within Circle. (Ela TC2:11)

Guilt is analyzed by Ela as a contributor to resistance:

I think students also felt that they were being put on the spot with all their guilt and their defensiveness, and were blaming themselves and projecting that onto other people. (TC2:11)

People [were] talking about the issue behind the scenes with their colleagues and stuff because they all feel guilty, so they try to find somebody else outside the class who thinks the same way that they do so that they can feel justified in the guilt! . . . I think some people . . . go through the whole course and block out much of the learning, unfortunately because of the guilt, which leads to defensiveness. What you see as a manifestation of that guilt, is defensiveness. (TC4:16)

Trickster Teaches
Can Whites Be Invested
in Challenging Hegemony?
Later in Circle Hattie proposes another interpretation of the interconnectedness of personal comfort
and the resistance of other students. She links it to
how the Model-In-Use challenges the cultural hegemony to which Whites are accustomed.

> ... White people feel very out of control when they're not in charge. And that's the kind of emotions that I sense from the course: is that they're not in control now, the different cultures are allowed to present their self, their thoughts, what they feel, express their cultures with respect and honor ... that they are too important being here .... (Hattie TC2:20)

Having mandatory equity courses in every program is seen as desirable by some but also contributes to levels of resistance:

> And some of the things that I looked at in the Circle is that people were there because they had to take the course. It was required. Some, I felt, were willing to learn and were really caring, but others were there because they had to be. So they would do what they had to do and get out. I looked at it, I'll never be able to do what I have to do and get out of my race. I'll always have to live that. I'll always endure pain because I'm a mother, because I'm a grandmother, and because I'm a woman. (Hattie TC2:20)

The struggle to gain and maintain an identity not rooted in Eurocentric acceptance is "life work" for members of visibly racial Communities. As Cal suggests, this is a reality little understood by those immersed in White privilege:

> However the real issue here right now is the point that whites have not been prepared to do the work to understand the lies or the distortions that they have been fed for most of their lives at a personal level or a structural level. I am also disappointed because unless it is understood at a personal level I don't think that it could be possibly understood from a perspective of racialism. I have spent about 25 years working on this and trying to understand these issues and I am not sure that most whites are prepared to undergo this type of intense self reflection not for as long a period of time. The most profound point is that I have just begun to scratch the tip of the iceberg as far as my own awakening is concerned. This like many struggles requires lots of focused work. (94-j)

Can Whites be expected to be seriously invested in challenging internalized and external forms of White domination? Cindy feels the level of commitment for participants from different cultural locations can be analyzed by noting the composition of "voluntary" Circles for Circle Talk on CCI:

> In the class the atmosphere is mostly good, but after the class when I have another kind of relationship with them, then I can hear a culture of resistance to what we are learning in the class. So when I came to the Talking Circle last time, and this time, one thing that came into my mind is, OK!, when the Talking Circle is not required, it is not for mark, what is the composition of the Talking Circle? Just like today, I can see the same things happen . . . not too many white classmates will come. I really regard this as a kind of resistance. (TC2:33)

Resistance is expressed by physical or emotional absence from the process. Cindy also makes the link between identity, privilege and depth of feelings stirred and shared in the classroom:

> And I find that during the class what they share with me . . . as compared to other minority or immigrants, when we shared a story, it really sticks in our hearts, but for them, sometimes, I feel, it's a bit superficial. Though I appreciate that they are aware of the Whites' domination. But what they would talk about is . . . whether the pampers have the face of the Black people? What's wrong after they leave the classroom? Does nothing push them to understand the White privilege? And they can go back to their own shell and they're not required to do anything. (TC2:33)

Trickster reveals that White participants are not encouraged by peers, family or their community around them to engage in reflective action on racial issues. This means that many can afford to remain uncommitted to processes designed to challenge their supremacy. I continue to interrogate my role as guide. I wonder what I contribute to producing resistance. I re-emphasize the part that culture and context play in our understanding of behaviour:

> Somehow when I hear students complain, particularly White students, complain about how they didn't get to say everything they wanted to say and how they didn't really get to share all the feelings that they had, and how they had to feel that they had to go and talk outside of class, or they chose to go and talk outside of class; and in one way I feel, well, maybe I should be doing something different, maybe I should be acting different, maybe I should be making more effort to embrace them in this process and how I'm teaching this process. (Fyre TC2:23)

My Elders teach that we can offer a learning opportunity but it is up to the learner to take responsibility for the lessons that apply to him or her. Trickster teaches that if I take responsibility for participants' feelings and acts of resistance, this solidifies them as "personal." This detracts from learning to interrogate them as manifestations of structural reality. I am learning to reframe resistance as part of the whole experience.

> I do really see that whole thing about talking outside of class .... Sitting on a pile of something that's going on in your body, and not putting it out—as an act of resistance. Like the Native people resisted hundreds of years of colonization through silence! Through just keeping it to yourself. To me, if students are wanting to keep it to themselves, if they embody that as their act of resistance, I'd really like to work at that in terms of at least having them acknowledge it as resistance. Instead of them just being passively doing it and thinking that they're hiding it or it's not visible, because to me when that's happening in Circle, it is visible. (Fyre TC2:23)

Resistance is visible in embodied cues of eye-rolling, defensive posturing and "superficial" contributions to Circle. What is "invisible" but detectable to experienced Circle practitioners is the difference between the feeling of doing Circle when the group understands and practices the values in the Traditional way and the energy produced when participants in the Circle are resisting the process.

> When you're doing Circle in a Traditional way you get a feeling that people are moving in around you, that they're closing in and they're supporting you in your story, and you get the feeling of community support for your story and a support for that. Even though the story . . . has negative things or hard things, that is Circle talk. We share from our depth of experience. In Traditional ways when we are able to do that and we are able to see that our community supports us, even in that position of weakness, even in that position of pain, then this intensifies our feeling of being together. But when people react this way from our pain, when people move back from our stories, when they don't want to hear them, or see the pain or react to it, then that can have an opposite effect. We feel our story is making people move away from us, which is not really what we want. We want to share our pain in a way that people can comfort us and care for us. (Fyre TC3:25)

The resistance of students to absorbing and relating to people's pain is a major challenge to using Aboriginal pedagogies to produce community in the classroom. Caring and sharing are foundational values of any Circle work and the depth to which people are acculturated to feel is a cultural difference. It is really a struggle to get people to respond differently than they would customarily.

> You can set the Circle, you can bring the people there, you can do the smudge, you can do all the things that you would do to create that Circle environment as a safe place, as you would do in a Native setting, but you'll get an entirely different result .... The most fundamental

difference is the ability to go in and the sense of responsibility of the sharing, that when I bring my pain out for you, when I tell my story to you, this is a gift . . . . My story is a gift to you . . . . When I cry about my experience, when I get to the point of having that heartfelt of a feeling, that it brings my tears out, that my tears are a gift to you! And this is a gift that builds community. Or when I tell a funny story and we all laugh about that story . . . we felt community in our laughing together. So pain is not the only way, or sorrow is not the only community felt feeling, but all of the feelings shared. If we could be open to them and send them out in to the Circle of caring together, then that's how Circle brings community. I do think a lot of times in trying to do Circle work here, there is that restriction of people really don't know their hearts. People haven't been able to connect to their hearts . . . . We're trained in so many ways to barrier ourselves from our feelings. (Fyre TC3:25)

A Speak-Out on Respect: A Trickster Tale

The resistance, expressed and veiled, embodied in the classroom context has had impacts on my experience of sharing feelings, experiences and stories and on my will to share the gifts of Aboriginal culture in this context and to non-Native peoples. I feel and have expressed this concern on several occasions throughout teaching courses and at Circle Talk on CCI:

Sometimes that's been really positive and I felt really good and powerful about using Circle that way. Other times I feel like . . . it really doesn't belong here . . . . And a couple of times there's been big conflicts in class because I've spoken about that, and said to people that I didn't like the way it was working and put that anger forward, and then people have had a backlash about that. (Fyre TC2:3)

Paradoxically, but true to the Trickster's form, when I target the resistance of students in a direct and honest way, anger, guilt and more resistance is often produced. The challenge is most frequently taken as imposition of authority of the "teacher," rather than the voice of the oppressed calling into question the tactics of the oppressor. In one class, I spoke out about what I perceived as students' lack of respect for the process. Their reactions serve to illustrate the complex relationship of authority and resistance in the classroom. These entries, when read together as descriptions of the same event, also illustrate a recurring theme: multiple interpretations of the "same" reality. Some students are able to recognize the structural dynamics that could lead to my speak-out in class. Others are more concerned that I might be expressing a "personal" reaction towards them or what they might have done:

I was not expecting to hear what was said in class tonight regarding the feelings surrounding the teaching of our class. I feel awful that these vibes were put out from my class. I did sense last week that things were feeling a bit scattered. I am very glad that this has been shared. It has raised my awareness of where I am in class and what exactly are the things I hope to gain from this experience. (Bejay Jan 20 93-j)

I feel terrible that you have been feeling so oppressed in this class. I can only imagine what it must be like for you to educate so many racist white people, and the energy coming from the students is not always positive. I hope that I didn't do anything to make it an awful experience for you. I am sort of glad that I am switching over because I feel like some of the white students take advantage of Circle and begin to talk about things that do not relate to the class. I feel guilty even writing these things but I really do feel that way sometimes. (Lena Feb 6 93-j)

Tonight Jean expressed her deep anger at the way this class is going. I felt shocked at the depth of her feeling about the lack of respect for her people's traditions, and general disrespect within the class.
It must have taken a huge amount of courage to do that and I certainly admire her for it. I also feel so *responsible* and guilty for whatever I have done that contributed to her pain. I feel scared now to say anything for fear of it being offensive.
I feel like an oppressor tonight—in a major way. Not a nice feeling. (Char Feb 3 93-j)

Sharing my feelings of being oppressed in the classroom is always an educational experience. Each time it has had multiple effects on students, many unintended.

During tonight's class Jean shared with us her feelings about this class so far via her journal. Jean was very open and honest in her feelings, which she stated are very similar to feelings associated with oppression. I commend anyone who has the guts to describe specifically when, where, and how they are oppressed. However I found Jean's style to be so open and honest that it left me feeling I was personally attacked. (Ken Feb 3 93-j)

Having my students feel "personally attacked" is certainly not an intended effect. Tia wrote an entry three days after my speak-out. She wanted to share with me the many feelings and emotions that arose: denial, anger and fear were acknowledged:

The first word to describe how I felt was *denial*. My immediate reaction was denial and that I could never be a part of a group or collective of people who could oppress another person. *Wrong!* When I look back at the size of the class itself and the fact that a majority of the people in the class are white and maintain a white culture, this is a form of oppression in and of itself. As a group we want to share and voice our experiences yet not being silent and learn/listen to other first person experiences. This act alone silences those who have so much to offer.

Another feeling I was experiencing was *anger*. I felt angry because I was being grouped with a bunch of people who were oppressing someone and we didn't even know it. This angers me the most, that I am so privileged that I couldn't even see/feel what was happening. I also felt angry because you thought enough of us as people to tell us how you were feeling, but all I could feel at the time was that I was at fault and being blamed for something I could not see or feel.

This is when I began to feel *scared* and afraid. Oppression is so deep and so interwoven that it has become a way of life. I am afraid because if you were feeling this way, others may also be feeling oppressed in a classroom with a majority of white students. I am also afraid that the words I voice may silence others and contribute to this damned oppressive society. I want to be part of change, not silencing people. (Tia 93j)

Tia concludes her entry recognizing the honesty and strength modeled when I heartfully shared my experience of oppression with them—the oppressors:

Finally, the word that stands out in mind is *strength*. It is not right that you have to explain you're being oppressed. Yet you shared this with a room full of strangers to assist in our awareness. You shouldn't have to explain anything. We should be able to see, feel what is happening in this classroom. I have a long way to go! But, I would like to thank you Jean for your honesty and strength in wanting [us] to know, see and feel what you were experiencing—*Awareness*. (TVM 93-j)

Awareness is definitely produced each time I use my own lived experience in the classroom to teach students how to "know, see and feel" oppression. As a tool of reversal, the teaching potential of these types of inside-out lessons is tremendous. I have also analyzed this experience as a breakdown of the consensual aspects of Circle work. According to Hart, consensual agreement is the outcome and the supporting structure of non-hierarchical relationships among the members of a group. Consensus is "a conscious, rational procedure orientated towards the creation of unity" (Hart 1985: 131). The contradiction arose because of the need to express criticism, which conflicted with "strong tendencies towards building harmonies, symbiotic relations" (Hart 1985: 131). I used Circle Talk, a pedagogy built on harmony and egalitarianism, to speak out as oppressed while in my role of teacher or oppressor. Trickster helps reveal that it was perceived by me and others as simultaneously an act of resistance to oppressive acts of privileged people and as an oppressive act. As Weedon reminds us, "[W]here existing power relations are under threat, initially consensual forms of discourse often employ coercion to govern the subjects in question should consent fail" (1987: 101). The issue of authority and resistance, and consensus and coercion, is definitely a contradictory one, especially when one envisions oneself as employing egalitarian methods. Balancing the power invested in the role of educator with the empowerment I seek for Aboriginal teachers, methods and students in this context is an ongoing struggle.

Trickster has taught me that working under the principle of voluntary cooperation as opposed to coercion is a constant challenge (Goodtracks 1973), especially when authority is structured into the educator's role and is a "commonsense" reality for most participants. As the teacher, how can I maintain the integrity of an egalitarian process in a hierarchical context? If our intentions as educators are to be inclusive and power-sharing, active attention must be given to the removal of barriers that may prevent community-building in the classroom. I continue to learn how I must interrogate my own role as teacher/ expert in maintaining the dominance already structured into the classroom setting. I agree with Hart and Holton, "[t]he teacher's consistent, respectful valuing of the differences existent in the classroom (be they cultural, social, racial or developmental differences) cannot be emphasized enough" (1993: 22).

The Northern Door

Backlash is In-Relation to Activism
Action Is Taken by Challenged Authorities.
Activism . . . Big or small has Risks.
Backlash is "personal assassination."
Failed . . . Fired.
Spiral into Hopelessness . . . Helplessness
Fear disempowers . . . deactivating Activism.

Be Aware of the larger political context
The institutional reality
"Freedom of speech" . . . "Political correctness"
"Academic freedom" . . . "Collegiality"
Code words for Hegemony . . . Supremacy.

Too few continuously Resist Acculturation
To the dominant forms of Authority and Knowledge
Present in Schools/Systems.
How do We sustain the struggling force?
Keep focus on the Politics behind the Personal attacks.
Remain part of the Struggle.
Support others as the way for Change.
Hold on to our Visions.

Anti-racism means "speaking out when we hear a stereotypic statement, when we feel excluded by what we are asked to accept as a reflection of our reality, and when we see the same old ruling-class models being presented as the norm" (Kalia 1991: 282). All anti-racist educators agree: racism needs to be challenged by the teacher and/or the students.

Trickster Teaches
Does Doing Activism Mean Being Done To?

Racism, paradoxically, is often not spoken about, even when directly visible. Racism in the School context in this decade has become "the R-word." I and others have been cautioned not to use it to describe discriminatory harassment or else credibility will be lost. Victims or activists naming racism are immediately called on to engage in a recounting of the explicit details of who offended whom. When it is left up to students, they are perceived as "having an attitude problem" (Carty 1991b: 36). Students, reprimanded for "intimidating" other students and told to be less "accusatory," are left wondering, like many who experience racial harassment, "Is it me, or is it them?" (Kalia 1991). Ng (1991) articulates parallels in our experience as teachers, as we are considered hostile and non-collegial for our efforts to directly challenge students and other faculty. Other forms of contextual backlash rely on a dispirited form of academic freedom and the legal defense of institutional reputation.

Backlash is often experienced as "personal" yet is decisively political. Kalia expresses what has become a commonsense reality for many struggling to survive within racist contexts.

> It is irrelevant, even if it could be proven, that all negative reactions I encounter are personal, not race related—what is relevant is that I am in the particular position of having to consider the possibility that how others treat me personally may be motivated by race politics. (1991: 281)

How we survive the very real challenge of backlash from our political efforts needs to be acknowledged as a critical issue. Backlash, Trickster has taught me, is an integral aspect of activism. Imperial authority and Aboriginal resistance have been theorized as In-Relation; so too are activism and backlash. Backlash is the action taken by the challenged authority. It occurs In-Relation to the resistance enacted.

If we recognize that we are In-Relation, we will notice that others around us react to a change in consciousness. They feel especially threatened if they believe that an attitude-change is being "forced" upon them. Inexperienced, yet inspired, students are quite often confrontational in style early on—feeling *all* should share their newfound insights. This can result in personal backlash within family, peer, teacher and workplace relations. Students' stories of family intervention illustrate the complexity of challenging racial "jokes" with those we love. Bejay tells the story of challenging her stepfather on the phone about his use of racial slurs about her ex-partner:

> At first I felt speechless and did not know how to respond to him. Then I felt very angry and, trying to remain calm, explained that what he said was racist. I was trying to show him that these awful labels and stereotypes hurt those they are named at. He just would not, or could not grasp what I was trying to tell him. He said he was only joking, and what was the big deal anyway? I ended up feeling very frustrated and had to hang up. I feel appalled and ashamed that someone I love who is very dear to me can be so disgusting. At the same time though, I felt good for speaking my view on this. I always stayed silent before but realize that I can no longer do this. The more I do this the easier it will become and I can only hope that the things I say will reach someone and make a difference. (Jan 13 93-j)

Bejay concludes her journal by summarizing her central learnings from challenging racism within her family context:

> Examining my own family, I have had to face the racism that exists and was passed on to me through my up bringing. The knowledge gained in this course has enabled me to openly call them on it, and to expect resistance. (93-jsum)

As Bejay expresses, addressing racism can produce resistance in many different forms and contexts. Other students report similar "unsuccessful" interventions on family members:

> I have also had the experience where my action to address a racist incident with a family member of mine did not turn out so positive. I made a point to address a particular comment with my uncle and he was *very* set in his ways . . . and his attitudes! My attempts at hoping to open his eyes to a few things pretty much failed—certainly not by lack of trying though! There is now quite a bit of tension between us—he insists on maintaining his attitude and I insist that he keeps it to himself when I am around. I have noticed that he makes a point to avoid me now . . . . I am still very respectful of him but I felt it was important to let him know where I stood. Perhaps he will see the light some day.
>
> Although this experience has not been a very positive one, I realize that I am doing the right thing in addressing these issues with him. Not everyone, or every situation will end up being positive—and some people may feel uncomfortable, but if it takes them to feel this way to start making changes . . . well then maybe that's a good thing. (Analee Nov 24 93-j)

Learning from the Trickster

Trickster Teaches Whose Comfort?

As Analee recognizes, people do feel "uncomfortable" when challenged to view themselves, their language and/or their behaviour as racist. These feelings can lead to an experience of backlash, the inevitable response to any act of resistance. Many who have had their racial consciousness raised find that they are influenced to "see" and "hear" others around them differently.

One African Canadian activist, Ela, reflects on the potential risk of loss of network members. This is often an early reaction to an enacted shift in personal consciousness.

> One of the biggest problems that people face when they start making changes is that it might mean changing your whole circle of friends because what locked you in place with the old circle of friends, now you no longer have in common . . . . Once I break out of that mold and all of a sudden decide that I see things differently and change my thinking, I see racism does exist, those friends are going to start either pulling me back in to the fold by trying to change my beliefs back to the old ones, or else they're going to reject me. Then I'm on my own and I have to create a new circle of friends . . . . It frightens people to see somebody change because they're still caught up in the old belief system and don't have the courage to make the change, so they feel threatened by somebody who has the courage to move on and try things, and look at things in a different way. (Ela TC4:15)

Critically interrogating the belief system of his peers, Mac exposes fatalism, as expressed through cynicism, as convenient to the privileged class and a major block to change:

> My friends say that nothing changes and I used to feel that they were right. However, they use it as a reason to do nothing (except analyze and come to comfortably smug opinions about the true and ugly nature of humanity). I can't write off everything they say but nowadays I feel like that is a luxurious position to be able to take. If you're the victim of racism, sexism, or other forms of oppression, that argument wouldn't be very comforting. In other words some people can afford to be jaded and cynical because they have very little at stake if no change took place. (92-j).

Trickster reminds us that it is important to critically reflect on the construct of "comfort." How far are we prepared to go to ensure the "comfort" of those around us? To whose comfort level are we consciously trying to adapt? While confronting racial slurs may create uncomfortable feelings for some, slurs themselves produce very uncomfortable feelings for those targeted. Discomfort can also be experienced through failure to address racism. In this story, the teller expresses both her oppressive experience and her growing discomfort regarding the need to challenge the labels that construct her:

> On the weekend, a couple I know and my partner and I drove together to a party when a racist remark was said . . . . While my partner immediately questioned this statement, I did only make a sound to indicate that I disagreed. I felt so uncomfortable and had so many thoughts that went through my head. Why did this man ruin the evening with this remark—should I ruin it even more? I had to spend the rest of the evening with him. Should I even want to spend the evening with him? When he attacked the "colored immigrants" I felt he was also talking to me. Often people say these statements without thinking they also attack me. I felt very uncomfortable, unwanted and conscious of my English. Even when I know that I am fluent in English, I often do not feel it. This statement made me question my abilities to speak English and enforced the pressure to improve my English.
>
> This episode made me feel uncertain about myself and my racism. When I did not act, I feel I reinforced the racism. I showed that it is ok to treat others that way. How can I effectively work with other immigrants and their issues when I cannot even handle this situation? (Vada Jan 31 93-j)

Acknowledging the reality of backlash means recognizing that the demand for action placed on the students can have contradictory aspects. Challenging co-workers, especially when a student is in a placement, can lead to "trouble," as Bejay found out:

> I sort of got myself into trouble at my field. I was taking part in a staff meeting and one of the staff [members] started to tell a joke about a black man who had gone fishing. I decided to speak out about this and so I did. I stated that the joke was racist, offensive, inappropriate, and just plain intolerable. There was instant silence in the room, but the joke was not told. I was feeling positive that I had spoken out but felt I still need to address this with the person. I started to talk about why I had spoken out when this staff member cut me off. She said that I really should be careful because I was "just a student" and that she could have some influence on the outcome of my field placement. Then she stormed out . . . .
>
> My initial reaction to this was anger! Who did she think she was threatening me? And why couldn't she discuss her racism! I felt like tearing a strip off her. However now I have calmed down a bit and can examine the situation a bit clearer. I am still mad. If I had to do it over, I would do the same thing. The joke was wrong and I had to call her on it. I recognize that I need to be careful because this person does hold some power over me in a sense. However I had committed myself to

being anti-racist. This includes challenging my own racism and that of others, I cannot be selective about who I wish to challenge or I am in essence defeating my own purpose. (Mar 1 93-j)

While the dangers of backlash are beginning to be visible to this student, it is clear that her commitment is unwavering in its youth. We all learn to be selective in who we challenge, but accepting the responsibility to confront, even with "risk" involved, is required of all committed activists. Bejay concludes her journal by restating her commitment to "an anti-racist lifestyle":

> I have committed myself to an anti-racist lifestyle. As I have learned through some of my encounters over the past term, this will not always be an easy thing. But to live this day in and day out at the receiving end is so much worse that I am inspired to continue this fight. I have learned that those in power do not want to give up what they have—Much work needs to be done . . . . (93-jsum)

Lena expresses a similar sentiment in one concluding entry: "I learned that it is scary to call people on their racism and although there will be resistance, anger and maybe even violence for practising anti-racism I am going to continue to do so" (Mar 7-14 93-j).

Taking action, no matter how big or small we are aiming, does have risks. Activism can pose challenges to others and often brings a counteraction to ourselves. I theorize about my own experiences as an activist:

> There's been more effort put out towards stopping or resisting any form of activism . . . than there has been to aid or add any energy to that work. I've been a bit shocked by the backlash. Then I say to myself: what's shocking about that? There's nothing really shocking about backlash. It happens almost routinely when somebody tries to make a difference or make a change, and it certainly happened to me a lot of times before. (Fyre TC4:2)

Backlash can cause us to spiral into hopelessness and helplessness. A critical approach to these feelings reveals fatalism recast in another form. Leonard proposes that fatalism has been "culturally constructed to serve the dominant order of things" (1990: 3):

> We resign ourselves to our role as agents of the state: Instead of acting with, we act upon them, instead of being subjects, they are reduced to objects—categorized, classified, planned for, evaluated, monitored, reviewed . . . . We may detect ourselves acting upon [others] as if they were objects, but we experience a similar objectification of ourselves. (Leonard 1990: 9)

As we continuously endeavour to theorize the experience of backlash in a complex relationship with activism, we can ask: how and when does it occur? The multiple tactics utilized in each specific context to procure compliance are as diverse as possibilities for challenging systemic oppression. I reflect on one experience that had a snowball effect—something that was perceived by me as "a little piece" but which had big repercussions. This story illustrates the spiral that creates and sustains the personal costs of activism:

> You think of it as a little piece when you first start taking it on, but then you get embroiled in the detail of what's going on with it, and you get emotionally hooked into what's going on, and then you start taking personal responsibility for what's happening, and then your little bit that you thought you were going to take on all of a sudden becomes something personally part of your own psyche, or your own will. Part of what you feel you need to do. And then sometimes you get locked and you can't really [en]vision how this is just a little bit, and how this little bit is just one more thing! And it's not really you, and it's not really the world, it's just one piece of the world that you're trying to change, and maybe it's not the end of the world. (Fyre TC4:3)

Trickster has taught me that it is this very sense of personal commitment to change that has left me open to become a target for backlash. I reflect on the role personal assassination plays in de-activating political activism. This "speak-out" is a lesson story, an effort to help myself and others learn to be self-preserving in our activist efforts:

> We have to keep our vision strong for what it is that we start with, and who we are in it, because one of the things that happens often is that when you're involved in a struggle, when people want this struggle to end, or they don't want it brought forward, then sometimes they use personal assassination to stop it. So to not take that seriously, to take it as backlash, to take it as . . . a political thing. It's hard to not feel personal when people are saying things about you, and to keep seeing it as part of the overall picture. (Fyre TC4:4)

Negative labelling has always been produced and escalated due to resistance. Blaut informs us that the necessity for dehumanizing arose out of the need to justify the actions taken by colonial powers to "maintain control in the face of Native resistance" (1993: 26).

Mohanty (1994) notes that for Schools to continue to conduct "business as usual" in the face of overwhelming challenges posed by the presence of "people of color," they have to enact policy and programs aimed at accommodation. To this end, conflicts are personalized and psychologized: the "problems" of race and difference are formulated into "narrow, interpersonal terms" and historical and contextual conflicts are rewritten as "manageable psychological ones"

(Mohanty 1994: 157). Through this process, "conflict resolution" is attempted in an effort to negotiate differences "between individuals who are dissatisfied as individuals" (Mohanty 1994: 157). Mohanty discloses that "[i]f complex structural experiences of domination and resistance can be ideologically reformulated as individual behaviours and attitudes, they can be managed while carrying on business as usual" (1994: 158). As in history, we continue to be "managed" by "divide and conquer" strategies: "Our voices are carefully placed and domesticated: one in history, one in English, perhaps one in the sociology department" (Mohanty 1994: 159). There is an erosion of "the politics of collectivity through the reformulation of race and difference in individualistic terms" (Mohanty 1994: 160).

For us as individuals, opportunities for anti-racist intervention are happening continuously. Regardless of the personal costs, activism can easily become our "life work," our daily lives become an embodied form. Surviving this takes a certain set of strategies.

> It's not something that really you step in to and just say, well, I'm going to do this little piece and that's all for me for the next year. It's continuous demands placed upon me, in my situation, continuously. You've got to carve out what it is that you want to do, and take that piece and do it. How do you decide what pieces are worthwhile and what pieces are to be left for somebody else to do? (Fyre TC4:4)

Many participants address the contradictory aspects of activism. One Aboriginal Elder, Dee, reflects on a commonly theorized theme among activists—why "certain people do things and others don't"? (TC3:10). Dee's analysis, based on recent activism in her Community, emphasizes the role fear plays in disempowering people from taking action to impact on the System:

> A lot of it is about fear and oppression because people don't feel they have any power . . . if we are scared to death, afraid of what's going to happen because we are speaking up. If we're afraid, what does that say for others who not only don't maybe have any education in the secondary system where does that leave them? What does that say to us as [professionals], of the power of people and what they have? When we're out there working we really need to be aware that they feel so powerless! And they will tell us whatever they need to tell us to survive. We need to look past that to see why it is they say what they say or don't say, or what they don't do. We really need to look past what we are normally aware of. One of the things that has become clearer to me in our Native community are all the fears that people have of coming forward to speak on anything! And even when there are those who have the strength and courage to come forward and speak, raise issues and fight for rights, other people in the community don't always stand behind them even though it's in their best interest, because of those fears! It's been a real enlightenment to me that people don't have

the courage because they are afraid. (TC3:10)

She brings the example much closer to home when she extends her analysis to include her experiences at School:

> I think it has come across also in the School here that people are afraid, very much afraid, even when we are supposedly in a safe place, we are afraid. I have found out that we have good reason to be afraid. I think that has been a learning experience for me, I will be less critical of those who are afraid to come and speak out, whether they're here at the School or whether they're in the outside community. (2 second hesitation). (Dee TC3:11)

She wisely concludes, "People have long years of experience of being afraid, and they have good reason" (Dee TC3:11).

Attending another Circle, Dee returns to the topic of fear, backlash and "protecting your butt" as an activist. She teaches from her lived experience as she tells of the risks of "taking a stand":

> It's really scary when . . . you're wondering who is going to support you when the crutch claw comes down on your head with all the backlash. But you've got to say, what's important here? Is it important that something is done, that you take the social action? Or is it important to protect your butt? If you're going to be out there working and you're too afraid to take any action because of protecting your butt, you'll never do anything. Nothing that really makes a big difference. Maybe you can make little tiny changes . . . . But unless you really take a stand and put yourself in jeopardy, it seems like you're not able to accomplish anything big . . . . How can we expect anybody else to come forward, when we're scared to come forward? And we shouldn't be, but we are! I felt that was one of my best learning lessons, and hopefully that will be my thing to look back on to gather my strength for motivation for future things. (Dee TC4:24–25)

In spite of her fear, Dee has intensified her activism in the Community. She sees the "roots" of her inner strength as coming from what she learned through the Model about the importance of activism:

> Today, or of late, I have been active in the community, and even though I still am afraid, which I'm sure most people I talk to are, and I like the honesty that they say they are afraid, but nevertheless fight and force issues and take a stand. I think that's really good, and I think a lot of that came from this class. The roots of my strength inside come from what I learned in this course about the importance of it. That's something that has been my real gain from this class. (Dee CC1:16)

Learning from the Trickster

Trickster asks: What does it take to keep us going? How do we stay motivated to want to continue to make a change? How do we sustain that struggling force in the midst of all the things that happen to us and in our lives to exhaust us, to keep us down, to keep our minds off our activist work? Keeping our focus on the politics behind the personal attacks is one strategy for survival. Many personal and collective survival strategies are learned and shared in story—offered as condolences and given reciprocally among activists. Learning that backlash is a very real and expectable part of activism is essential to helping one de-personalize the attacks when they come. Other Circle participants reinforce this theme. We need to remain strong in our activism, in supporting each other, even in the face of backlash. Free counsels us all to remain part of our Community and to support others as the way for change to occur:

> Change is really important, but I guess it's also important for us to feel that we can take our knocks! Because there is going to be backlash! There is going to be things that you don't feel are justified, but I think hanging in there and reaffirming in yourself and trying to hang on to your self-esteem through it, and remaining part of your community, is going to be important in change. Hanging on to that community and asserting yourself in it, and making yourself real and visible in it, as a supporter of other members in the community, I think that's the way for change. (TC4:33)

Change is occurring on a daily, weekly, monthly and yearly basis. Not all change is reflective of an inclusive agenda. The forces of hegemony exert a powerful erosion of any and all movements toward cultural diversity. We must learn our Trickster tales well and be continuously opening ourselves to the lessons embedded in our daily encounters with the Systems and with people who hold and enact power over us. In order to sustain our personal and collective spirit we must re-learn the Tradition of visioning.

Visioning: Our Future Path

To VISION is to transform
To see what Was . . . Is . . . Can be.
To have Hope for our children . . . our Future
In the midst of the struggles of our Present
The pain of our Past.
Draw energy from the Directions of the Medicine Wheel:
Knowing . . . Air from the East
Willing . . . Fire from the South
Feeling . . . Water from the West
Doing . . . Earth from the North.
Energy spirals to the Centre.
Balancing power in each of the Directions
Allows for Transformation.
Growth of new Ideas . . . Inspiration to Will

Visioning: Our Future Path

To get to the Heart of the matter . . .
To Act with full force.
Feel your power to end and begin anew
To create . . .
to give birth to new ideas
Awaken to new Visions of possibility,
To Transform yourself and others.
Feel your straight spine . . .
like our Sister the Tree
Roots growing down into the Ground . . .
Boughs reaching up to the Sky.
Let the energy of the Directions flow through you.
Ask to be Informed . . . Inspired
Connected . . . Moved.
Ask what you might do
Ask to be put to good use.

Teaching and learning is a process
A transformational cycle.
We must insist on a Healing one.
Power with . . . Not power over.
Revitalization . . . Not acculturation.
Control and manipulation
From the outside . . . from the top down
Has been the rule for many years
Created an intolerable level of disorder
In our Families and Communities.
We need to be responsible
To ourselves . . . For ourselves

Our visions are Rooted in our histories
Our daily struggles . . . Our Self-In-Relation.
We want Change for ourselves
For our Families . . . our Communities.
We want Change in the Systems
In the educational Models currently in place
In the Schools "for the next students coming in."
We want to Change the World.
How can our Visions become a reality?
Time . . . Patience . . . Doing together
Are essential.

Let us Vision Together

What can be done?
To move into a more hopeful Future.
Our Communities able to participate
Influence major decisions in our lives.
Respect . . . Integrity
Our cultural belief systems and practices
Promoted and enhanced.
How can all or part of this Teaching/Learning Model
Contribute to your Visions?
Come let us share our Visions
To create a greater Circle of Interconnectedness.
To contribute to a healthier and happier future for us All.

Visioning can take many forms. When we are silent, we can open to the still quiet voice within ourselves. We also can allow ourselves to receive guidance, inspirational thoughts or feel the direction we are to take in our lives. The doorway to the spirit lies in our imaginations. To vision is to allow ourselves to see the world, a time or space beyond our current lives and situations. What we think or put our energy into we can create. To begin, we can visualize a healthier life for our bodies, ourselves, our family, our community and all our relations. We can also hold a vision for our people. We may not always be able to do the physical work, however, the power of our thoughts or prayers can contribute to the energy to bring about change.

Spending time each day to "day dream" is a common visioning path. When we allow our minds to open and expand, our heart can lead the way from analytical thinking to spiritual awareness. The universe or teacher within ourselves can then direct us to new ideas, solutions or to entire new ways of being in the world. When visioning is combined with ceremony, we can overcome our physical selves for spiritual enlightenment. The power of fasting or vision questing lies in our ability to be free from physical processes in order to open ourselves to spiritual guidance. Spiritual guidance can come from ourselves or from other forms of consciousness: spirits of the earth, water, fire and air, four-legged, winged ones, swimmers and crawlers or other dimensions of reality. (Wolf Eagle 1997)

We "vision" to transform that which is, to actively create more potent lives for ourselves and our children. Through visioning we can tap into the strength of the Traditions of our Ancestors, the energy of our Earth Mother.

The Elders teach that if we hold in our hearts a "guiding sacred vision" we will be able to cope better and live well even in society's changing conditions (Beck and Walters 1977). We must seek vision to remember the ancient knowledge in our bodies, to find ways to actualize the Traditional ways in our daily lives. We vision to give ourselves a feeling of belonging again, to build our connections to the Earth, to others in our Community, to the spirit world and to ourselves.

Through visioning we can align ourselves with the past, the present and the ever-evolving future. We can collapse Eurocentric notions of time, space and relationship and will new options and alternatives into being. Through visions, we can access our warrior spirit, our ability to be "prophetic critics":

> We promote a prospective and prophetic vision with a sense of possibility and potential, especially for those who bear the social costs of the present. We look to the past for strength, not solace; we look at the present and see people perishing, not profits mounting; we look toward the future and vow to make it different and better. (West 1993: 217)

Visions can inform our thinking, willing, feeling and doing. Visions are products of a movement to change and act as change agents. As such, to be a visionary is to be reacting, enacting and proacting. We can vision how we can be active in the "creation of oppositional analytical and cultural spaces" (Mohanty 1994: 148). Visioning allows us to engage in the hopeful utopian thinking necessary for radical transformation (Benhabib 1992).

If we do not have a vision we do not know where we want to get to. Once we have access to a guiding vision, we can then plan strategies that will help us actualize it. We each have a responsibility to then do the work necessary to fulfill our visions. Many times we are not able to fully understand our visions at the moment we receive them. They often become clear later as we act in the world. What we do not understand, makes sense later in an "ah-ha" experience.

Our visions are personal, but what I vision or see comes out of who I am, my Self-In-Relation to myself, my family, my community, my agency and my world. Following Dion Stout's (1994) Model, I theorize that I might vision about: a) my core self—what my "medicine" or ability might be; b) how I might influence the values, attitudes and behaviours of my family; c) how I might extend my energy into the Communities of which I am a member; d) how I will develop agency to bring together diverse groups of people to challenge the Systems of which we are part; and e) how I will work with coalitions or other diverse Communities to challenge the imbalance between the peoples in the World. This cycle of visioning will allow me to recreate my Self "in solidarity with those who are, those who have been and those who are yet to be" (Dion Stout 1994: 15), and ultimately to fulfill my obligation to my Self and others.

Self

I express my Self-In-Relation to visioning in my opening remarks for Visions Circles:

> My visioning comes out of a place of wanting it to be different! Of reflecting back upon my own past, my own struggles, and the pain of my own experiences within the system. And my daily lived experience now as a teacher here in a White [School]. Where most of what I see around me, and most of what I experience on a day to day basis, has very little to do with anything I understand to be Native Tradition and reality. I would really like that to be different. I know from talking to other people, Native people that have been in the [School] System and burnt out, and who have left, that the experience of coming here, for many Native people, and for many Black people, and people from other groups, is that we can't see ourselves anywhere here. We can't feel ourselves anywhere here. We can't make that connection. It's so hard to make that connection. So my vision is to create space for myself within this institution to work and feel happy and connected to my work. And also to begin to create a space in the [School] System for Native and Black and other students to feel connected at some level. To feel that there is a space for honesty and a space for our Traditions. (Fyre VC2:6)

I teach that we have to regain our visioning as a strategy essential to our survival in these Systems:

> So many of us have so little opportunity to really get in touch with what our lifework is. What our real vision or our heart work is. What our connection to the Earth is. What our connection to our work is. Many of us end up working day in and day out, but haven't, or don't and can't, and are unable to really take the time to vision. To take the time to, as we used to in Ancestral days, go out on the earth and spend time, maybe days, waiting to hear, waiting to find out, waiting for a message that would guide us and lead us into our future path. So that we could move forward in the future with a certain knowingness that we were on the right path. I think that one of the losses, through acculturation, that we have to seriously work to regain, is the power of vision! Is the power of visioning. To not get so caught up, and I do this myself, caught up, bogged down, oppressed, beat up, by everything that's going on in our day to day. (Fyre VC2:7)

Some participants find their voices to share their personal life visions in the Circle process.

> What I think is my vision of the world, and I think about an egalitarian society, I'm not even used to dreaming about. It's nothing we dreamed

about in school. They never asked about our dreams and our visions. You would think that would be the first thing that would be taught so that you would know where you're going with your life. (Bea VC1:22)

One Native youth envisions a future for herself: "Speaking about visions, I'm probably someday, hopefully, going to be a student of Jean's. If I can make it through high school! (laughs)" (El VC1:11). Tia's vision is to continue to validate her own experiences, to continue to heal from the scars of oppression:

> One of my steps for my healing is writing this on paper and recognizing that it happened to me. The next step that I am working on is being good to myself and validating my experiences. In doing so I am able to get rid of that pouch that I have buried so deeply and have carried on my back for so long. (93-j)

Liz recognizes how visioning can re-inspire self-love:

> I can claim back my own sense of spirituality that way too. That I am loved and I am capable of being, of giving love, and I am entitled to receive love, if not from anyone else, but from myself. So when I vision I think of all those parts of who I am and loving myself completely. (VC1:19)

Family

As Aboriginal contributors, we often express visions In-Relation to our families and Communities. These visions are often rooted in our histories. My opening remarks at one Vision Circle illustrates this theme:

> I'm hoping, or my vision is, not necessarily in my lifetime, but over time, if we keep working at it, if we keep putting it out, that there will be some change. That there will be some change for our children and our grandchildren. That they can feel hopeful and happy about being Native. And feel really strong about this. (Fyre VC1:16)

It is Traditional to express one's Self-In-Relation to one's children and one's community. Free expresses this wish:

> I see visions through my children! I see them still struggling living in their communities with their university degrees. Two of them! I see them giving to the community. I see them going to the schools and speaking and using Talking Circle. And Jean has also inspired that. They are now following the example. They use a rainstick, they use a feather, they use Talking Circles. And through me I encourage them also . . . . This is a gift of our culture. A gift that we hope will help create peace between the societies. (VC1:20)

Circle Works

Community

In Traditional form, Free expresses connection to Community, working over time and across generations as essential to manifesting her visions:

> The answer is not in learning and then leaving. The answers are in learning and then building within the community with it. With our learning and standing strong within the community. That's where I see the change taking place. I don't see a big change in my time, but I'm hoping that the influence of my children doing this work, and my grandchildren standing strong on it, and making that circle of connectiveness—interconnectiveness, bigger, as they go along, by extending their children and their relations and their friends, their non-native friends and supporters, the circles will get bigger and they will get stronger. (VC1:21)

African Canadian participants also express community-mindedness in their visioning. Unicorn expresses concern for the youth:

> My vision is at present in the initial stages; is to try and do things with my life, my work, everything that I do, and everyone that I'm connected with that will be a role model for the younger people to come. I stress that it is geared mostly to under-represented groups. (three second pause) In which my main two have always been Black, mainly because I am Black, and Native. (VC2:8)

Agency

Visioning is a necessary aspect of building the connection to Self and others required for agency. Liz, an African Canadian participant, acknowledges the loss of visions as a political act:

> When I think of visions I think of how easy it is to be robbed of our visions; as a Black woman, as people of First Nations, or Native culture, or even as a woman, that we are robbed at birth of our visions! Or that we are denied access to them in some way or another. But most ways it's through living in a white predominant male, patriarchy, racist, sexist, homophobic society. And in that, I think reclaiming our visions is very painful . . . . In taking back what belongs to us, or oneself . . . we are connecting parts of our sense of who we are, at least I feel I am, that have been robbed or taken away from me. In doing that, that's very powerful. In doing that, I'm stating, I feel, to someone else, that you're not going to get rid of me that easily. That I'm not going to be that disjointed so that you can pick apart every bone or be that parasitic, or the vulture and pick away at the last bit of flesh that I can reclaim as my own. In visioning I think of happier times too! And that I can be visioning by myself or I can be visioning with others like I am today in a Circle, and in that Circle we have that sense of sharing. I have that sense of

> sharing! And the sense that every territory can be walked on. That every part of one's self can be exposed without having to be judged at all times by other people. I think Circle work allows people to feel connected. And I think in that connectiveness, that we're allowed to be exposed and feel that we can claim back what is taken away from us . . . . (VC1:19)

Unicorn notes the positive impacts she sees on White peers and hopes they enact what they say—that they will continue their learning process:

> In closing circle it was evident that your teaching methods gave my classmates student access to new knowledge. Although they are at different levels of awareness it is much more than they had before (positive). Your class has triggered a desire, to learn more and/or to take action, in some of my classmates. I have observed this transition from September. I hope they continue their pursuit of awareness and sensitivity with respect to how you have introduced them to cross-cultural issues. (Dec 2 93-j)

Cal recognizes his "personal" growth and visions for greater focus and balance in his future activist endeavours:

> It is obvious that my consciousness and my person have grown a great deal . . . . I will continue to get myself focused and create a greater balance in my life. I need to select my struggles much more carefully, as it is my responsibility to defend the dignity of all peoples and fight the inhumanity of racism. (Apr 7 94-j)

Several Eurocentric students also express the sentiment that although the class was over they hope to continue their learning. Mac is inspired to reflect his visions around the Medicine Wheel. He enacts West's (1993) Model of prophetic visioning by connecting the strengths gained through learning in the past with present realities and a future commitment to change:

> All that I learn here is just a beginning. It remains with me to continue my own learning to open my own doors, and to see with my own eyes. I feel like I have glimpsed the dawn but want to feel the warmth of the noon day sun. The North, the strength of acting and seeing will be my guide. A guide to new levels of understanding and knowledge which return me to the East and my awareness that my learning is not yet complete. (Mac 92-j)

Gela's description of methods planned to continue her learning provides a valuable summary of lessons embedded in the process. Her vision demonstrates her understanding and commitment to the material presented in the Model:

I intend to continue learning about cultures that differ from mine and look forward to learning ways in which to promote the equality and value of all people. I also plan to continue reading books and attending cultural events. As I become more and more culturally aware I would like to educate other white people about the privileges their skin color and status guarantee them. I hope to continue learning by listening to first voice, I now realize that important issues and experiences are often distorted if they are not presented in first voice. (Gela Apr 93-jsum)

In their journals, some participants vision changes to be made at the School, and many of these changes are realized in the following School year:

I'm hoping that as a collective group we can make a difference by starting with a students' handbook. In this handbook I would like to see an anti-racist statement which the school embraces. I would also like to see a racial harassment policy in place. What is happening at this school really angers me and I believe that we as [professionals] must start practising what we preach in our code of ethics. For me this is also a way of working through the anger I am presently feeling. (Tia 93-j)

Visioning strategies for change gives us direction and hope. It is also a creative outlet for the anger, which is always present once the many forms of oppression and injustice become more visible. Phil, who realized many and varied opportunities for action, "en-vision-ed" a Traditional wish to "change things for the next students who are coming in":

I am also going to write up all my experiences, and encourage others to do the same and find a way of presenting them to the [School] in a way that will document them, teach staff, and change things for the next students who are coming in.
I want to help to organize a support group for Aboriginal students at the School. This will help students who meet with racism to get support and not to feel that they are alone and being personally victimized. It will provide a system of advocacy for students who need to address racism issues without feeling that if they say something there will be a lot of backlash. (Apr 15 93-t4)

Phil is wise to recognize that raising consciousness through First Voice about her own lived experiences within the School will require collective validation and support. The Native Support and Action Circle is a vision now enacted. Meetings of Aboriginal students are held regularly and these students lobby for changes in the School.

Free expresses a desire to use Circle in achieving her visions for Aboriginal people in the School community:

What I would like to look at, is the idea of Talking Circle giving voice to

Native people in being able to speak their experiences of discrimination across the campus, across the [School], in the different disciplines. To be able to speak their voice of how they feel themselves being treated and the vision idea of what would they like to see changed to make them feel more comfortable in this very White learning environment? I think that's really important for our people. I hope to carry these messages to my community as well. (VC1:6)

Randi also sees Circle as part of her visionary work in the field of Aboriginal mental health:

The vision for me in the Circle certainly is to work on the mental component of our lives. And mental health, to be able to get some control over our own destiny as Native people in Native communities. To say that we aren't going to take it any more. We're going to do what's right for us. (VC1:18)

Unicorn reflects on her own isolation and need for more contact, more support and more allies within the School context:

Even though I feel isolated, I'm just learning about those members of the Native communities. My need for knowledge and exposure—is based on working relationships and friendships in school . . . when you meet someone in situations, things draw you closer. My immediate vision is to work to find new ways to support other people's work in terms of Jean's, with Circle work. And [Sarah] in her work. Ways of supporting so that we don't feel so isolated when we're in a White environment. No matter what the differences and the struggles are, we need to have allies. (VC2:8)

World

We can all learn to extend our visions to embrace world change. A vision can be expressed at its most radical and simple level as a "wish." Lena expresses her deepest feelings in this entry . . . "if I had one wish":

If I had one wish it would be that we could go back in time and change all the wrongs done by white people. I am not going to be like other white people, I am going to change and try to fix and change some of the things that have been done throughout history by the white culture so this kind of horrific abuse does not continue to happen. (Jan 16 93-j)

Van speaks in a manner that addresses solidarity and alliance-building:

I learned a lot in this class, and the structure [was such that] I wouldn't have learned what I did or have been as touched as I was if the class hadn't been structured the way it was. With the Circle and First Voice.

First Voice really spoke to me . . . . You have to hear from people, their experiences, their lives, and to see it, to know it, to feel it. Feel or try to empathize with their situation . . . . It made me feel instead of just hear! It was a total learning . . . . For me. For my heart and body. (TC4:4)

Another student, Gracie, has this to say:

I feel very appreciative to Jean for giving me one of the very few kinds of opportunities I would have in an academic setting. If I could do all those courses, go through the pain, join with people, do something constructive, it would be worth a whole lot more than three letters after my name, and a whole bunch of bull that goes along with it. (TC2:27)

These student visions interconnect with Redbird and her desire that the Model will help change the System for future generations:

I just hope that the System changes for the better for everyone. For Native people and everyone that needs it! I always feel apologetic for asking someone for anything, any kind of a favour, help, anything at all. So that's why I don't bother much any more. But for the coming up generations, I hope the System will change, and I hope that you, who took the course, will understand this and treat people with dignity and sympathy and give what they need. This is what I feel. (Redbird TC3:3)

Charlotte reflects on her struggles as an activist. She emphasizes time, patience and doing together as essential considerations when trying to enact our visions for world change:

I see movement happening. It's just hard to be patient. I know that one of my struggles on this particular journey is to come to grips with time. Not to try to do too much too fast all the time. Too many things at once. To just understand that when you're in the version of time that we're all living in at the moment one thing happens and then another thing happens, and then another thing happens, and that's all you can do. (three second pause) It's very important to take one step and then take the next step, and then take the next step, and understand that that's enough. Understand that lots of other people are doing the same thing. You're not alone. (Charlotte VC2:16)

Jan expresses similar ideas about the relationship of time, collectivity and hope by using a gardening metaphor:

I try to be hopeful when dealing with someone who just seems overwhelming . . . . Maybe you're just planting an idea at this point, that really down the road more people will plant this same idea. But I think it is hopeful that change happens in time. (TC4:30)

Conclusion

Within these pages and my classroom, I have planted many seeds of change. Despite the contradictions, I remain hopeful for the Model.

> I think that there are a lot of people trying to do this work right now. Cross-cultural issues work, anti-racist work, educational work, and I don't really think there's a lot of real good models for how to do it, and I am very hopeful for my Model. I've seen it work, not only here at the School, but in short workshops around various locations, and I really am hopeful for it as a good Model for other people to use and not just one that works only for myself. That's my hope, that this Model does get out in the right way that other people will be able to be inspired from it and try to do their own thing with it. (Fyre TC4:4)

My vision is re-inforced by participants who desire a longer course:

> Cross-cultural can be a very affirming place to people who are silenced elsewhere. I think cross-cultural should be lengthened to a year; because looking at Black, Acadian, and Native experiences, one semester isn't enough for that! But people are also saying, well, let's do something on deaf culture . . . on gay and lesbians . . . on seniors, and issues around AIDS, and it's . . . *exploding*, and it needs to!! But it needs a year for that! (Kate TC1:2)

> When I finished the course, I was just ready to learn more. I had just come to the point where I got started with the questions more in depth. There was just, more and more, it went on. And, I was just ready. Then it was up to me to try to find another place for that, and it would be nice if the course was longer. (Vada TC2:36)

Phil, and others, express a desire for continued Circle work:

> Hopefully when this is finished it would be nice to continue our Saturday morning Traditions (laugh) in spite of having finished this particular project. It would be really interesting if we could have a Talking Circle every so often so that people who wanted to participate through the project would still be able to have a Healing Circle. (TC3:15)

Our visions reflect our past histories, our current struggles, our life visions. This work is in progress; it is my life work, a guiding vision yet to be fully revealed. Sarah, a Mi'kmaq Elder, speaks of her vision, which has become her "life work":

> I had a vision, and I still have that vision, and I believe it was established when I was thirteen. That was the time when I was leaving residential school. When I left that place I said, I hope this place will never exist for

any other First Nations people to come to this place again. (sigh) It was a horrible place. I swore when I left that place; I knew I would get into education, and that was the only way I could fight. (VC2:17)

We are fighting to actualize our visions for change in the School Systems and models. I remain convinced that a revolutionized world will not "come into existence in a linear way, as the result of a single-minded drive, but in a cyclic, circular way, working in all dimensions of a culture, moving from one position to another, not in reaction but in interaction with other forces" (French, in Gould 1987: 18). The movement from linear models to acknowledgment of the strength of the interconnectedness of the Circle is truly a revolutionary position, one that guides the development of my pedagogy and my vision for the future. I hope that my work contributes to the vision expressed in this Trickster dialogue by Keeshig-Tobias:

> M. The prophecy says the four colours of the people will live together as one, side by side, respecting each other's differences, celebrating those differences.
> E. And sharing the beauty of this creation, and making sure it will be around for lifetimes to come. But how do you love someone who won't listen, who refuses to see?
> M. Well, I guess, you just got to put your arms around him, hold him tight and say "I love you" over and over again until he stops struggling.
> E. And who's strong enough to do that? Who? (1992: 110)

I stand strong on my Ancestors' belief in personal responsibility for sustaining Tradition and I recognize the need to create educational change: "You have to realize and believe that one person can make a difference. I was brought up to believe that" (Cardinal-Schubert 1992: 135).

To all my Relations, Megwetch.

Appendix
Cross Cultural Issues (CCI)
Course Outline

This core course provides an opportunity to: critically examine theoretical frameworks for viewing racial, ethnic and cultural groups in society; broaden students' understanding of those different from themselves and examine their personal/cultural values as they relate to these groups; explore building a relationship to oppressed populations; and emphasize strategies being taken to effect personal and social change. Students will be expected to become more aware of their own culture and open themselves to experiences with peoples of other cultures in order to be more able to work cross-culturally.

These broad objectives will be approached using an Aboriginal framework to enhance the opportunity for cross-cultural understanding, encouraging students to recognize and appreciate differences in both the process and content of the course. Emphasis is placed on learning through experience and voice: *First Voice,* "Don't talk about what you don't know"; *Storytelling,* Transmission of the "Gifts of the Cultures"; *Talking Circle,* "Speaking from the Heart/Listening Respectfully"; and *Taking Action,* "Doing More Than Saying" are some of the lessons emphasized through process.

The Medicine Wheel, a Model/philosophy originating in the Plains tradition, promotes the values of balance, interconnectedness and unity—those things believed by Aboriginal Healers and Elders to be necessary for the health and well-being of peoples. Following this vision, the course, the readings and the assignments are grouped into four sections, the four Directions. As is the custom, we will begin in the East with what we need to know to understand cross-cultural practice. We will follow the path of the Wheel, exploring in the South, the peoples and their *cultures*; in the West, their/our *relationship*; and in the North, *strategies* for change.

Whenever possible, we will hear "First Voice," the voices of the groups themselves: Aboriginal/First Nations/Mi'kmaq, Blacks/African Nova Scotians and Acadians are highlighted as indigenous to the region. Other populations, Lesbians and Gays, Immigrant peoples and Disabled consumers may also receive attention, acknowledging the racial and cultural diversity within these groups. Interaction with the Communities is highlighted through inviting Community guests to class and through tasks involving direct contact with individuals and groups within the School, city and region.

Active involvement on the part of all students is expected, both through in-class participatory learning methods and out-of-class reading, journal writing and involvement in cross-cultural experiences. Students are expected to be reading each week, completing a section of materials every three weeks. The materials have been copied for your convenience and include a selection of articles, stories and poetry relevant to each section/Direction.

Circle Works

Proposed Course Progression
Class 1: Introductions, Medicine Wheel Meditation, Outline

Class 2, 3, 4: The East: Knowing/Thinking, the Air
What do we need to *know* to be effective in cross-cultural practice? Theories of oppression, racism and White privilege and culture will be explored. Task I: Who am I? What is my culture? How am I the Oppressor? How am I the Oppressed? Connect personal experiences to structural realities.

Class 5, 6, 7: The South: Spirit/Culture, the Fire
Who are the oppressed peoples? What are their histories, their present struggles, their visions for the future? How can we begin to see beyond the pains and struggles of victimization to the strength and endurance of survival and resistance, the gifts of our cultures? What sustains our peoples in the face of the structures of oppression?

Task II: Explore a culture other than White culture. Interview a person(s); attend an event(s); read a book(s); open yourself to learning opportunities. How do these persons see social issues and daily life? When you compare their views/experiences with yours, how do you describe the differences and similarities? How is this related to culture? Whose will, whose culture guides your work, your life, their work, their lives?

Class 8, 9: The West: Relationships/Emotions, the Water
What has been the relationship to oppressed populations? What are the feelings and experiences of oppressed persons in relation to professionals? This relationship is often acted out through specific fields of practice. How can we recognize when we are acting *on,* rather than acting *with,* someone?

Task III: Examine a field of practice, either in relation to a specific population (i.e., African Canadian, Aboriginal, Acadians, Lesbian and Gay or Asian peoples), or take a particular issue and explore it across populations. Explore historical context (what has been done in the past, what is currently being done and what are the visions for the future) or explore around the Medicine Wheel. Place emphasis on how the Community/ population serviced views the problem and the "solutions."

Class 10, 11: The North: Doing/Acting, the Earth
What interventions can assist oppressed individuals and groups in their struggles for empowerment? Feminist therapy, applied meditation, ritual action, advocacy, political analysis and political action are all possible tools to be explored. Explore methods developed by the Communities themselves: what are we doing to help ourselves, what do we want help with, what is a viable, respectful and helpful role?

Task IV: Do something about it! Take an action. Some examples include anti-racist community work (join a local organization and work with them on a project); an analysis of racism in an organization or a piece of policy; a class project on racism or cultural diversity could be organized. Open Circles on various issues have been done to complete this task. We will talk further. Please consult me or my teaching assistant for ideas or to review strategies before enacting them. Due at Talking Circle on Action.

Class 12: Closing Circle and Cross Cultural Feast

Evaluation

All students are expected to complete *all four tasks* and provide evidence of learning in each of the four Directions. An indepth reading of the materials supplied as well as in-class participation will be necessary to be able to successfully complete the tasks.

Students are able to choose how they are going to represent their learnings: a well-developed journal entry; an academic paper; a story; an in-class presentation; a "speak-out" in Circle time: a piece of artwork; a dialogue transcript; or a video production.

Each student is encouraged to commit to a different style of representation for *each* of these four tasks. Each task is equally weighed at 20 percent. Tasks can be submitted in combined form and group work is encouraged. It is each student's responsibility to ensure that evidence of his or her learnings is submitted to the professor for all four tasks. A short paper (3–5 pages) clearly outlining learnings gained in undertaking the task is the minimal expectation for any non-written form (i.e., presentation, artform).

Journalling

The remaining 20 percent will be allocated to the journal. Journal writing is expected weekly and it is to be course specific. That is, specify what impacted on you with respect to your development as a more culturally aware person: something you have read; something someone said in class; a gut feeling; a memory from your past; a racist incident you observed/experienced; a taste of power/powerlessness. How were you affected? Discuss the details in depth. End by commenting on how this relates to your past and what you now know or want to do differently in the present/future.

Journals are expected to reflect:
a) processing of in-class learning;
b) highlights of readings; and
c) participation in community learning (racism logs, events, conversations, media, etc.)

All journals are to be submitted midterm for feedback and are due at term end.

Each student is expected to review their journal. Use the Medicine Wheel to provide a summary of your most important learnings and your plans for continued work. Students will self-assign a letter grade, providing rationale for their choice.

Bibliography

Absolon, Kathy. 1994. "Building Health from the Medicine Wheel: Aboriginal Program Development." Paper presented at Native Physicians Association Meeting, Winnipeg, Manitoba. March 6–8.

Acker, Joan, Kate Barry, and Joke Esseveld. 1983. "Objectivity and Truth: Problems in Doing Feminist Research." *Women's Studies International Forum* 6(4):423–35.

Armstrong, Jeannette. 1987. "Traditional Indigenous Education: A Natural Process." *Canadian Journal of Native Education* 14(3):14–19.

———. 1988. *Slash*. Penticton, BC: Theytus.

———. 1990a. "Real Power: Aboriginal Women—Past, Present and Future." *The Phoenix* (Summer):4–7.

———. 1990b. "The Disempowerment of First North American Native Peoples and Empowerment through Their Writing." *Gatherings: The En'owkin Journal of First North American People* 1(Fall):141–46.

Assembly of First Nations. 1988. *Tradition and Education: Towards a Vision of Our Future*. Ottawa: Assembly of First Nations.

Bannerji, Himani. 1991. "Re: Turning the Gaze." *Resources for Feminist Research/ Documentation sur la Recherche Féministe* 20(3/4):5–1.

Barman, Jean, Yvonne Hebert, and Don McCaskill, eds. 1986. *Indian Education in Canada, Volume 1: The Legacy*. Vancouver: University of British Columbia Press.

———. 1987. *Indian Education in Canada, Volume 2: The Challenge*. Vancouver: University of British Columbia Press.

Barsh, Russell Lawrence. 1986. "The Nature and Spirit of North American Political Systems." *The American Indian Quarterly: Journal of American Indian Studies* 10(3):181–96.

Battiste, Marie. 1986. "Micmac Literacy and Cognitive Assimilation." In Jean Barman, Yvonne Hebert and Don McCaskill (eds.), *Indian Education in Canada, Volume 1: The Legacy*. Vancouver: University of British Columbia Press.

Battiste, Marie, and Jean Barman. 1995. *First Nations Education in Canada: The Circle Unfolds*. Vancouver: University of British Columbia Press.

Beck, Peggy, and A.L. Walters. 1977. *The Sacred*. Tsaile, AZ: Navajo Community College.

Benhabib, Seyla. 1992. *Situating the Self: Gender, Community, and Postmodernism in Contemporary Ethics*. New York: Routledge.

Berger, Peter, and Thomas Luckmann. 1967. *The Social Construction of Reality*. New York: Doubleday.

Blaut, James M. 1993. *The Colonizers' Model of the World*. New York: Guilford.

Bowers, C.A. 1983. "Linguistic Roots of Cultural Invasion in Paulo Freire's Pedagogy." *Teachers College Record* 84(4):935–53.

Brah, Avtar, and Jane Hoy. 1989. "Experiential Learning: A New Orthodoxy." In Susan Warner Weil and Ian McGill (eds.), *Making Sense of Experiential Learning: Diversity in Theory and Practice*. Milton Keynes: Open University Press.

Brand, Dionne, and Krisantha Sri Bhaggiyadatta. 1986. *Rivers Have Sources, Trees Have Roots: Speaking of Racism*. Toronto: Cross Cultural Communication Center.

Brandt, Godfrey. 1986. *The Realization of Anti-Racist Teaching*. Philadelphia: Falmer.

Bibliography

Briskin, Linda. 1990. *Feminist Pedagogy: Teaching and Learning Liberation.* Toronto: York University Press.

Broden, Adrienne, and Steve Coyote. 1991. "Sacred Herbs: The Smudging Ceremony." *Native Friendship Centre of Montreal Newsletter* January.

Brown, Phillip. 1990. "Biracial Identity and Social Marginality." *Child and Adolescent Social Work* (7):319–37.

Buffalo, Yvonne Rita Dion. 1990. "Seeds of Thought, Arrows of Change: Native Storytelling as Metaphor." In Toni Laidlaw, Cheryl Malmo and Associates, *Healing Voices: Feminist Approaches to Therapy with Women.* San Francisco: Jossey-Bass.

Cahill, Sedonia, and Joshua Halpern. 1992. *Ceremonial Circle.* San Francisco: Harper.

Cardinal-Schubert, Joane. 1992. "Portfolio." In Gerald McMaster and Lee-Ann Martin (eds.), *Indigena.* Vancouver: Douglas and McIntyre.

Carniol, Ben. 1990. *Case Critical.* Toronto: Between the Lines.

Carnoy, Martin. 1974. *Education as Cultural Imperialism.* New York: David McKay.

Carr, Edward. 1961. *What Is History?* New York: St. Martin's.

Carroll, Mary. 1986. "The Carrier Role of Social Work: Learning from Alaskan Native Americans." *Social Casework: The Journal of Contemporary Social Work* 67(3).

Carty, Linda. 1991a. "Black Women in Academia: A Statement from the Periphery." In Himani Bannerji, Linda Carty, Kari Dehli, Susan Heald and Kate McKenna (eds.), *Unsettling Relations: The University as a Site of Feminist Struggles.* Toronto: Women's.

———. 1991b. "Women's Studies in Canada: A Discourse and Praxis of Exclusion." *Resources for Feminist Research/Documentation sur la Recherche Féministe* 20(3/4):12–18.

Charnley, Kerrie. 1990. "Concepts of Anger, Identity and Power and the Vision in the Writings and Voices of First Nation's Women." *Gathering: The En'owkin Journal of First North American People* 1(Fall):10–22.

Chau, Kenneth. 1989. "Sociocultural Dissonance among Ethnic Minority Populations." *Social Casework* (70):224–30.

Clifford, James. 1988. *The Predicament of Culture: Twentieth-Century Ethnography, Literature and Art.* Cambridge, MA: Harvard University Press.

Collins, Patricia Hill. 1991. *Black Feminist Thought.* New York: Routledge.

Colorado, Pam. 1988. "Fire and Ice: Natives, Alcohol and Spirituality: A Northern Health Paradigm." *Arctic Medical Research* 47(1):598–603.

Conners, Edward. 1994. "The Role of Spirituality in Wellness or How Well We Can See the Whole Will Determine How Well We Are and How Well We Can Become." Paper presented at the Native Physicians Conference, Winnipeg, Manitoba. March 6–8.

Cruikshank, Julie. 1992. *Life Lived Like a Story.* Vancouver: University of British Columbia Press.

Culley, Margo. 1985. "Anger and Authority in the Women's Studies Classroom." In Margo Culley and Catherine Portuges (eds.), *Gendered Subjects: The Dynamics of Feminist Teaching.* Boston: Routledge and Kegan Paul.

Currie, Noel Elizabeth. 1992. "Jeannette Armstrong and the Colonial Legacy." In W.H. New (ed.), *Native Writers and Canadian Writing.* Vancouver: University of British Columbia Press Press.

David, Joe. 1992. "Portfolio." In Gerald McMaster and Lee-Ann Martin (eds.), *Indigena.*

Vancouver: Douglas and McIntyre.

Deloria, Vine, Jr. 1986. "American Indian Metaphysics." *Winds of Change.* Boulder, CO: American Indian Science and Engineering Society.

———. 1992. "Ethnoscience and Indian realities." *Winds of Change* 7(3):12–18.

———. 1994. *God Is Red: A Native View of Religion.* Golden, CO: Fulcrum.

Devault, Marjorie. 1990. "Talking and Listening from Women's Standpoint: Feminist Strategies for Interviewing and Analysis." *Social Problems* 37(1):96–116.

Dion Stout, Madeleine. 1994. "An Indigenous Perspective on Healing and Wellness." Paper presented at the Native Physicians Conference, Winnipeg, Manitoba. March 6–8.

Dominelli, Lena. 1988. *Anti-Racist Social Work Practice.* London: Macmillan.

Ellsworth, Elizabeth. 1989. "Why Doesn't This Feel Empowering? Working Through the Repressive Myths of Critical Pedagogy." *Harvard Educational Review* 59(3):297–324.

———. 1992. "Teaching to Support Unassimilated Difference." *Radical Teacher* (42):4–9.

English-Currie, Vicki. 1990. "The Need for Re-Evaluation in Native Education." In Jeanne Perreault and Sylvia Vance (eds.), *Writing the Circle.* Edmonton: NeWest.

Erasmus, George. 1989. "Twenty Years of Disappointed Hopes." In Boyce Richardson (ed.), *Drumbeat: Anger and Renewal in Indian Country.* Toronto: Summerhill.

Essed, Philomena. 1991. *Understanding Everyday Racism: An Interdisciplinary Theory.* Newbury Park: Sage.

Fay, Brian. 1987. *Critical Social Science: Liberation and Its Limits.* Ithaca, NY: Cornell University Press.

Fife, Connie. 1992. *Beneath the Naked Sun.* Toronto: Sister Vision.

Fiske, Jo-Anne. 1991. "Gender and the Paradox of Residential Education in Carrier Society." In Jane Gaskell and Arlene McLaren (eds.), *Women and Education.* Calgary: Detselig.

———. 1992. "A Conceptual Lexicon for Teaching Cross Cultural Courses in Women's Studies." Paper presented at Makerere University, Kampala, Uganda.

Forbes, Jack. 1979. "Traditional Native American Philosophy and Multicultural Education." In *Multicultural Education and the American Indian.* Los Angeles: American Indian Studies Centre, University of California.

Fox-Genovese, Elizabeth. 1991. *Feminism without Illusions: A Critique of Individualism.* Chapel Hill: University of North Carolina Press.

Freire, Paulo. 1972. *Cultural Action for Freedom.* Harmondsworth: Penguin.

———. 1973. *Education for Critical Consciousness.* New York: Seabury.

———. 1985. "Rethinking Critical Pedagogy: A Dialogue with Paulo Freire." In *The Politics of Education: Culture, Power and Liberation.* South Hadley, MA: Bergin and Garvey.

Frye, Marilyn. 1983. *The Politics of Reality: Essays in Feminist Theory.* Trumansburg, NY: Crossing.

Fulani, Lenora. 1988. *The Psychopathology of Everyday Racism and Sexism.* New York: Harrington Park.

Galper, Jeffry. 1980. *The Politics of Social Services.* Englewood Cliffs, NJ: Prentice-Hall.

Gatens, Moira. 1991. *Feminism and Philosophy: Perspectives on Difference and Equality.* Bloomington: Indiana University Press.

Bibliography

Geo, David. 1993. Guest lecture at Native Spirituality Colloquium, Maritime School of Social Work, Halifax, January 21.

Gilroy, Joan. 1990. "Social Work and the Women's Movement." In Brian Wharf (ed.), *Social Work and Social Change in Canada.* Toronto: McClelland and Stewart.

Godard, Barbara. 1992. "The Politics of Representation: Some Native Women Writers." In W.H. New (ed.), *Native Writers and Canadian Writing.* Vancouver: University of British Columbia Press.

Goodtracks, Jimm. 1973. "Native American Non-Interference." *Social Work* November:30–34.

Gordon, Edmund, Fayneese Miller, and David Rollock. 1990. "Coping with Communicentric Bias in Knowledge Production in the Social Sciences." *Educational Researcher* 19(3):14–19.

Gotowiec, Andrew, and Morton Beiser. 1994. "Aboriginal Children's Mental Health: Unique Challenges." *Canada's Mental Health* (Winter):7–10.

Gould, Ketayun. 1987. "Feminist Principles and Minority Concerns: Contributions, Problems, and Solutions." *Affilia* 2(Fall):6–19.

Grant, Agnes. 1992. *Our Bit of Truth: An Anthology of Canadian Native Literature.* Winnipeg: Pemmican.

Graveline, Fyre Jean. 1994. "Lived Experiences of an Aboriginal Feminist Transforming the Curriculum." *Canadian Woman Studies* 14(2):52–55.

Gresko, Jacqueline. 1986. "Creating Little Dominions within the Dominion: Early Catholic Indian Schools in Saskatchewan and British Columbia." In Jean Barman, Yvonne Hebert and Don McGaskill (eds.), *Indian Education in Canada, Volume 1: The Legacy.* Vancouver: University of British Columbia Press.

Griffin, Virginia R. 1988. "Holistic Learning/Teaching in Adult Education: Would You Play a One String Guitar?" In Thelma Barer-Stein and James A. Draper (eds.), *The Craft of Teaching Adults.* Toronto: Culture Concepts.

Gunn Allen, Paula. 1986. *The Sacred Hoop: Recovering the Feminine in American Indian Traditions.* Boston: Beacon.

Haig-Brown, Celia. 1988. *Resistance and Renewal: Surviving the Indian Residential School.* Vancouver: Tillicum.

Hall, Stuart. 1991. "Ethnicity: Identity and Difference." *Radical America* 23(4):9–20.

Hampton, Eber. 1995. "Towards a Redefinition of Indian Education." In Marie Battiste and Jean Barman (eds.), *First Nations Education in Canada: The Circle Unfolds.* Vancouver: University of British Columbia Press.

Harding, Sandra. 1990. "Feminism, Science, and the Anti-Enlightenment Critiques." In Linda Nicholsen (ed.), *Feminism/Postmodernism.* New York: Routledge.

Harris, Olivia. 1991. "Time and Difference in Anthropological Writing." In Lorraine Nencel and Peter Pels (eds.), *Constructing Knowledge: Authority and Critique in Social Science.* London: Sage.

Hart, Mechthild. 1985. "Thematization of Power, the Search for Common Interests, and Self-Reflection: Towards a Comprehensive Concept of Emancipatory Education." *International Journal of Lifelong Education* 4(2):119–34.

———. 1991. "Liberation through Consciousness-Raising." In Jack Mezirow (ed.), *Fostering Critical Reflection in Adulthood.* San Francisco: Jossey-Bass.

———. 1992. *Working and Education for Life.* New York: Routledge.

Hart, Mechthild, and Deborah Wood Holton. 1993. "Beyond God the Father and the Mother: Adult Education and Spirituality." In Peter Jarvis and Nicholas Walters (eds.), *Adult Education and Theological Interpretations*. Malabar: Krieger.

Henry, Jane. 1989. "Meaning and Practice in Experiential Learning." In Susan Warner Weil and Ian McGill (eds.), *Making Sense of Experiential Learning: Diversity in Theory and Practice*. Milton Keynes: Open University Press.

Hodgson, Maggie. 1990. "Shattering the Silence: Working with Violence in Native Communities." In Toni Laidlaw, Cheryl Malmo and Associates, *Healing Voices: Feminist Approaches to Therapy with Women*. San Francisco: Jossey-Bass.

Holloway, Wendy. 1992. "Gender Difference and the Production of Subjectivity." In Helen Crowley and Susan Himmelweit (eds.), *Knowing Women*. Cambridge: Polity.

hooks, bell. 1984. *Feminist Theory: From Margin to Center*. Boston: South End.

————. 1987. Presentation at a public forum sponsored by the Congress of Black Women at the Ontario Institute for Secondary Education, Toronto, September 21.

————. 1988. *Talking Back: Thinking Feminist, Thinking Black*. 1st ed. Toronto: Between the Lines.

————. 1990. *Yearning: Race, Gender and Cultural Politics*. Toronto: Between the Lines.

Hope, Anne, and Sally Timmel. 1989. *Training for Transformation: A Handbook for Community Workers*. Gweru, Zimbabwe: Mambo.

Horwitz, Lucy. 1989. "Learner Autonomy: A Case Study." In Susan Warner Weil and Ian McGill (eds.), *Making Sense of Experiential Learning: Diversity in Theory and Practice*. Milton Keynes: Open University Press.

Howse, Yvonne, and Harvey Stalwick. 1990. "Social Work and the First Nation Movement: Our Children, Our Culture." In Brian Wharf (ed.), *Social Work and Social Change in Canada*. Toronto: McClelland and Stewart.

Ibrahim, Farah. 1985. "Effective Cross-Cultural Counselling and Psychotherapy: A Framework." *The Counselling Psychologist* 13(4):625–38.

James, Carl. 1994. "The Paradox of Power and Privilege: Race, Gender and Occupational Position." *Canadian Woman Studies* 14(2):47–51.

Jansen, Theo, and Jumbo Klerq. 1992. "Experiential Learning and Modernity." In Danny Wildemeersch and Theo Jansen (eds.), *Adult Education, Experiential Education and Social Change: The Postmodern Challenge*. Driebergen: VTA Groep.

Jansen, Theo, and Danny Wildemeersch. 1992. "Bridging Gaps between Private Experiences and Public Issues: An Introduction to the Theme." In Danny Wildemeersch and Theo Jansen (eds.), *Adult Education, Experiential Education and Social Change: The Postmodern Challenge*. Driebergen: VTA Groep.

Jarvis, Peter. 1985. *The Sociology of Adult and Continuing Education*. London: Croom Helm.

Jay, Gregory. 1995. "Taking Multiculturism Personally: Ethnos and Ethos in the Classroom." In Jane Gallop (ed.), *Pedagogy: The Question of Impersonation*. Bloomington: Indiana University Press.

Joe, Rita. 1989. "The Gentle War." *Canadian Woman Studies* 10(1 & 2):27–29.

Johnston, Basil. 1992. "One Generation from Extinction." In W.H. New (ed.), *Native Writers and Canadian Writing*. Vancouver: University of British Columbia Press.

Kahn, Si. 1991. *Organizing: A Guide for Grassroots Leaders*. Toronto: McGraw-Hill.

Kalia, Seema. 1991. "Addressing Race in the Feminist Classroom." In Jane Gaskell and Arlene McLaren (eds.), *Women and Education*. Calgary: Detselig.

Bibliography

Katz, Judith. 1985. "The Sociopolitical Nature of Counselling." *The Counselling Psychologist* 13(4):615–24.

Katz, R., and V. St. Denis. 1991. "Teacher as Healer." *Journal of Indigenous Studies* 2(2):24–36.

Kearney, Michael. 1984. *Worldview.* Novato, CA: Chandler and Sharp.

Keeshig-Tobias, Lenore. 1992. "Trickster beyond 1992: Our Relationship." In Gerald McMaster and Lee-Ann Martin (eds.), *Indigena.* Vancouver: Douglas and McIntyre.

Kenway, Jane, and Helen Modra. 1992. "Feminist Pedagogy and Emancipatory Possibilities." In Carmen Luke and Jennifer Gore (eds.), *Feminism and Critical Pedagogy.* New York: Routledge.

Khosla, Punam. 1991. "From the Navel to the Fist: Feminists Working against the Tides of Individualism, Abstraction and Victimization." *Resources for Feminist Research/Documentation sur la Recherche Féministe* 20(3/4):98–108.

King, C. 1991. "Indian Worldview and Time." In Ernest J. McCullough and Robert Lorin Calder (eds.), *Time as a Human Resource.* Calgary: University of Calgary Press.

Kirby, Sandra, and Kate McKenna. 1989. *Experience Research Social Change: Methods from the Margins.* Toronto: Garamond.

Kleinfeld, Judith. 1975. "Effective Teachers of Eskimo and Indian Students." *School Review* (February):301–44.

Knockwood, Isabelle. 1992. *Out of the Depths: The Experiences of Mi'kmaw Children at the Indian Residential School at Shubenacadie.* Lockport, NS: Roseway.

Kolb, David. 1984. *Experiential Learning.* Englewood Cliffs, NJ: Prentice Hall.

LaDuke, Winona. 1986. "The Indigenous Women's Network Gathering: A Meeting of Spirits and Healing." *Fireweed* 22(Winter):23–27.

Laenue, Poka. 1987. "Culture in Contemporary Society." *Canadian Journal of Native Education* 14(3):4–13.

LaRocque, Emma. 1991. "Racism Runs through Canadian Society." In Ormond McKague (ed.), *Racism in Canada.* Saskatoon: Fifth House.

Lather, Patricia. 1991. *Getting Smart.* London: Routledge.

Leonard, Peter. 1990. "Fatalism and the Discourse on Power: An Introductory Essay." In Linda Davies and Eric Shragge (eds.), *Bureaucracy and Community.* Montreal: Black Rose.

Longfish, George. 1992. "Portfolio." In Gerald McMaster and Lee-Ann Martin (eds.), *Indigena.* Vancouver: Douglas and McIntyre.

Lorde, Audre. 1992. "Age, race, class and sex: Women redefining difference." In Helen Crowley and Susan Himmelweit (eds.), *Knowing Women.* Cambridge: Polity.

Lorler, Marie-Lu. 1989. *Shamanic Healing within the Medicine Wheel.* Albuquerque, NM: Brotherhood of Life.

Lutz, Hartmut. 1991. *Contemporary Challenges: Conversations with Canadian Native Authors.* Saskatoon: Fifth House.

Macias, Cathaleene. 1989. "American Indian Academic Success: The Role of Indigenous Learning Strategies." *Journal of American Indian Education* (August):43–52.

Mama, Amina. 1989. "Violence against Black Women: Gender, Race and State Responses." *Feminist Review* (32):31–48.

Manuel, George. 1974. *The Fourth World: An Indian Reality.* New York: Free.

Maracle, Lee. 1988. *I Am Woman.* North Vancouver: Write On.

McCaskill, Don. 1987. "Revitalization of Indian Culture: Indian Cultural Survival Schools." In Jean Barman, Yvonne Hebert and Don McCaskill (eds.), *Indian Education in Canada, Volume 2: The Challenge.* Vancouver: University of British Columbia Press.

McIntosh, Peggy. 1990. "White Privilege: Unpacking the Invisible Knapsack." *Independent School* (Winter):31–36.

McKay, Eva. 1992. "We Are Here." In Agnes Grant (ed.), *Our Bit of Truth: An Anthology of Canadian Native Literature.* Winnipeg: Pemmican.

McLaren, Peter. 1989. *Life in Schools.* New York: Longman.

———. 1994. "Multiculturalism and the Postmodern Critique: Towards a Pedagogy of Resistance and Transformation." In Henry Giroux and Peter McLaren (eds.), *Between Borders: Pedagogy and the Politics of Cultural Studies.* New York: Routledge.

McMaster, Gerald, and Lee-Ann Martin. 1992. *Indigena.* Vancouver: Douglas and McIntyre.

Mead, Margaret. 1942. "Our Educational Emphasis in Primitive Perspective." *American Journal of Sociology* (48):633–39.

Means, Russell. 1980. "Fighting Words on the Future of the Earth." *Mother Jones* (December):22–28.

Medicine, Beatrice. 1987. "My Elders Tell Me." In Jean Barman, Yvonne Hebert and Don McCaskill (eds.), *Indian Education in Canada, Volume 2: The Challenge.* Vancouver: University of British Columbia Press.

Medicine Eagle, Brooke. 1991. *Buffalo Woman Comes Singing.* New York: Ballantine.

Meili, Dianne. 1991. *Those Who Know: Profiles of Alberta's Native Elders.* Edmonton: NeWest.

Merchant, Carolyn. 1989. *Ecological Revolutions.* Chapel Hill and London: University of North Carolina.

Miller, James Roger. 1991. *Skyscrapers Hide the Heavens.* Toronto: University of Toronto Press.

Minh-ha, Trinh. 1989. *Women Native Other.* Bloomington: Indiana University Press.

Mohanty, Chandra Talpade. 1994. "On Race and Voice: Challenges for Liberal Education in the 1990's." In Henry Giroux and Peter McLaren (eds.), *Between Borders: Pedagogy and the Politics of Cultural Studies.* New York: Routledge.

Mussell, Bill. 1994. "Rethinking Institutional Response and Support Services for First Peoples." Paper presented at the Native Physicians Conference, Winnipeg, Manitoba. March 6–8.

Ng, Roxanna. 1991. "Teaching against the Grain: Contradictions for Minority Teachers." In Jane Gaskell and Arlene McLaren (eds.), *Women and Education.* Calgary: Detselig.

———. 1994. "Sexism and Racism in the University: Analyzing a Personal Experience." *Canadian Woman Studies* 14(2):41–46.

Nicholson, Linda. 1990. *Feminism/Postmodernism.* New York: Routledge, Chapman and Hall.

Paul, Lawrence. 1992. "Portfolio." In Gerald McMaster and Lee-Ann Martin (eds.), *Indigena.* Vancouver: Douglas and McIntyre.

Peshkin, Alan. 1988. "In Search of Subjectivity—One's Own." *Educational Researcher* (October):17–21.

Pictou, Phillipa. 1993. Personal communication, March 17.

Piven, Frances Fox, and Richard Cloward. 1977. *Poor People's Movements: Why They Succeed, How They Fail.* New York: Pantheon.

Raes, Koen. 1992. "Critical Theory in a 'Disenchanted World': The Challenge of Anti-Theoreticism." In Danny Wildemeersch and Theo Jansen (eds.), *Adult Education, Experiential Learning and Social Change: The Postmodern Challenge.* Driebergen: VTA Groep.

Raymond, Janice. 1985. "Women's Studies: A Knowledge of One's Own." In Margo Culley and Catherine Portuges (eds.), *Gendered Subjects: The Dynamics of Feminist Teaching.* Boston: Routledge and Kegan Paul.

Razack, Sherene. 1991. "Issues of Difference in Women's Studies: A Personal Reflection." *Resources for Feminist Research/Documentation sur la Recherche Féministe* 20(3/4):45–46.

Redwine, Marie. 1989. "The Autobiography as a Motivational Factor for Students." In Susan Warner Weil and Ian McGill (eds.), *Making Sense of Experiential Learning: Diversity in Theory and Practice.* Milton Keynes: Open University Press.

Regnier, Robert. 1994. "The Sacred Circle: A Process Pedagogy of Healing." *InterChange: A Quarterly Review of Education* 25(2):129–43.

Richardson, Boyce. 1989. Drumbeat: Anger and Renewal in Indian Country. Toronto: Summerhill.

Russell, Michele. 1985. "Black-Eyed Blues Connection: Teaching Black Women." In Margo Culley and Catherine Portuges (eds.), *Gendered Subjects.* Boston: Routledge and Kegan Paul.

Said, Edward. 1978. *Orientalism.* New York: Pantheon.

———. 1993. *Culture and Imperialism.* New York: Knopf.

Sanchez, Carol Lee. 1988. "Sex, Class and Race Intersections: Visions of Women of Color." In Beth Brant (ed.), *A Gathering of Spirit.* Toronto: Women's.

Saulis, Malcolm. 1994. "Considerations and Gaps in the Development of Mental Health Worker Programs for First Nations Populations." Paper presented at the Native Physicians Conference, Winnipeg, Manitoba. March 6–8.

Schenke, Arleen. 1991. "The 'Will to Reciprocity' and the Work of Memory: Fictioning Speaking Out of Silence in ESL and Feminist Pedagogy." *Resources for Feminist Research/Documentation sur la Recherche Féministe* 20(3/4):47–55.

Schutz, Alfred. 1967. *The Phenomenology of the Social World.* George Walsh and Frederick Lehnert. Trans. Evanston: Northwestern University Press.

Silko, Leslie. 1981. *Storyteller.* New York: Seaver.

Sioui, Georges E. 1992. "The Discovery of Americity." In Gerald McMaster and Lee-Ann Martin (eds.), *Indigena.* Vancouver: Douglas and McIntyre.

Spelman, Elizabeth V. 1988. *Inessential Woman: Problems of Exclusion in Feminist Thought.* Boston: Beacon.

Starhawk. 1987. *Truth or Dare: Encounters with Power, Authority and Mystery.* San Francisco: Harper.

Steiger, Brad. 1984. *Indian Medicine Power.* West Chester, PA: Schiffer.

Sterling, Robert, and Yvonne Hebert. 1984. "Non-Authority in Nicola Valley Indian Culture and Implications for Education." *Canadian Journal of Native Studies* (2):293–301.

Thomas, Barb. 1984. "Principles of Anti-Racist Education." *Currents: Readings in Race Relations* 2(3):20–24.

Thompson, Edward Palmer. 1991. *Customs in Common.* London: Merlin.

Todd, Loretta. 1992. "What More Do They Want?" In Gerald McMaster and Lee-Ann Martin (eds.), *Indigena.* Vancouver: Douglas and McIntyre.

Trend, David. 1992. *Cultural Pedagogy: Art/Education/Politics.* New York: Bergin and Garvey.

Usher, Robin. 1989. "Locating Experience in Language: Towards a Poststructuralist Theory of Experience." *Adult Education Quarterly* (40):23–32.

Van Den Bergh, Nan, and Lynn Cooper, eds. 1986. *Feminist Visions for Social Work.* Silver Spring, MD: National Association of Social Workers.

Wallace, Michelle. 1991. "Multiculturalism and Oppositionality." *Afterimage* (October):6–9.

Weatherford, Jack. 1988. *Indian Givers: How the Indians of the Americas Transformed the World.* New York: Fawcett Columbine.

Webster, Gloria Cranmer. 1992. "From Colonization to Repatriation." In Gerald McMaster and Lee-Ann Martin (eds.), *Indigena.* Vancouver: Douglas and McIntyre.

Weedon, Chris. 1987. *Feminist Practice and Poststructuralist Theory.* New York: Basil Blackwell.

Weil, Susan Warner, and Ian McGill. 1989. *Making Sense of Experiential Learning: Diversity in Theory and Practice.* Milton Keynes: Open University Press.

Weiler, Kathleen. 1991. "Freire and a Feminist Pedagogy of Difference." *Harvard Educational Review* 61(4):449–74.

Weir, Lorna. 1991. "Anti-Racist Feminist Pedagogy, Self-Observed." *Resources for Feminist Research/Documentation sur la Recherche Féministe* (3/4):19–26.

West, Cornel. 1993. "The New Cultural Politics of Difference." In Simon During (ed.), *The Cultural Studies Reader.* New York: Routledge.

Whitehead, Ruth Holmes. 1988. *Stories from the Six Worlds: MicMac Legends.* Halifax: Nimbus.

Wicker, Diane Goldstein. 1986. "Combatting Racism in Practice and in the Classroom." In Nan Van Den Bergh and Lynn Cooper (eds.), *Feminist Visions for Social Work.* Silver Spring, MD: National Association of Social Workers.

Wolf Eagle, Veronica Moonstream. 1997. Personal communication, July 21.

York, Geoffrey. 1990. *The Dispossessed: Life and Death in Native Canada.* London: Vintage.

Young Man, Alfred. 1992. "The Metaphysics of North American Indian Art." In Gerald McMaster and Lee-Ann Martin (eds.), *Indigena.* Vancouver: Douglas and McIntyre.

Index